Development and Policy Concerning Children with Special Needs

The Minnesota Symposia
On Child Psychology

Volume 16

edited by
MARION PERLMUTTER
University of Minnesota

LAWRENCE ERLBAUM ASSOCIATES, PUBLISHERS
1983   Hillsdale, New Jersey   London

Copyright © 1983 by Lawrence Erlbaum Associates, Inc.
All rights reserved. No part of this book may be reproduced in
any form, by photostat, microform, retrieval system, or any other
means, without the prior written permission of the publisher.

Lawrence Erlbaum Associates, Inc. Publishers
365 Broadway
Hillsdale, New Jersey 07642

Library of Congress Cataloging in Publication Data

Development and policy concerning children with special
 needs.

 "The Minnesota Symposia on Child Psychology,
volume 16."
 Papers presented at the 16th Minnesota Symposia on
Child Psychology, Oct. 22-24, 1981, University of
Minnesota, Minneapolis, sponsored by the Institute of
Child Development.
 Bibliography: p.
 Includes index.
 1. Child development—Congresses. 2. Child
psychology—Congresses. 3. Children—Government policy
—Congresses. 4. Parent and child—Congresses.
5. Adaptability (Psychology)—Congresses. 6. Child
psychopathology—Prevention—Congresses. I. Perl-
mutter, Marion. II. University of Minnesota. Institute
of Child Development. III. Minnesota Symposia on
Child Psychology (16th: 1981: University of Minnesota,
Minneapolis)
HQ767.82.D48 1983   305.2'3   83-1676
ISBN 0-89859-261-5

Printed in the United States of America

Contents

Preface vii

1. **Early Interactions and Interaction Coaching of High-Risk Infants and Parents**   1
   Tiffany Field

   Disturbed Interactions of High-Risk Infants
      and Their Parents   2
   Attentive, Affective, and Physiological Behaviors of
      High-Risk Infants During Early Interactions   5
   Thresholds for Stimulation During Infant Games   15
   Interaction Coaching of High-Risk Infants and
      Their Parents   20
   Summary   29

2. **Comments on Field's Chapter**   35
   Megan R. Gunnar

3. **Infant-Caregiver Attachment and Patterns of Adaptation in Preschool: The Roots of Maladaptation and Competence**   41
   L. Alan Sroufe

   History of the Problem   44
   Description of the Preschool Project   52
   Assessment of Adaptation in the Preschool   54
   Findings   58
   Distinguishing Among Patterns of Maladaptation   63
   The Power of the Attachment Assessments   68
   Attachment and Temperament   70
   The Difficulty of Predicting Specific Patterns of Maladaptation   72
   Further Research   74
   Conclusion: May Patterns of Maladaptation be Altered?   76
   Appendix: Minnesota Preschool Affect Checklist   80

4. **Comments on Sroufe's Chapter**   85
   William D. Erickson

5. **Patterns of Self-Control in Young Handicapped Children**   93
   Claire B. Kopp, Joanne B. Krakow, and Brian Vaughn

   The Literature   96
   The Clinical Literature   100
   The Present Study   106
   Conclusion   124

6. **Comments on Kopp, Krakow, and Vaughn's Chapter**   129
   Byron Egeland

7. **Toward a Model for the Attention Deficit Disorder**   137
   Marcel Kinsbourne

   Neurological Models of Hyperactivity   139
   Laboratory Study of Add Characteristics   141
   Hyperactivity, Impulsivity, Inattentiveness   142
   Determinants of the Vigilance Decrement   151

CONTENTS v

    Arousal During Vigilance Decrement   152
    Arousal in Add   153
    Summary   162

8. **Comments on Kinsbourne's Chapter**   **167**
    Anne D. Pick

9. **A Longitudinal View of a Preschool Research Effort**   **175**
    David P. Weikart

    Does Preschool Education Make a Difference in the Lives of Children?   178
    Is Preschool Education Cost-Effective?   182
    Have We Found the Answer?   184
    Of the Theoretically Diverse Systems of Preschool Education, is One Most Effective?   187
    What Are the Elements of a Successful Preschool Program?   191
    Can Longitudinal Work Survive Changes in Society?   193
    What is the Challenge of the 80's?   195

10. **Comments on Weikart's Chapter**   **197**
    Shirley G. Moore

11. **Intervention to Protect Abused and Neglected Children**   **207**
    Michael Wald, Merrill Carlsmith, P. Herbert Leiderman, and Carole Smith

    Introduction   207
    What Type of Intervention Should Occur?   210
    Developing Research to Guide Courts and Legislatures   214
    The "Bay Area" Study   219
    Conclusions   228

12. **Comments on Wald, Carlsmith, Leiderman, and Smith's Chapter**   **233**
    June Louin Tapp

Preface

This volume contains the papers presented at the sixteenth Minnesota Symposia on Child Psychology, held October 22-24, 1981, at the University of Minnesota, Minneapolis. As has been the tradition for this annual series, the faculty of the Institute of Child Development invited six internationally eminent researchers to present their own research, and to consider problems of mutual concern to scientists studying children and development. For the sixteenth symposium, six members of the University of Minnesota community were also asked to comment on the papers, and their reactions are included in the volume.

The theme of the past symposium, and the present volume, was development and policy concerning children with special needs. This topic is particularly timely. The field of child psychology is coming to a new appreciation of individual differences, and is raising new questions concerning plasticity of development. Knowledge about special populations promises to enrich our general understanding of development. In addition, policy makers increasingly are valuing the contributions of developmental scientists. Such societal impact perhaps has been most obvious with regard to special populations.

The main presenters at the symposium were Dr. Tiffany Field (Mailman Center for Child Development, University of Miami), Dr. Marcel Kinsbourne (Eunice Kennedy Shriver Center for Mental Retardation, Walter E. Fernald State School), Dr. Claire Kopp (Graduate School of Education, University of California at Los Angeles), Dr. Alan Sroufe (Institute of Child Development, University of Minnesota), Dr. Michael Wald (Stanford Law School, Stanford University), and Dr. David Weikart (High/Scope

Education Research Foundation). Each of these distinguished scholars discussed significant research on the development of a different population of children with special needs. Field's research involves investigation of infants at high risk, and Sroufe's preschool children at high risk. Kopp has studied handicapped children, and Kinsbourne hyperactive children. Weikart's paper addressed issues concerning early childhood education policy, and Wald's children's legal policy. I believe the symposium thus provided a useful synthesis of understanding of these several important developmental problems, and also stimulated thought about the relevance of atypical development for the understanding of normal development.

Financial support for the sixteenth Minnesota Symposia on Child Development was provided by a Public Health Service grant from the National Institute of Child Health and Human Development, and by the Institute of Child Development. Many individuals at the Institute of Child Development provided help in carrying out the symposium, and their dedication was greatly appreciated. They include Margarita Azmitia, Eddie DeAngelo, Lonnie Behrendt, Andy Collins, Helen Dickison, Virginia Eaton, Rebecca Eder, Sue Fust, Carl Granrud, Bill Hartup, Liz Haugen, Judy List, Bill Merriman, Frosso Motti, Carolyn Palmer, Maria Pastuszek, Anne Pick, Herb Pick, Martha Robb, Chris Todd, and Maria Wolf.

Finally, the contributors who presented their research, and the discussants who critiqued this work, are gratefully recognized. Their insights about development and policy concerning children surely are a credit to our field.

Marion Perlmutter
University of Minnesota

# 1 Early Interactions and Interaction Coaching of High-Risk Infants and Parents

Tiffany Field
University of Miami Medical School

Interactions between young infants and their parents typically feature the parents "infantizing" their behavior or slowing down, exaggerating, and repeating their behaviors, contingently responding by imitating or highlighting the infants' behaviors, taking turns or not interrupting, and respecting the infants' occasional breaks from the conversation. The infant, in turn, looks and sounds attentive and content. An interaction of this kind is illustrated in Fig. 1.1. Atypical or disturbed interactions feature instead a gaze averting, squirming, fussing infant and an anxious or depressed looking, controlling and frustrated parent. Although all infant-parent dyads experience occasional disturbed interactions, high-risk and handicapped infants are noted to experience disturbed interactions with some frequency. Because patterns or styles of interaction appear to get established at an early age and because there is some evidence for continuity between early interaction behaviors and later communication skills, intensive efforts are being made to understand the dynamics of early interactions and to find strategies which might facilitate the development of early interaction skills. Interaction coaching is a term we have used for our attempts to modify disturbed interactions. In this chapter I will review some of the literature on the disturbed interactions of high-risk infants, including data from our own studies on infants' attentive, affective, and physiological behaviors during early interactions as well as manipulations or interaction coaching techniques which seem to facilitate the interactions of high-risk infants and their parents.

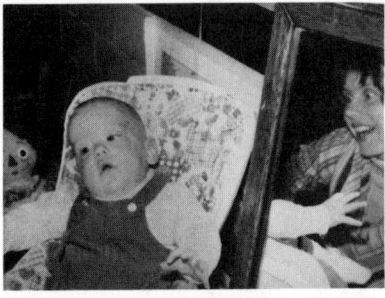 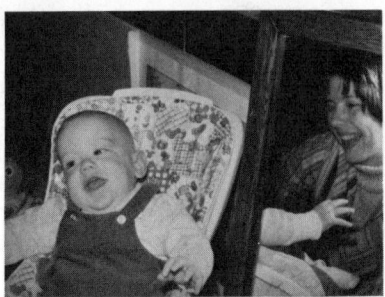
 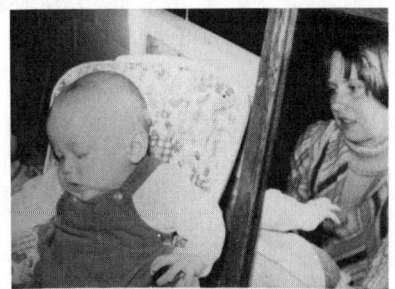

FIG. 1.1 A typical sequence observed during early interactions of normal infants and their mothers—(a) the infant looks at its mother and the mother shows an exaggerated facial expression (mock surprise here); (b) the infant and mother smile; (c) the infant laughs, the mother "relaxing" her smile; and (d) the infant looks away, the mother ceases smiling and watches her infant.

DISTURBED INTERACTIONS OF HIGH-RISK INFANTS AND THEIR PARENTS

Infants and adults appear to respond very similarly to interaction disturbances. Two of the most disturbing adult-adult interaction patterns, that of "interrupting" and that of "latent responding" have been demonstrated by Chapple (1970) in laboratory manipulations. For the "interrupting" disturbance, an adult experimenter continued to make initiations to an adult subject without letting the subject "get a word in edgewise;" this ultimately eventuated in the subject's inactivity. In the "latent responding" manipulation, the experimenter remained silent, unresponsive or slow to respond; this was increasingly stressful for the subject who continued to make initiations to the experimenter without response and ultimately became inactive.

Similar manipulations have been tried with infants and mothers such as asking the mother to remain still or stone-faced (Fogel, Diamond, Langhorst, & Demos, 1981; Stoller & Field, 1982; Trevarthen, 1974;

Tronick, Als, Adamson, Wise, & Brazelton, 1978). As in the nonresponsive experimenter condition of the adult study by Chapple (1970), the infants were distressed by a nonresponsive partner; they showed excessive gaze aversion and fussing. The mother, like the "slow to respond" experimenter in Chapple's study, was probably equally disturbed. Similarly, some have presented a "non-stop, stimulating" mother to the infant by merely asking her to "keep her infant's attention" (Callaghan, 1981; Field, 1977a). The mother in this situation no longer attends to her infant's gaze signals and "interrupts" the activity of the infant. This manipulation usually results in infant gaze aversion and fussiness.

These types of interactions occur naturally with some frequency among high-risk infants and their parents. For example, mothers of preterm infants are frequently extremely active or controlling and their infants are inattentive and unresponsive during early interactions (Brown & Bakeman, 1979; DiVitto & Goldberg, 1979; Field, 1977a, 1979b; Goldberg, Brachfeld, & DiVitto, 1980). For the mothers of unresponsive infants these interactions may feel like the "latent responding" manipulation of Chapple (1970), and for the infants of "overactive, controlling" mothers the interactions must feel like the "interrupting" manipulation of Chapple. Lower socioeconomic status mothers respond quite differently to their inattentive, unresponsive preterm infants, usually with inactivity or passivity (as in the "latent responding" manipulation of Chapple) (Bee, VanEgeren, Streissguth, Nyman, & Lockie, 1969; Field, 1980a, Field, Widmayer, Stringer, & Ignatoff, 1980; Tulkin & Kagan, 1972). That these disturbances are stressful for both infants and mothers is apparent in their overt behaviors and elevated heart rate and blood pressure levels (Field, 1979b, 1980a, Field et al., 1980). Overstimulating, controlling behavior has also been reported for mothers of Down's syndrome infants (Dunst, 1980; Jones, 1977; McQuiston, McCarthy, MacTurk & Vietze, 1980), cerebral palsied infants (Kogan, 1980), autistic infants (Kubicek, 1980; Stern, 1971), schizophrenic infants (Massie, 1980), failure-to-thrive infants (Greenberg, 1971), blind infants (Als, Tronick & Brazelton, 1980) and deaf infants (Walker & Kershman, 1981).

Multiple interpretations have been offered for the frequently observed hyperactivity and intrusiveness of the mothers of unresponsive high-risk or handicapped infants. The most vague interpretation is that the "frustration" of receiving minimal responses from the infant leads to a kind of "aggressivity" on the part of the mother (Berkowitz, 1974). Aggressivity often occurs in an aroused person who is presented with an aversive stimulus. The relative unresponsiveness of the preterm infant, the less developed repertoire of coos and smiles, frequent gaze aversion, and fussiness may be perceived as aversive by the mother. In addition, the "fragility" and "difficult" temperaments of these infants (as evaluated by the parents; Field,

Hallock, Dempsey, & Shuman, 1978) may be perceived as aversive. Another possibility is that the mothers are more active to compensate for the relative inactivity of their infants, perhaps "to keep some semblance of an interaction going." A third interpretation is that the mother may want her child to perform like his or her peers, and she attempts to encourage performance by more frequent modeling of behaviors. Still another explanation is that the mothers view their infants as fragile and delayed and, as a result, tend to be overprotective. Overprotectiveness in the extreme is construed as overcontrolling behavior. Because these infants are less responsive than their normal peers, parents may need to work harder at generating responses such as attention, smiles, and contented vocalizations. However, finding the optimal level of stimulation is a problem because low levels do not seem to arouse or elicit responses from these infants while high levels eventuate in gaze aversion and fussiness. Because of the seemingly higher thresholds to stimulation noted in preterm infants (Field, Dempsey, Ting, Hatch, & Clifton, 1979), Down's syndrome infants (Cicchetti & Sroufe, 1978) and retarded infants (Kogan, 1980), the stimulation requirements may be greater for these infants than for normal infants. But since these infants are also more difficult to console once thresholds are exceeded (and fussing and crying ensues) the parent may be dealing with a more difficult stimulation modulation problem than are the parents of normal infants.

Direction of effects or causality cannot be determined from these studies of early interactions. However, the data have evoked considerable concern, since the behaviors of these dyads appear to persist beyond the period of their early interactions. Follow-up studies of preterm infants, for example, have reported relationships between early interaction disturbances and later communication problems and developmental delays. In a two year longitudinal follow-up of a group of preterm infants, the best predictor of developmental status at two years was the pattern of interaction observed during the first few months (Sigman, Cohen, & Forsythe, 1981). Similarly, Bakeman and Brown (1980) reported that interactions as early as three months are significantly correlated with teacher ratings of peer interaction as late as three years. Our data suggest that the mothers who were more active and less sensitive to their infants' gaze signals at four months, issued more imperatives and were over-protective or controlling during interactions at two years. The preterm infants of these mothers showed more gaze averting and fussiness at four months and manifested behavioral problems such as hyperactivity, short attention span and language production delays at two (Field, 1979b) and three years (Field, Dempsey, & Shuman, 1981). For other high-risk infants Jones (1977), reporting on Down's syndrome infants, and Kogan (1980), reporting on cerebral palsied children, suggest similar continuities. Thus, there is some disconcerting evidence for continuity between early interaction disturbances and later developmental delays. Outlined, in the following pages are some basic exploratory studies in which we analyzed the attentive, affective, and physiological behaviors of high-risk infants and their parents in an attempt to understand the dynamics of these early interaction-disturbances.

ATTENTIVE, AFFECTIVE, AND PHYSIOLOGICAL BEHAVIORS OF HIGH-RISK INFANTS DURING EARLY INTERACTIONS

Our early studies on interaction disturbances focused on the activity level of the adult and the gaze and gaze aversion patterns of the infant. The recent development of a system for coding the facial expressions of infants (Oster & Ekman, 1978) has added a significant dimension to the analyses of early interactions. Although we have argued elsewhere that attentive and affective behaviors should be analyzed together as they occur in time (Field, 1981), we will first provide some simple descriptive data on the frequency with which affective displays occurred during the early interactions of high-risk and normal infants.

For these descriptive purposes the videotaped interactions of 20 normal and 40 high-risk infants were coded. The infants called "normal" had experienced an uncomplicated delivery at term age. The high-risk infants included a group of 20 postterm, postmaturity syndrome (M GA = 42 weeks, M birthweight = 3600 grams) and 20 preterm, respiratory distress syndrome (RDS) infants (M GA = 32 weeks, M birthweight = 1800 grams). These infants were considered at high-risk for disturbed interactions because they had presented atypical interactive behaviors at birth. For example, the preterm RDS infants were less alert, less attentive to stimulation, and less active than term, normal infants on the interaction items of the Brazelton Scale (Brazelton, 1973). The postterm, postmaturity syndrome babies were conversely hyperactive, very easily aroused and irritable during the Brazelton assessment (Field, Hallock, Ting, Dempsey, Dabiri, & Shuman, 1978). Although these infants appeared to be on opposite ends of an activity/irritability continuum, they presented similar problems to their parents during early interactions (Field, 1977a, 1977b).

When these infants were approximately 4-months-old (corrected age), they were videotaped with their mothers for 3 minutes of spontaneous face-to-face interactions. In addition, heart rate was recorded via telemetry for both the infants and mothers. The videotapes were coded using an electronic event recorder for infant gaze and gaze aversion (for looking at and looking away from mother), vocalizing, laughing, crying, and the basic eight facial expressions—happy, sad, interested, surprised, afraid, angry, disgusted, and ashamed (Ekman & Friesen, 1975). Because all of these expressions except happy, sad, and interested, occurred at very low frequencies, only these three were included in analyses of group differences. Similar facial behaviors were coded for the mothers. In addition, we coded the amount of time during which they tactilely stimulated their infants and played "infant games" such as "peek-a-boo," "pat-a-cake," "I'm gonna get you," "itsy bitsy spider," and "tell me a story." The infants' contingent responses to their mothers' smiles, vocalizations, and smiles plus vocalizations were also coded using the criterion that the infants' responses (smile, vocalization, or smile plus vocalization) occur within three seconds of the mothers' behaviors. Finally, the coders, who were unaware of the risk conditions, rated the overall expressivity of the infants and their mothers on a 5-point Likert-type scale with a five representing a positive expression and a one, a negative expression.

Analyses of these data revealed that the normal term infants exhibited significantly more happy faces than the postmature and RDS infants (see Fig. 1.2). The RDS infants exhibited significantly more sad faces than the

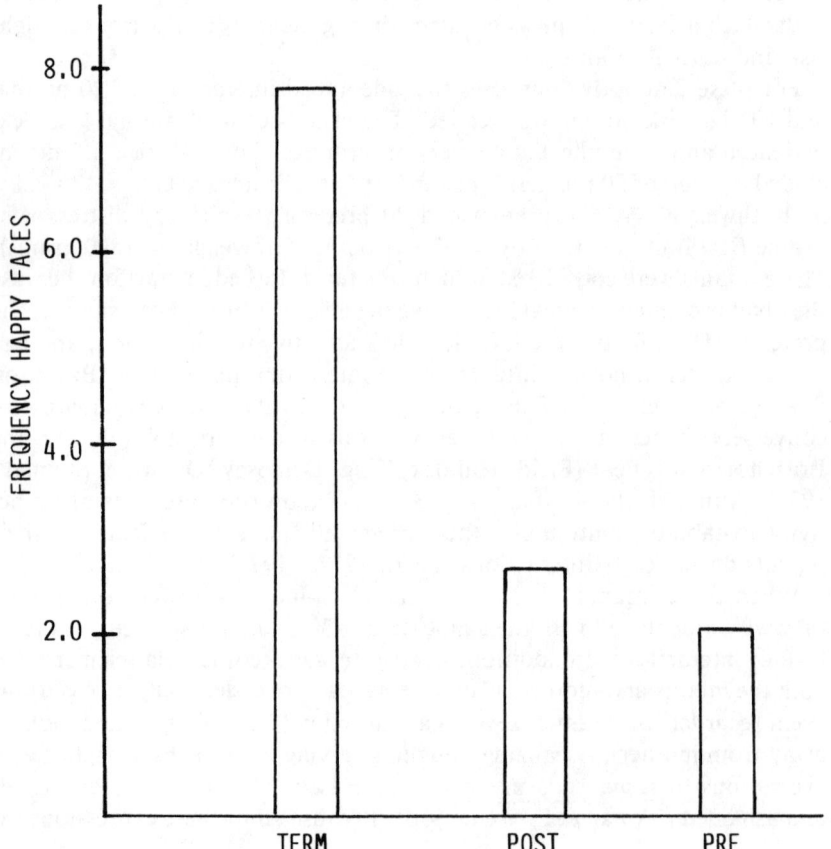

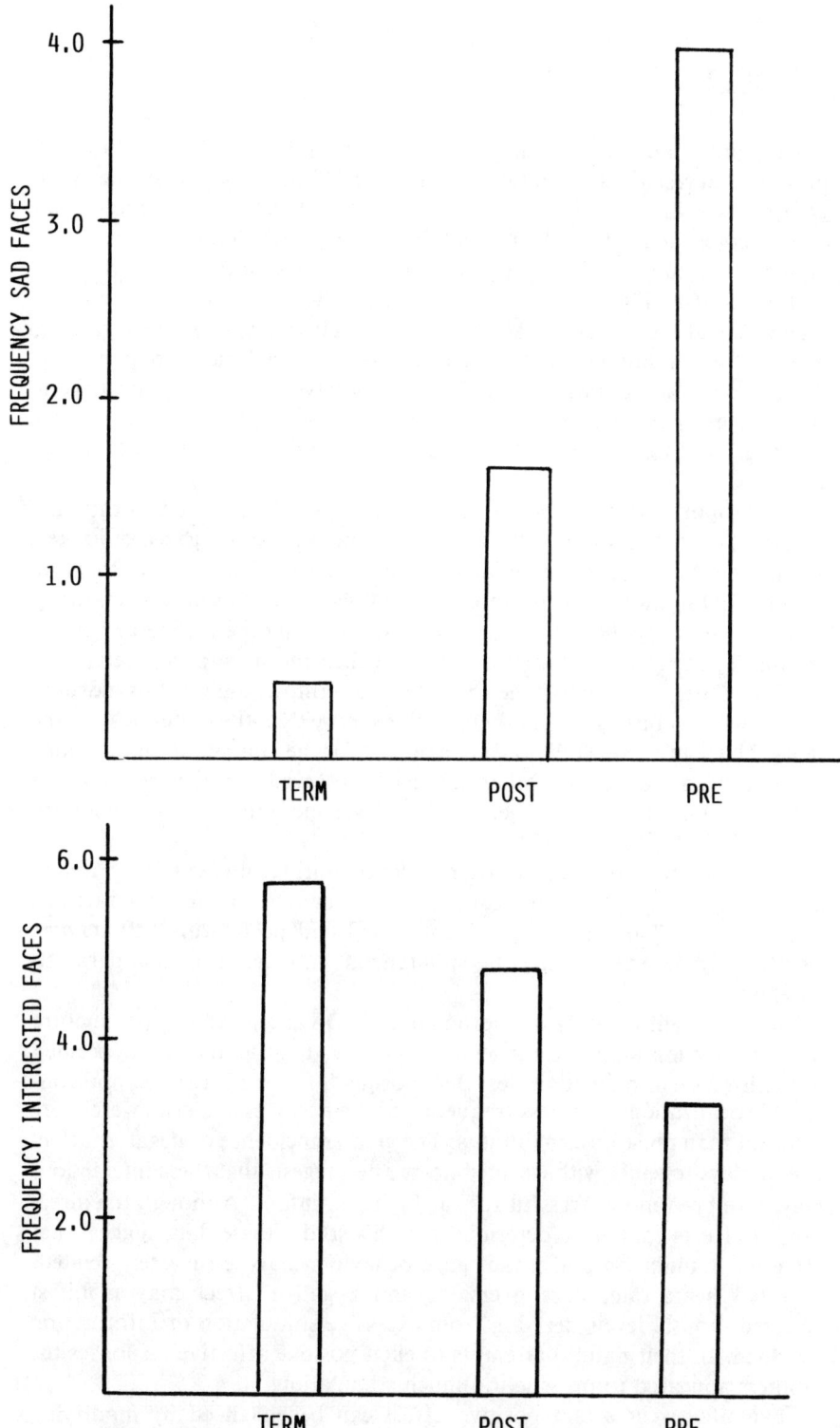

FIG. 1.2 Frequency of happy, sad, and interested facial expressions emitted by normal, postterm, and preterm infants during a 3-minute spontaneous face-to-face interaction with their mothers.

postmature infant who, in turn, looked sad more frequently than the term infants. Interested faces occurred with equal frequency across the three groups. Analyses of the data on vocalizations suggested that cooing occurred more often among the normal than the high-risk infants. Conversely, crying occurred more frequently among the high-risk infants than the normal infants (see Fig. 1.3). Contingent vocalizations occurred with approximately equal frequency for all three groups. However, contingent smiling and contingent smiling/vocalizing responses occurred more frequently in the group of normal infants (see Fig. 1.4). Analyses of the 5-point Likert-type ratings of expressivity suggested that the group of term normal infants received more positive expressivity ratings, as did their mothers (see Fig. 1.5).

The proportion of interaction time that the mothers talked to their infants and the proportion of interaction time that the infants gazed or looked at their mothers also differentiated the groups (see Fig. 1.6). Mothers of preterm RDS infants talked more than mothers of postterm, postmaturity syndrome infants who, in turn, talked more than mothers of term normal infants. The term normal infants looked at their mothers for a greater proportion of the interaction time than the postterm, postmaturity syndrome infants who, in turn, gazed at their mothers more than the preterm, RDS infants. Thus, an inverse relationship emerged for the amount of mother talking and infant gazing at mother. We have observed a similar relationship for interactions in which mothers' activity level and infant gaze behavior are modified (Field, 1977a; 1979b).

For an analysis of tonic heart rate levels during interactions, baseline heart rate was compared to mean heart rate for the 3-minute interactions (see Fig. 1.7). The heart rate of both RDS and postmature infants was significantly elevated during the spontaneous interaction as compared to baseline.

Thus, the high-risk infants, both preterm RDS and postterm, postmature infants, were less attentive and less responsive to their mothers, they seemed to "enjoy" their interactions less than normal infants; their smiles and contented vocalizations were less frequent and their frowns and cries were more frequent than those of term infants. The greater incidence of negative affective displays together with elevated heart rate suggests that these interactions may have been more stressful for the high-risk infant. Although the direction of effects cannot be determined in this study, these data suggest that maternal stimulation and infant gaze behaviors may be inversely related. Elevated heart rate, gaze aversion, and negative affect may manifest elevated arousal levels deriving from excessive stimulation or information overload. In their natural attempts to elicit positive affective responses the mothers appeared to provide too much stimulation.

That attentiveness and positive affect can be enhanced by modifying the mother's behavior is demonstrated by a manipulation in which we

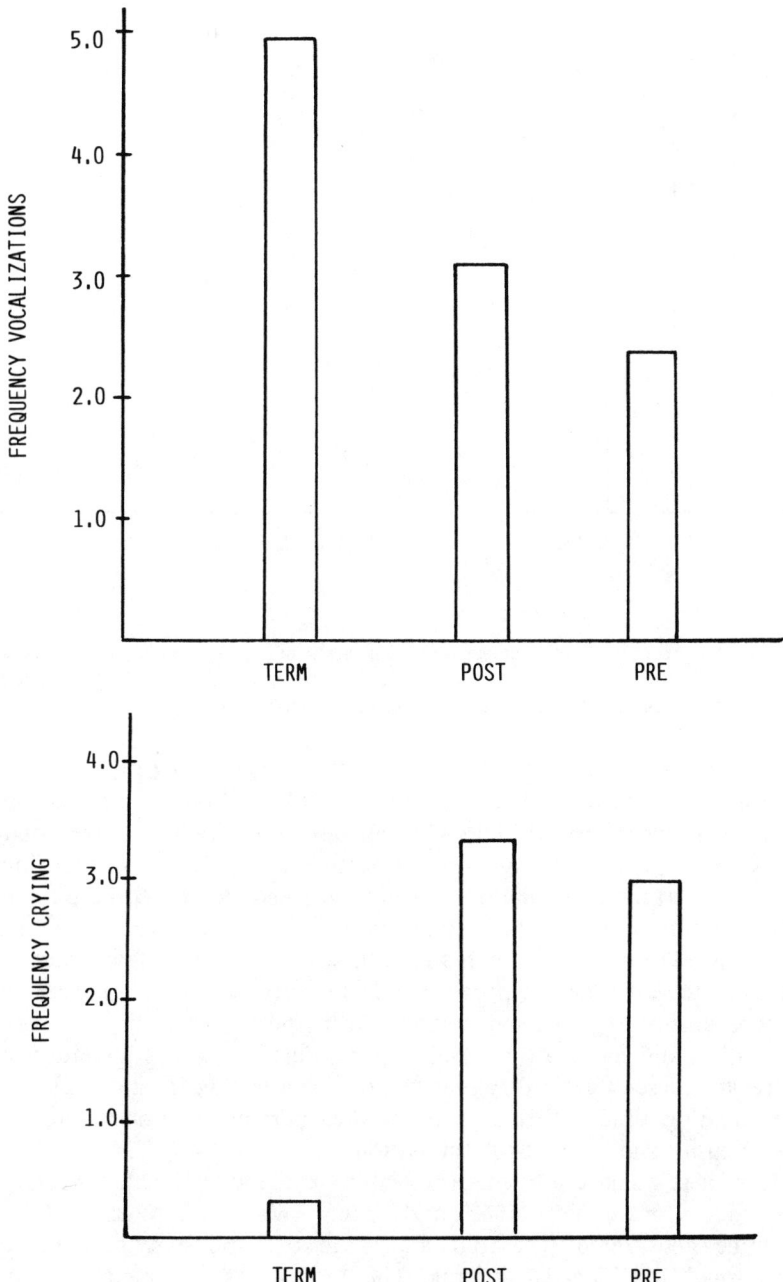

FIG. 1.3 Frequency of contented vocalizations and cries by normal, postterm, and preterm infants during a 3-minute spontaneous face-to-face interaction with their mothers.

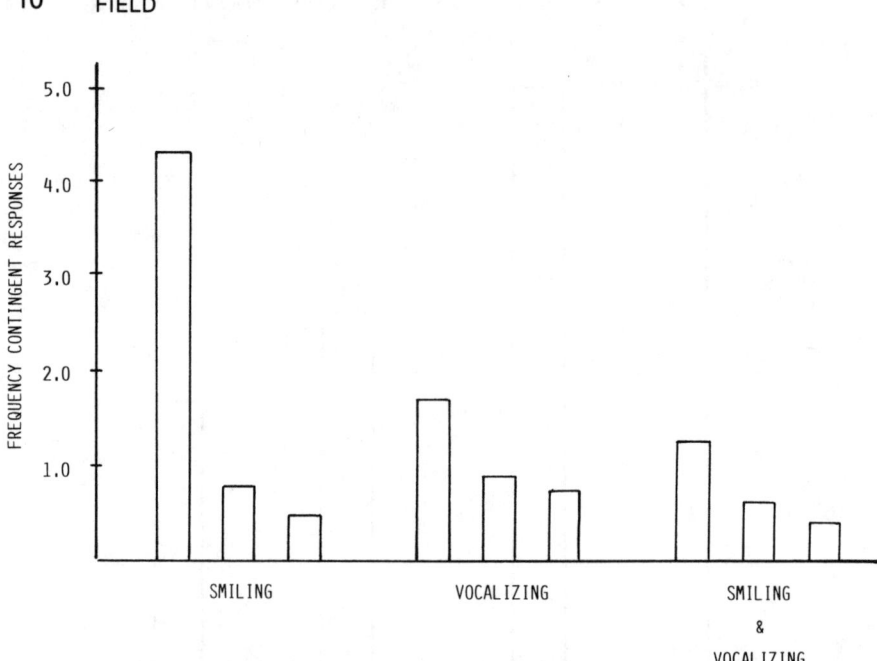

FIG. 1.4 Frequency of smiling, vocalizing, and smiling and vocalizing contingent responses of term, (left bars), postterm (middle bars), and preterm infants (right bars) during a 3-minute spontaneous face-to-face interaction with their mothers.

asked mothers to imitate the behaviors of their infants (Field, 1977a; 1977b). The mothers became less active and their infants became more attentive than they had been during spontaneous interactions. Corresponding decreases were noted in tonic heart rate (see Fig. 1.8). Conversely, during an attention-getting manipulation in which we asked mothers to keep their infants' attention, mother activity increased as did infant gaze aversion and heart rate. The interpretation made of these data was that these infants may have limited information processing and/or arousal modulation abilities, thus requiring more frequent "breaks" from the conversation to process information and modulate arousal. Appropriate levels of stimulation may differ for these infants; they may respond to a narrower range of stimulation creating a more difficult task for their parents, who must finely tune the intensity and amount of stimulation.

Elsewhere we have posited an activation band model (Field, 1981c) based on models by Sokolov (1963) and Sroufe, Waters, & Matas, (1974) to describe the different thresholds and ranges of responsivity to stimulation by normal and high-risk infants. This model was presented as follows: (Field, 1981c).

1. Attentiveness and positive affect during early interactions may occur within a range or band of activation that has as its lower limit an attention

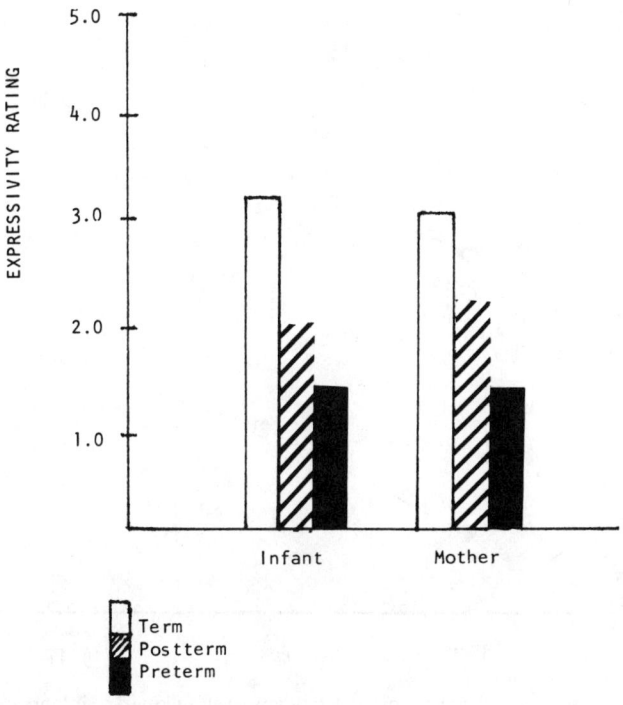

FIG. 1.5 Expressivity-rating (1 = negative expressivity, 5 = positive expressivity) of term, postterm, and preterm infants and their mothers during spontaneous face-to-face interaction.

threshold and as its upper limit an aversion threshold. An hypothetical activation band for normal infants is depicted by the dotted lines in Fig. 1.9. The lower limit reflects a threshold for accepting or attending to stimulation and the upper limit a threshold for rejecting or averting stimulation.

2. The upper and lower thresholds of this activation band may shift and the band width vary as a function of the infant's rest-activity and arousal cycles.

3. An intrinsic curvilinear relationship between stimulation and arousal/attention-affect processes suggests that only moderate stimulation (be that quantitatively moderate or moderately discrepant stimulation) would fall within the activation band. As the thresholds of the band shift, the relative discrepancy or amount of stimulation perceived by the infant may also shift.

4. Within the activation band positive affect may occur and vary in form and energy (e.g., from smiling to laughing) as a function of both the parameters of stimulation and the arousal level and attentive/affective response energy of the infant.

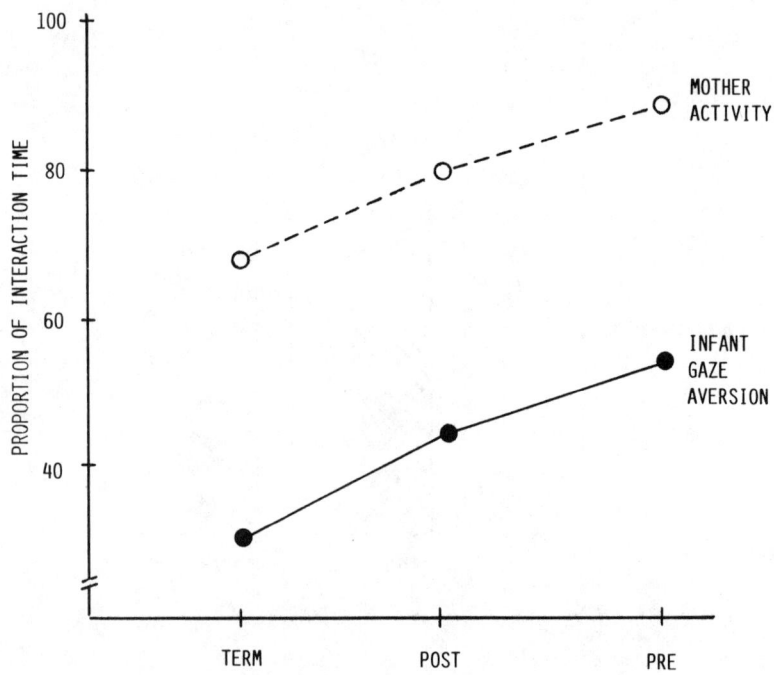

FIG. 1.6 Proportion of interaction time mothers spent talking and infants spent gazing at their mothers during spontaneous face-to-face interaction.

5. Moderate levels of positive affect such as smiling and laughing may serve to modulate arousal and sustain attention (Sroufe & Waters, 1976).

6. If and when stimulation and/or affective responsivity exceed moderate levels, the upper limit of the activation band is approached, at which point the infant will manifest an inattentive response (e.g. gaze aversion). If that limit or threshold is exceeded, an aversive reaction or negative affect (e.g. fussing or crying) will occur.

7. As the infant develops, arousal cycles may lengthen and the proposed activation band may widen as manifested by longer periods of attentiveness and more modulated affective responses.

8. The activation band width and thresholds vary as a function of individual differences.

9. The activation band may be narrower and the arousal cycles shorter in infants experiencing developmental delays or deficits (be they perceptual, motor, cognitive, or physiological delays or deficits). More specifically, as depicted in the upper solid curve of Fig. 1.9, there may be a narrower band for hypo-responsive infants such as preterm RDS, Down's syndrome, and

1. INTERACTION COACHING   13

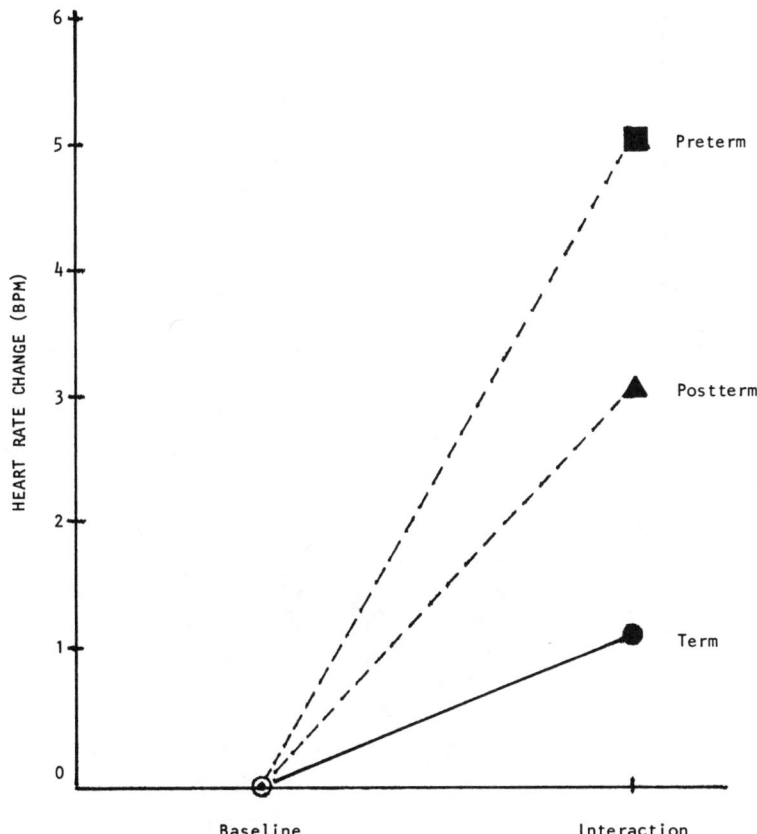

FIG. 1.7 Mean tonic heart rate change in beats per minute from baseline to spontaneous interaction for term, postterm, and preterm infants.

autistic infants, which may feature a higher-than-normal attention threshold and a lower-than-normal aversion threshold. Similarly, there may be a narrower band for hyper-active infants (e.g., postmature, hyperactive, and autistic infants). In contrast to the posited activation band of hyporesponsive infants, the band of hyper-reactive infants may be delimited by both lower attention and lower aversion thresholds (p. 58–59).

Based on Brazelton neonatal data on these infants (Field, et al., 1978), on neonatal responsivity and habituation to tactile and auditory stimulation (Field, Dempsey, Ting, Hatch, & Clifton, 1979; Rose, Schmidt, & Bridger, 1976), on data from interaction studies of these infants, (Field, 1977a, 1979b, 1981b), and on data from this study, we would hypothesize that preterm RDS infants have higher thresholds to stimulation and postterm, postmature infants have lower thresholds to stimulation, and both groups

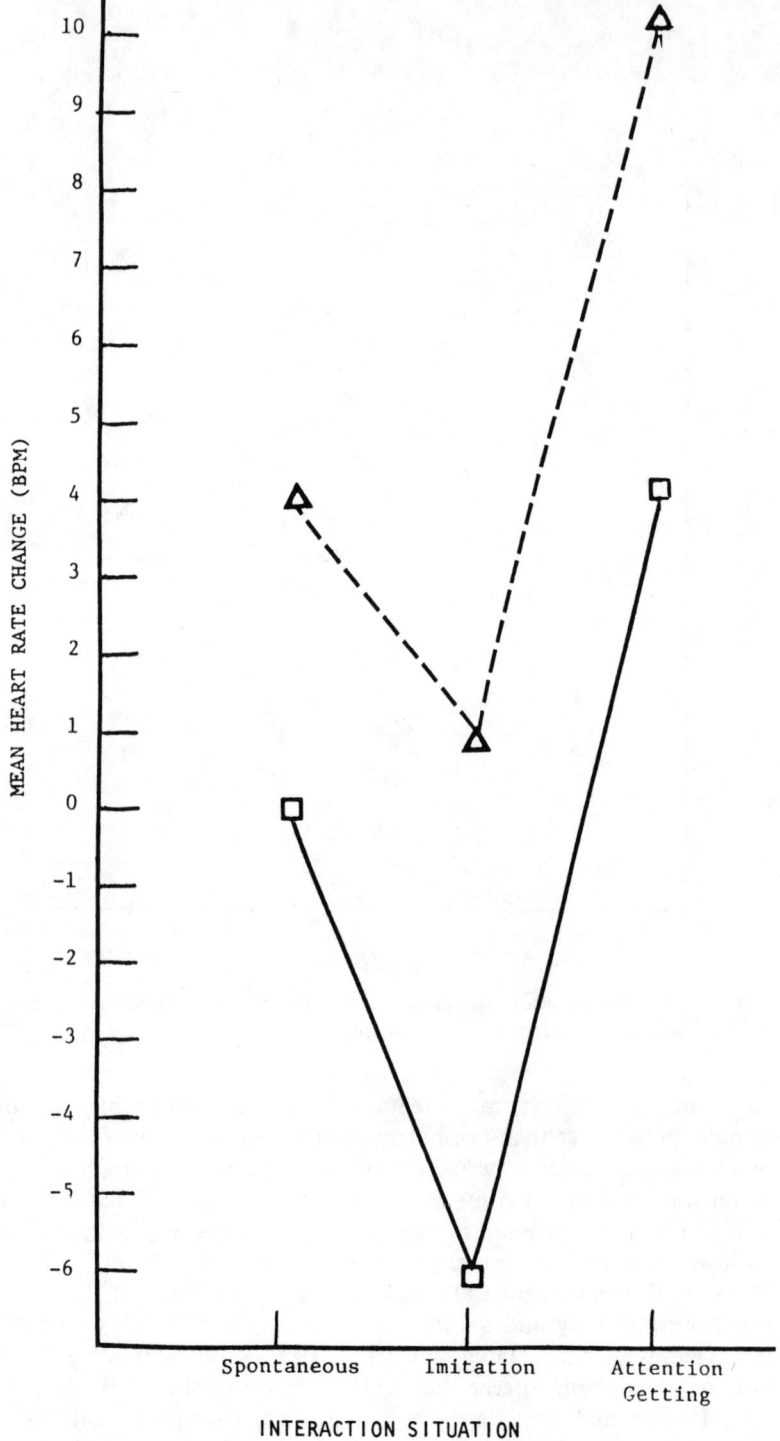

FIG. 1.8 Mean tonic heart rate change in beats per minute from baseline situation to spontaneous, imitation, and attention-getting manipulated interactions for normal infants (□ — □) and for high-risk infants (△---△).

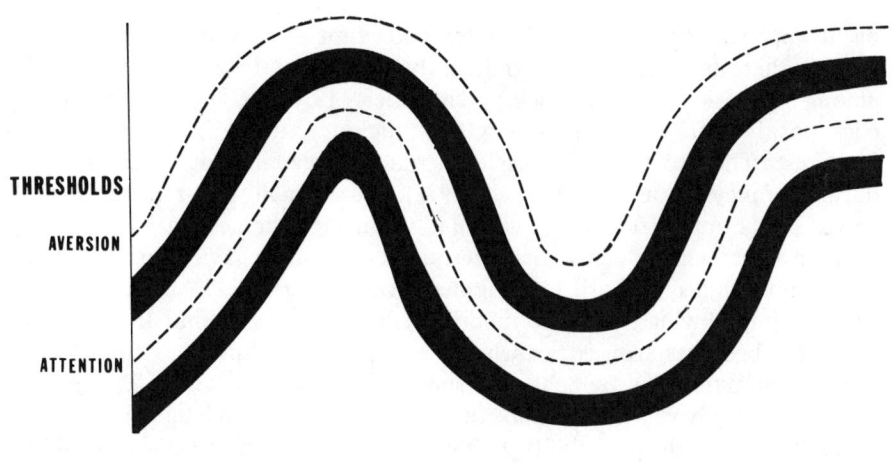

REST-ACTIVITY/AROUSAL CYCLES

FIG. 1.9 Posited activation band model. Upper solid line is posited activation band for preterm infants, broken line band for term infants and lower solid band for postterm infants. Lower and upper limits of band represent attention and aversion thresholds respectively and bands represent range of stimulation to which infant responds attentively and with positive affect.

have more delimited activation bands within which they show attentive and positive affective behaviors. The mother of the preterm RDS infant would need to provide more intense or variable stimulation to elicit her infant's attention whereas the mother of the postterm postmature would need to provide less intense or variable stimulation to elicit her infant's attention. But both groups may have narrower activation bands or a narrower range of stimulation to which they respond with attentiveness and positive affect. The mothers of these infants would, thus, be "walking a narrow line" in gauging their stimulation so as not to exceed the upper or aversion thresholds and elicit gaze averting or fussy behavior. The following study on gameplaying between these infants and their mothers was an attempt to study that question.

THRESHOLDS FOR STIMULATION DURING INFANT GAMES

Infant games such as "peek-a-boo," "pat-a-cake," "I'm gonna get you," "itsy bitsy spider," "so-big," and "tell me a story" have been noted to occur approximately 39% of the interaction time for normal infants and their mothers and fathers, but significantly less frequently (28% of the time) among high-risk infants and their parents (Field, 1979a). Games of this kind elicit positive affect such as smiling and laughing, and have been used by some researchers to assess the developmental course of smiling and laughter during infancy (Sroufe & Wunsch, 1972). Occasionally the repetition of games or the intensification of stimulation during a game that is eliciting positive affect will suddenly elicit averting and crying behaviors, as in "the child who laughed so hard his laughter turned to crying." An important rule of game playing may be to modify, reduce, or cease stimulation when the infant becomes aroused, or when the infant is attempting to modulate arousal, as manifested by behaviors such as smiling or laughter. The purpose of this study was to determine the infant's threshold to laughter during gameplaying and the probability with which gaze aversion and crying would closely follow laughter, or, the attention and aversion thresholds of these infants in the context of natural interaction activity such as gameplaying.

The gameplaying manipulation followed the spontaneous three-minute interactions described earlier. The mothers were given a demonstration of the game "I'm gonna get you." That game was selected because it is among the more popular games for this age infant (Field, 1979a). The mother's eyes widen and her head looms forward and contacts the infant's stomach. As the mother looms forward she repeatedly says, with increasing intensity, "I'm gonna get you", "I'm gonna get you." She then shakes her head on the infant's stomach as if tickling the infant with her head. The mothers were instructed to pause a few seconds between trials of the game and to cease playing the game at the point at which the infant began to laugh.

The mothers of the high-risk infants engaged in significantly less gameplaying and less variety of games during spontaneous interactions with their infants (See Table 1). Judging from the data on the gameplaying manipulation, the mothers may have played games less often because they were less effective in eliciting and sustaining positive affect in their infants. The preterm, RDS infants required a greater number of game trials before laughing, which may relate to their hypothesized higher thresholds, and the postmature infants required very few trials, which may relate to lower thresholds. However, both RDS and postmature infants were more likely than term infants to gaze avert subsequent to their laughter and cry subsequent to gaze aversion. Thus, once the high-risk infants began to laugh, they were also more likely to gaze avert and cry. Given that infant gaze aversion and crying are aversive to mothers, that is mothers often look distressed and show elevated heart rate during those behaviors (Field, 1979b), they will play games less frequently.

When the high-risk infants laughed during spontaneous interactions their mothers were less likely to decrease or cease stimulation (see Table 1.1).

TABLE 1.1
Means for gameplaying measures

	GROUPS		
	Term	RDS	Postmature
Spontaneous interactions			
1. Gameplaying time (%)	39	22	21
2. Different games (#)	4.2	2.3	1.9
3. Probability of mother decreasing or ceasing stimulation			
- Post laughter (%)	62	38	41
- Post gaze aversion (%)	71	57	53
- Post crying (%)	84	64	67
"I'm gonna get you" Game			
1. Trials to laughter (#)	4.6	2.1	7.3
2. Probability gaze aversion (%)	18	47	57
3. Probability crying (%)	07	43	41

Perhaps because laughter was a rare event, they wanted to prolong their infant's laughter when it occurred. Unfortunately, sustaining the stimulation that had elicited laughter appeared to have the opposite effect. Instead of prolonging laughter, continued stimulation led to gaze aversion and in some cases, crying. The mothers of these high-risk infants seem to be faced with the task of providing only the necessary amount of stimulation to elicit a response, and having a narrower range within which they can behave without "driving" the infant to aversive behaviors. Upon eliciting a positive affective behavior, the mother may have to realize that "more of the same stimulation" may not sustain that positive affective behavior. The infants' "high arousal" behaviors such as laughter, gaze aversion, and crying must be read as signals that the infant may need a break to process information and modulate arousal.

Elevated heart rate during these interactions suggests that the infant may be aroused autonomically during smiles, laughter, gaze aversion, and crying. Although heart rate increases surrounding these behaviors typically have been attributed to movement artifacts, a number of studies have reported that the heart rate accelerations occur prior to these behaviors. For example, in a study by Stoller and Field (1981), heart rate acceleration occurred prior to gaze aversion with heart rate returning to baseline during the gaze aversion period (Field, 1981d). Similarly, heart rate acceleration preceded crying behavior in a study by Vaughn and Sroufe (1979). Thus, smiling, laughter, gaze aversion, and crying may be the affective components of autonomic arousal. They may serve as signals to the mother that the infant is aroused and thereby may function as effective "cut-off" behaviors or behaviors which serve to minimize incoming stimulation. During laughter, for example, the eyes are often closed and the ears may also be unreceptive to external stimulation as the peals of one's own laughter predominate. Gaze aversion and crying may even more effectively block external stimulation.

Smiles and laughter may be tension release behaviors which enable the infant to modulate arousal while still maintaining attention to the stimulation (Fogel, Diamond, Langhorst & Demos, 1981; Sroufe et al., 1974). Mothers, at least, treat these behaviors as signals to modulate their own behavior. For example, most of the mothers of normal infants reduced stimulation at the point at which infants laughed, and fewer mothers waited until the infant gaze averted or cried. There appears to be a relationship between the infant's ability to modulate arousal with smiles and laughter without reverting to gaze aversion and crying and the mother's immediate reduction in stimulation following the smiling and laughter behaviors. A schematic illustration of this progression of behaviors during gameplaying can be seen in Fig. 1.10. The X axis depicts sustained attention of the infant and variation or modulation of stimulation by the mother. The Y axis depicts heart rate. Within the figure the solid ascending curve represents increasing heart rate and the dotted descending curves represent decreasing heart rate. The hatched bars represent variation in the mothers' use of stimulus modalities or varying intensity of stimulation (the "adding on" and "dropping out" of behaviors by mothers). Heart rate is depicted as progressively increasing prior to smiling, laughing, gaze averting, and crying behaviors. As the behaviors occur, the level of maternal stimulation decreases, heart rate peaks and gradually returns to baseline. Thus, the affective displays may enable the infant to modulate arousal and may serve as signals to the mother to modulate stimulation. If the infant is less able to modulate arousal or has a more limited repertoire of affective displays, or if the mother is not responsive to the affective displays by modulating stimulation, the infant's aversive threshold may be exceeded and the infant may gaze avert and cry, essentially terminating the game.

High-risk infants such as preterm RDS and postterm postmature infants may have more difficulty modulating arousal, as is suggested by the lower incidence of positive affective displays in these infants and the greater probability with which they progress from laughter to gaze aversion to crying during the "I'm gonna get you" game. The mothers of these infants may have more difficulty reading their infants' signals (in part because they occur less frequently) and greater difficulty modulating stimulation (perhaps

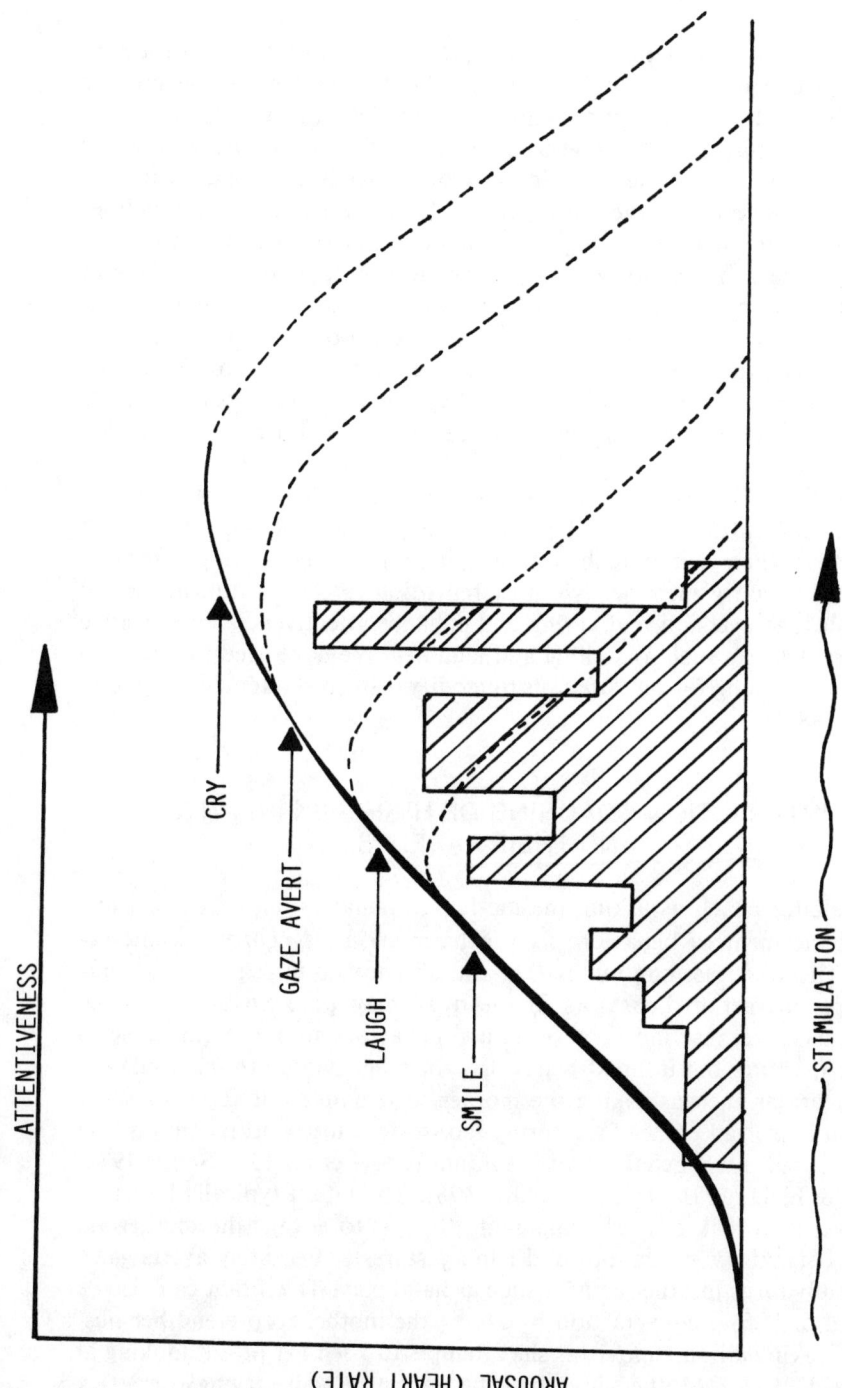

FIG. 1.10 A schematic illustration of the progression of infant and mother behaviors during gameplaying. The X axes depict sustained attention of the infant and variation or modulation of stimulation by the mother. The Y axis depicts heart rate. Within the figure the solid ascending curves represent increasing heart rate and the dotted descending curves represent decreasing heart rate. The hatched bars represent variation in the mother's use of stimulus modalities or varying intensity of stimulation.

because they are "seeking more of the pleasure" associated with their infants' infrequent smiling and laughter). This is suggested by their lower probabilities of decreasing stimulation following infant laughter, gaze averting, and crying. The hypothesized differences between the behavioral curves of normal and high-risk infant-mother dyads are depicted in Fig. 1.11. The uppermost curve represents the high-risk dyad with the mother starting her stimulation at a high enough level to attract her infant's attention, as appears necessary with a preterm RDS infant, for example. But then, she sustains that level despite infant gaze aversion and crying. In contrast, the lower curve, representing the interaction of the normal infant-mother dyad, shows varied or modulated stimulation provided by the mother in response to the infant's affective signals and a cessation of her behavior as the infant gaze averts and before the infant reaches a crying state.

Determining the origins of interaction problems in these complex streams of behavior is difficult at best. However, manipulations of interactions such as asking mothers to imitate their infants, maintain silence during gaze aversion, and simplify their behaviors by repetition (Field, 1981e), appear to diminish gaze aversion and crying and enhance attentiveness and positive affective displays such as smiling and laughter. We have used the term interaction coaching for our attempts to modify disturbed interactions (Field, 1978a, 1981e).

INTERACTION COACHING OF HIGH-RISK INFANTS AND THEIR PARENTS

Manipulations such as asking the mother to remain stone-faced or show the enhancement of behaviors seen in harmonious, synchronous interactions. The basic assumption is that the absence or infrequency of harmonious interaction behaviors in the dyad may be contributing to the disturbance. Because mothers' or adults' behaviors are more amenable to change than are the infants' behaviors, their behaviors are manipulated. Manipulations such as asking the mother to remain stone-faced or show her profile instead of her face during face-to-face interaction demonstrate the effects of adult behavior on the infant (Fogel et al, 1981 Stern, 1974; Stoller & Field, 1981; Tronick et al., 1978). The infant typically looks inquisitive, then makes several apparent attempts to engage the mother via greeting signals (vocalizations and hand gestures), alternately averts gaze, and finally turns to other activity such as hand play. The infant can also be "turned-off" to a conversation by asking the mother to pretend her husband is taking a home movie as she attempts to keep her infant looking at her (Field, 1977a). Mothers invariably became more active trying every trick

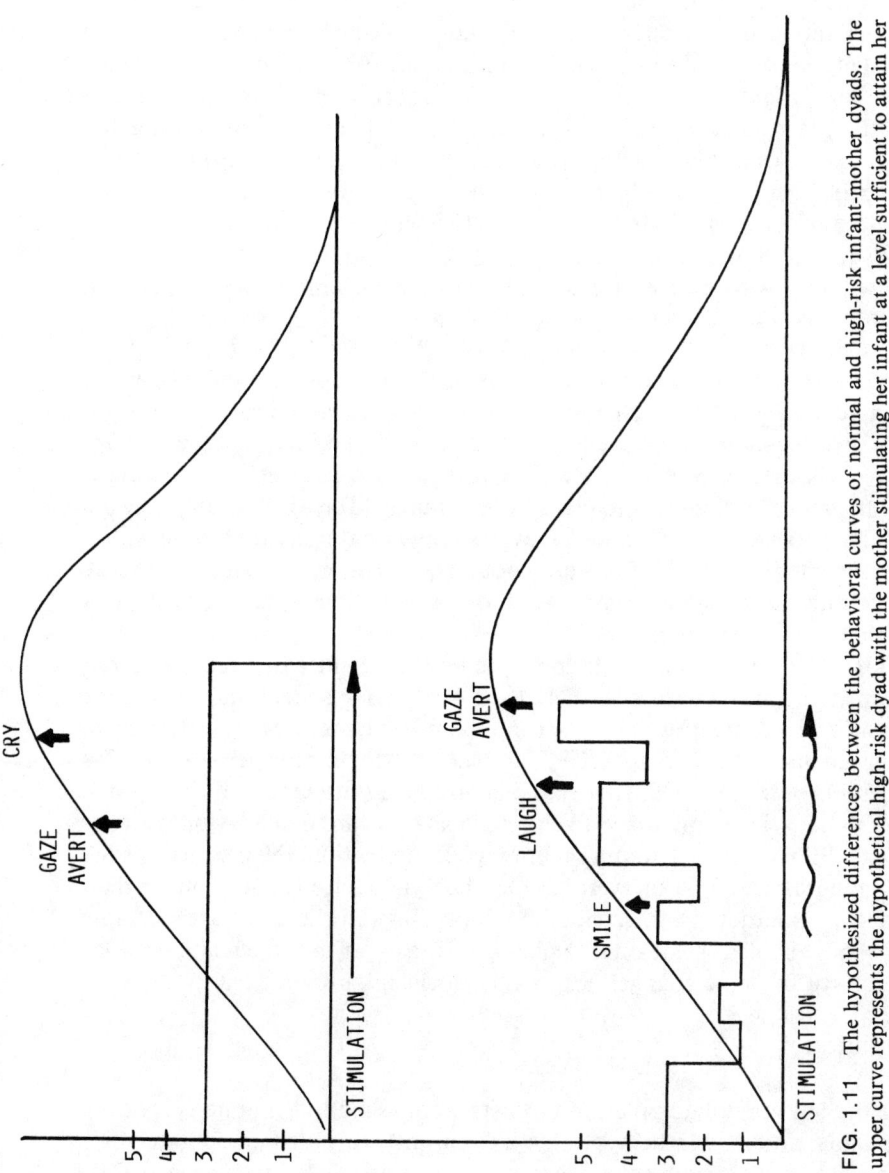

FIG. 1.11 The hypothesized differences between the behavioral curves of normal and high-risk infant-mother dyads. The upper curve represents the hypothetical high-risk dyad with the mother stimulating her infant at a level sufficient to attain her infant's attention but then sustaining that level rather than modulating stimulation during infant gaze aversion and crying. The lower curve depicts the normal infant-mother dyad, showing varied or modulated stimulation by the mother in response to the infant's affective signals and a cessation of her behavior as the infant averts with the infant never reaching a crying state.

in their repertoire to sustain the infant's eye contact. The infant, in turn, was given no time to respond, and subsequently averted gaze, squirmed, and fussed for the duration of the interaction.

Facilitative manipulations have included asking the mother to count slowly to herself as she interacts (Tronick et al., 1978), asking her to imitate all of her infant's behaviors (Field, 1977a) repeat her words slowly (Field, 1977b; Stern, Beebe, Jaffe, & Bennett, 1977,) or be silent during her infant's sucking and looking away periods (Field, 1977b, 1978a). These manipulations vary in their effectiveness. However, each of them has resulted in longer periods of eye contact, fewer distress vocalizations, and less squirming on the part of the infant (Field, 1981e).

I will review data here for manipulations in which mothers were asked to imitate their infants' behaviors, to repeat their own verbal expressions, and to remain silent when their infants looked away from them. These types of manipulations were intended to simplify and "slow down" the interactive behaviors of mothers. Other manipulations were intended to introduce variety and complexity in the mother's behaviors. Techniques used here included asking the mother to "keep her infant looking at her" (an attention-getting manipulation) and to play "infant games" for which examples were provided. Because all of these behaviors appear naturally during the spontaneous interactions of infants and mothers, we merely intended to increase the occurrence of these behaviors and observe the effects of these increases on the infant's behavior.

For all of these manipulations preterm RDS infants were observed because, as was described earlier, they were less attentive and responsive during early interactions and their middle income mothers were overactive resulting in somewhat disturbed interactions (Field, 1977a, 1979b). The general procedure was to first film a spontaneous interaction during which the mother was simply asked to "pretend she was at home playing with her infant." Following a 3-minute spontaneous interaction, the instructions for a 3-minute manipulation were given. The dyads were given no more than two manipulations per session. Multiple sessions and a large sample ($N = 60$) enabled the counterbalancing of the order of these manipulations to control for state changes across time spent in an infant seat.

Imitation

For the imitation manipulation mothers were asked to "imitate everything the baby does." Mothers of this age infant are noted to imitate their infant's behaviors with some frequency (Pawlby, 1977; Trevarthen, 1974). Although some of the mothers expressed that they felt "a bit silly imitating hiccups and cry behaviors," they otherwise did not feel uncomfortable with this activity.

1. INTERACTION COACHING   23

The tapes were continuously coded for imitations by the mother, the criterion being behaviors of the same form and modality of the infant's behavior and occurring within three seconds of the behavior of the infant. The tapes were also coded for infant gaze at mother, defined as head aligned on the same horizontal and vertical plane as the mother's head.

Although the incidence of imitative behavior on the part of the mother was relatively high during the spontaneous interactions, there was a significant increase in imitative behavior during this manipulation (See Fig. 1.12). The amount of infant gaze at mother, as predicted, increased significantly during the imitation manipulation.

The infant may look longer or require less "time-out" or breaks in the conversation to process the mother's imitative behaviors, because they are by definition behaviors which are similar to behaviors already in the infant's repertoire and thus more easily assimilated or processed by the infant. Many of the imitations evolved into repetition or chains of the same

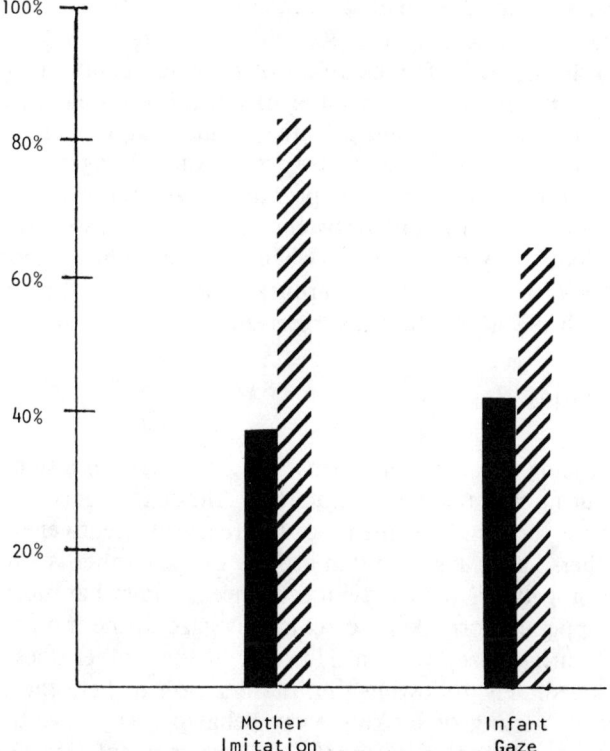

FIG. 1.12   Percentage of infant behaviors imitated by the mother during spontaneous interaction and imitation manipulation and percentage of interaction time infants gazed at mother during those interactions (■ spontaneous, ▨ manipulation).

behaviors with the mother imitating the infant's behavior followed by the infant's repetition of his own behavior (or his imitation of the mother's imitation) as in a secondary circular reaction or in an infant game.

Repetition of Phrases

Fogel (1977) and Stern et al, (1977) have noted the frequent occurrence of repetitions by mothers of this age infant. Repetition of phrases such as "Hi ya.", comprised approximately 64% of the mothers' phrases. This behavior was also noted to occur with some frequency during spontaneous interactions as can be seen in Fig. 1.13. The percentage figure here refers to the proportion of all verbal phrases (a phrase typically being two to three words followed by a pause) which were immediately repeated and closely approximated the initial phrase without considering intonation curves. As expected, the mother's repetition of phrases increased during the manipulation, and the mean proportion of interaction time the infants spent looking at the mother also increased. The same interpretation made for the effectiveness of imitation may apply here. Repetition of phrases may simplify the processing of information for the infant. Although, the infant's processing of the content of phrases or the meaning of words is not well understood, at least the intonation quality and affective displays accompanying phrases may be more readily assimilated if they are repeated. Longer looking by the infant during a manipulation which presumably simplifies the information processing task of the infant is consistent with the notion we have advanced that infants look away or gaze avert when stimulation has exceeded the infant's capacity to modulate the arousal and process the information associated with the stimulation just received.

Silencing During Pauses

Mothers' silencing during infants' pauses or gaze aversions also occurs quite frequently during spontaneous interactions. Although silence during infant gaze aversion is thought by some to lead to renewed attentiveness of the infant, and others have suggested that activity of the mother is a more effective "attention-getter," the behavior sequence is somewhat more complex. The infant appears more likely to return his gaze to the mother if she remains silent during gaze aversion. However, if the mother does not emit a behavior immediately following the infant's gaze at her, the infant will revert to gaze averting or looking away behavior. This reverting to gaze aversion is frequently noted during the still-face manipulation (Fogel et al., 1980; Stoller & Field, 1981; Trevarthen, 1974; Tronick et al., 1978). The proportion of the pausing time that the mother remained silent increased

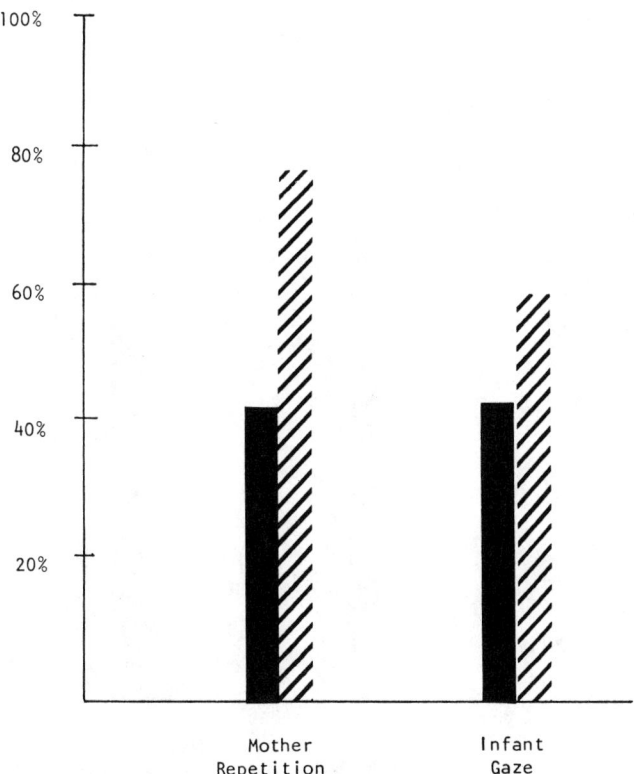

FIG. 1.13 Percentage of mothers' verbal phrases which were repeated during spontaneous interaction and repetition manipulation and percentage of interaction time infants gazed at mother during those interactions (■ spontaneous, ▨ manipulation).

during this manipulation (See Fig. 1.14). A parallel decrease was noted in the proportion of interaction time the infant spent pausing.

Similar interpretations were made for the effectiveness of each of these manipulations. The mothers' behaviors were simplified; the infants were faced with a simpler arousal modulation and information processing task and thus could sustain visual attentiveness to the mother for longer periods without requiring breaks in the interactions. Other types of manipulations, for example, asking the mother "to get her infant's attention" or to engage in stimulating infant games such as "I'm gonna get you," have been noted to elicit increases in infant gazing-away or gaze aversion behaviors (Field, 1977a; Field, 1979b). Those manipulations, that of "attention-getting" and gameplaying were included in our interaction coaching series. We expected that these might be effective for the interactions of mothers who were naturally very quiet and inactive during spontaneous interactions.

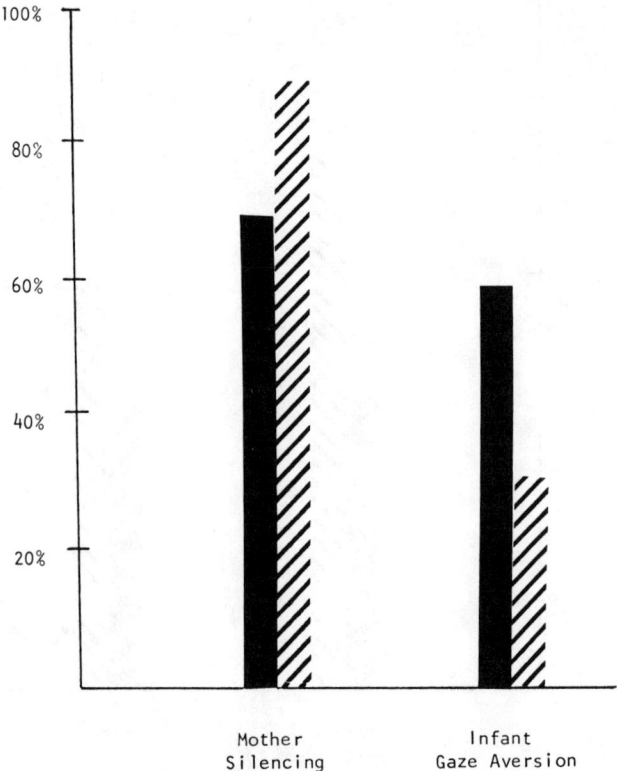

FIG. 1.14 Percentage of infant pauses or gazes away from the mother during which the mother remained silent during the spontaneous interaction and during the silencing manipulation and percentage of interaction time infants gaze averted during those interactions (■ spontaneous, ▨ manipulation).

Attention-getting

Because this manipulation had been noted previously to result in excessive gaze aversion on the part of the infant (Field, 1977a), it was always presented last. The mothers were simply asked to keep their infants looking at them. Most of the mothers immediately began to talk, to make funny sounds, make exaggerated facial expressions, to wave their hands about, and to realign their face in front of the infant's face whenever the infant gaze averted. As can be seen in Figure 15, there were dramatic increases in mother vocalization and decreases in infant gazing at mother. Several behaviors which frequently occur during spontaneous interactions such as imitation, silencing during pauses, were no longer present. An exception occurred for mothers who received the imitation manipulation prior to the attention-getting manipulation. These mothers appeared to have learned that imitation is an effective attention-maintaining strategy. Typically, the mothers, in their attempts to sustain their infants' attention, provided excessive amounts of stimulation in all modalities. In addition, they no longer appeared to attend to their infants' gaze signals. This was a stressful manipulation for the infant because it constituted a "stimulus overload" and because the infants were not given any pauses or breaks in the conversation to process the stimulation or modulate their apparently high arousal levels.

Gameplaying Manipulation

The game, "I'm gonna get you," was used for this manipulation because of its popularity among the sample of infants and mothers described earlier in this chapter. As would be expected the incidence of gameplaying increased

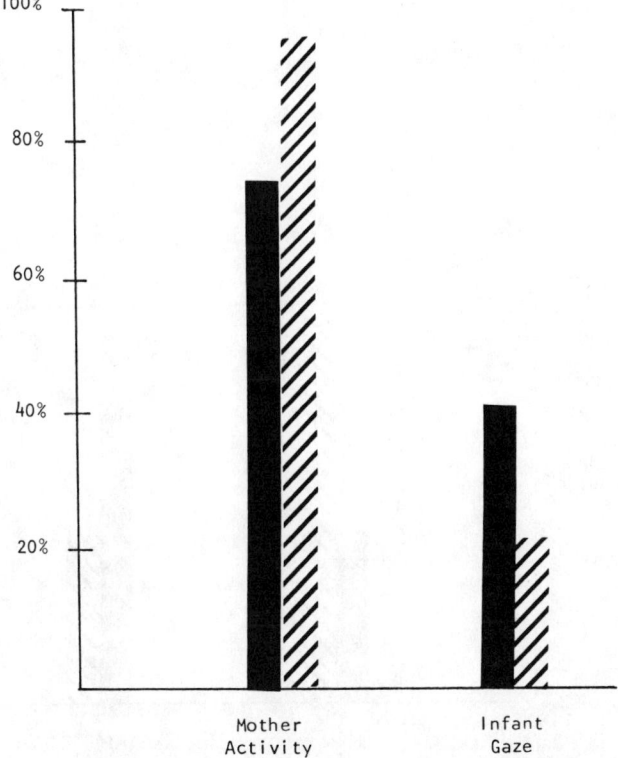

FIG. 1.15 Percentage of interaction time that mother was active during spontaneous interaction and attention-getting manipulation and percentage of interaction time infants gazed at mother during those interactions (■ spontaneous, ▨ manipulation).

during this manipulation. In turn, the infants showed less gazing at the mothers (see Fig. 1.16), although the incidence of their affective displays (e.g. smiling and laughing) was considerably elevated during this manipulation. This suggests that arousal levels of the infants were increased. Had the mothers varied the game or its intensity or simply paused for periods of time between bouts of the game, the infants may have had sufficient time to modulate arousal. However, in compliance with the instructions to repeat the game, mothers persisted in playing the same game. Although the infants may have habituated to the particular game, "I'm gonna get you," it appeared rather that their high arousal levels derived from their being given no pauses or breaks in the repetitions of the game.

Despite greater gaze aversion for most of the infants during the "attention-getting" and gameplaying manipulations, approximately 11 of the 60 infants showed increases in gazing at mother during these manipulations. When we examined the spontaneous interactions of these infants and

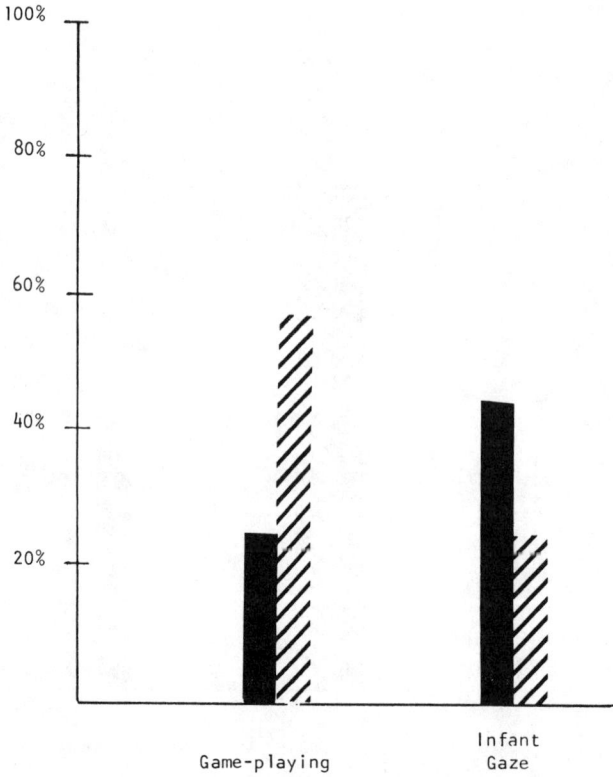

FIG. 1.16 Percentage of interaction time that mother engaged in infant games during spontaneous interaction and during gameplaying manipulation and percentage of time infant gazed at mother during those interactions (■ spontaneous, ▨ manipulation).

their mothers, we noted that the mothers were active for less than half of the interaction time ($M = 39\%$). However, during these manipulations they became more active (M = 63% for the attention-getting manipulation and 58% for the gameplaying manipulation). Thus, although these manipulations typically increased the activity levels of the mothers and decreased their infants' visual attentiveness, there were some dyads for which an increase in mothers' activity level contributed to an increase in infant attentiveness. This result highlights the need to first assess the baseline interactions of the individual dyad. While belonging to a group of middle income mothers of preterm, RDS babies, who have been noted to be extremely active during interactions (Field, 1977a), these 11 mothers were clearly less active than the larger group. The earlier manipulations for simplifying and slowing down the activity of these mothers who were already extremely inactive would have clearly been inappropriate and ineffective. In this same vein, careful consideration in tailoring individual interaction coaching techniques for mothers of high-risk infants must be given to socioeconomic and cultural group differences. Dramatic differences in early interactions have been observed both within and across cultures (Field, Sostek, Vietze, & Leiderman, 1981; Field & Widmayer, 1981) and even among groups who have similar native language and lifestyles (Field & Pawlby, 1980).

Because most mothers who are experiencing difficult interactions with their infants are aware of and concerned about those difficulties, they are usually willing to try anything. However, although the manipulations used in these interaction coaching sessions were effective and were well-received by the infants' mothers, the degree to which these manipulations facilitated their ongoing interactions is not clear. Nonetheless, these data suggest that mothers and high-risk infants can be taught other ways to interact.

SUMMARY

Two of the most disturbing adult-adult interaction patterns, that of "interrupting" and that of "latent responding", appear to occur during the early interactions of high-risk infants and their middle income mothers. The high-risk infant is relatively unresponsive as is a "latent-to-respond" adult and the mother appears to be overstimulating not unlike an "interrupting" adult. Although the direction of effects is unclear and interpretations of these behaviors are somewhat speculative, high-risk infant–mother dyads appear to be ineffectual in sustaining a reciprocal, harmonious interaction.

Our studies on the attentive, affective, and physiological behaviors of two groups of high-risk infants, the preterm, respiratory distress syndrome and the postterm, postmaturity syndrome infant, suggest that these infants are less attentive, show fewer positive affective responses such as smiling and laughing and more distress behaviors such as gaze averting, fussing, and elevated heart rate than normal term infants. Their mothers, while also showing fewer positive affective behaviors, provide more verbal and tactile stimulation during interactions.

A model was presented suggesting that attention and aversion thresholds may differ in these infants. The mothers of preterm RDS infants, for example, may have to provide more stimulation than mothers of term infants to elicit their infants' attention and affective responsivity. However, they then may have to carefully modulate their behaviors so as not to approach the infants' aversion thresholds manifested by gaze aversion, crying, and elevated heart rate. The activation band, or range of stimulation to which the preterm RDS infants will attend and respond positively may be narrower than that of the normal term infant, placing the constraint on the mother of having to carefully modulate her stimulation. Data were presented on a game-playing manipulation which revealed that preterm, RDS infants required more trials and postterm, postmaturity infants required fewer trials of an "I'm gonna get you" game to respond with laughter, suggesting that their thresholds to laughter were higher and lower respectively. Their mothers had more difficulty modulating (decreasing or ceasing) their stimulation as the infants' laughter turned to gaze aversion and crying. Mothers of these infants appeared to be "walking a narrow line" in gauging their stimulation so as not to exceed the aversion thresholds of their infants and elicit gaze averting or fussy behavior.

Elevated heart rate of the infants suggested that they may be autonomically aroused during smiling, laughter, gaze aversion, and crying. Smiling, laughter, gaze aversion, and crying may be the affective components of antonomic arousal. These affective displays may serve as signals to the mother that the infant is aroused and thereby may function as effective "cut-off" behaviors or signals to the mother to modulate or minimize the amount of stimulation she provides in order that the infant may process the information just received. Information processing and/or arousal modulation abilities of these high-risk infants may be less developed, as outlined in our activation band model. Thus, the stimulation modulation task of their mothers may be more difficult.

That high-risk infants and their mothers can interact more harmoniously is illustrated by the interaction manipulations or interaction coaching exercises we have investigated. Simple exercises such as asking the mother to imitate her infant's behaviors, to repeat her phrases, or to remain silent during her infant's pauses or "breaks" in the conversation proved effective in reducing the amount of stimulation she provided (and probably also in increasing her sensitivity to the infant's interaction signals and in increasing her contingent responsivity). In turn her infant's attentiveness and affective responsivity was enhanced. Thus, it would appear that mothers and high-risk infants can be taught more effective ways to interact with each other.

REFERENCES

Als, H., Tronick, E., & Brazelton, T. B. Stages of early behavioral organization: The study of a sighted infant and a blind infant in interaction with their mothers. In T. Field, S. Goldberg, D. Stern & A. Sostek (Eds.), *High-risk infants and children: Adult and peer interactions.* New York: Academic Press, 1980.

Bakeman, R., & Brown, J. Early interaction: Consequences for social and mental development at three years. *Child Development,* 1980, *51,* 437–477.

Bee, H. L., VanEgeren, L. F., Streissguth, A. P., Nyman, B. A., & Lockie, M. S. Social class differences in maternal teaching styles and speech patterns. *Development Psychology,* 1969, *1,* 726–734.

Berkowitz, L. Some determinants of impulse aggression: Role of mediated associations with reinforcements for aggression. *Psychological Review,* 1974, *81,* 165–176.

Brazelton, T. B. *Neonatal Behavioral Assessment Scale.* London: Spastics International Medical Publications, 1973.

Brown, J. M., & Bakeman, R. Relationships of human mothers with their infants during the first year of life: Effect of prematurity. In R. W. Bell & W. P. Smotherman (Eds.), *Maternal influences and early behavior.* New York: Spectrum, 1979.

Callaghan, J. Face-to-face interaction styles: A comparison of Anglo, Hopi, and Navajo mothers and infants. In T. Field, A. Sostek, P. Vietze, & A. H. Leiderman (Eds.), *Culture and early interactions.* Hillsdale, N.J.: Lawrence Erlbaum Associates, 1981.

Chapple, E. D. Experimental production of transients in human interaction. *Nature,* 1970, *288,* November, 14.

Cicchetti, D., & Sroufe, L. A. An organizational view of affect: Illustration from the study of Down's Syndrome infants. In M. Lewis & L. A. Rosenblum (Eds.), *The development of affect,* Vol. 1. New York: Plenum, 1978.

DiVitto, B., & Goldberg, S. The effects of newborn medical status on early parent-infant interactions. In T. Field, A. Sostek, S. Goldberg, & H. H. Shuman (Eds.), *Infants born at risk.* New York: Spectrum, 1979.

Dunst, C. J. Developmental characteristics of communicative acts among Down's syndrome infants and nonretarded infants. Paper presented at the biennial meeting of the Southeastern Conference on Human Development, Alexandria, VA, April, 1980.

Ekman, P., & Friesen, W. V. *Unmasking the face.* Englewood Cliffs, N.J.: Prentice-Hall, 1975.

Field, T. Effects of early separation, interactive deficits and experimental manipulations on infant-mother face-to-face interaction. *Child Development,* 1977, *48,* 763–771. (a)

Field, T. Interactions of high-risk infants with various social partners. Paper presented at the Biennial Meeting of the Society for Research in Child Development, Denver, April, 1977. (b)

Field, T. The three Rs of infant-adult interactions: Rhythms, repertoires, and responsibility. *Journal of Pediatric Psychology,* 1978, *3,* 131–136. (a)

Field, T. Games parents play with normal and high-risk infants. *Child Psychiatry and Human Development,* 1979, *10,* 41–48. (a)

Field, T. Interaction patterns of high-risk and normal infants. In T. Field, A. Sostek, S. Goldberg, & H. H. Shuman (Eds.), *Infants born at risk.* New York: Spectrum, 1979. (b)

Field, T. Interactions of preterm and term infants with their lower and middle class teenage and adult mothers. In T. Field, S. Goldberg, D. Stern & A. Sostek (Eds.), *High-risk infants and children: Adult and peer interactions.* New York: Academic Press, 1980. (a)

Field, T., & Pawlby, S. Early face-to-face interactions of British and American working and middle class mother-infant dyads. *Child Development,* 1980, *51,* 250–253. (b)

Field, T. Fathers' interactions with their high-risk infants. *Infant Mental Health Journal,* 1981, *2,* 249–256. (a)

Field, T. Gaze behavior of normal and high-risk infants during early interactions. *Journal of the American Academy of Child Psychiatry,* 1981, *20,* 308-317.

Field, T. Infant arousal, attention, and affect during early interactions. In L. Lipsitt & C. K. Rovee-Collier (Eds.), *Advances in infant development.* Vol. 1. Hillsdale, N.J.: Lawrence Erlbaum Associates, 1981. (c)

Field, T. Infant gaze aversion and heart rate during face-to-face interactions. *Infant Behavior and Development,* 1981, *4,* 307-316.

Field, T. Interaction coaching for high-risk infants and their parents. In H. Moss (Ed.), *Prevention and Human Sciences.* New York: Haworth Press, 1981. (e)

Field, T., Dempsey, J., & Shuman, H. Developmental follow-up of pre- and postterm infants. In S. L. Friedman & M. Sigman (Eds.), *Preterm birth and psychological development.* New York: Academic Press, 1981.

Field, T., Dempsey, J., Ting, G., Hatch, J., & Clifton, R. Cardiac and behavioral responses to repeated tactile and auditory stimulation by preterm and full term infants during the neonatal period. *Developmental Psychology,* 1979, *15,* 406-416.

Field, T., Hallock, N., Dempsey, J., & Shuman, H. Mothers' assessments of term infants and preterm infants with respiratory distress syndrome: Reliability and predictive validity. *Child Psychiatry and Human Development,* 1978, *9,* 75-85.

Field, T., Hallock, N., Ting, G., Dempsey, J., Dabiri, C., & Shuman, H. H. A first year follow-up of high-risk infants: Formulating a comulative risk index. *Child Development,* 1978, *49,* 119-131.

Field, T., Sostek, A., Vietze, P., & Leiderman, P. H. *Culture and early interactions.* Hillsdale, N.J.: Lawrence Erlbaum Associates, 1981. (c)

Field, T., & Widmayer, S. Mother-infant interactions among lower SES Black, Cuban, Puerto Rican, and South American immigrants. In T. Field, A. Sostek, P. Vietze, & A. H. Leiderman (Ed.), *Culture and early interactions.* Hillsdale, N.J.: Lawrence Erlbaum Associates, 1981.

Field, T., Widmayer, S., Stringer, S., & Ignatoff, E. Teenage, lower class black mothers and their preterm infants: An intervention and developmental follow-up *Child Development,* 1980, *51,* 426-436.

Fogel, A. The role of repetition in the mother-infant face-to-face interaction. In H. R. Schaffer (Ed.), *Studies in mother-infant interaction.* London: Academic Press, 1977.

Fogel, A., Diamond, G. R., Langhorst, B. H., & Demos, V. Affective and cognitive aspects of the two-month-old's participation in face-to-face interaction with its mother. In E. Tronick (Ed.), *Joint regulation of behavior.* Cambridge, England: Cambridge University Press, 1981.

Goldberg, S., Brachfeld, S., & DiVitto, B. Feeding, fussing, and playing: Parent-infant interaction in the first year as a function of prematurity and prenatal problems. In T. Field, S. Goldberg, D. Stein, & A. Sostek (Eds.), *High risk infants and children: Adult and peer interactions.* New York: Academy Press, 1980.

Greenberg, N. H. A comparison of infant-mother interactional behavior in infants with atypical behavior and normal infants. In J. Hellmuth (Ed.), *Exceptional infant,* Vol. 2, N.Y.: Brunner/Mazel, 1971.

Jones, O. H. M. Mother-child communication with pre-linguistic Downs' syndrome and normal infants. In H. R. Schaffer (Ed.), *Studies in mother-infant interaction.* London: Academic Press, 1977.

Kogan, K. L. Interaction systems between preschool aged handicapped or developmentally delayed children and their parents. In T. Field, S. Goldberg, D. Stern, & A. Sostek (Eds.), *High-risk infants and children: Adult and peer interactions.* New York: Academic Press, 1980.

Kubicek, L. Mother interactions of twins: An autistic and non-autistic twin. In T. Field, S.

Goldberg, D. Stern, & A. Sostek (Eds.), *High-risk infants and children: Adult and peer interactions.* New York: Academic Press, 1980.

Massie, H. N. Pathologic interactions in infancy. In T. Field, S. Goldberg, D. Stern, & A. Sostek (Eds.), *High-risk infants and children: Adult and peer interactions.* New York: Academic Press, 1980.

McQuiston, S., McCarthy, M. E., MacTurk, R. H., & Vietze, P. Mother-infant face-to-face interaction in 3- and 6-month-old Down syndrome infants. Paper presented at the annual meeting of the American Association on Mental Deficiency, San Francisco, May, 1980.

Oster, H., & Ekman, P. Facial behavior in child development. In *Minnesota Symposium on Child Psychology,* Vol. 11. Minneapolis, M.N.: University of Minnesota Press, 1978.

Pawlby, S. Imitative interaction. In H. R. Schaffer (Ed.), *Studies in mother-infant interaction.* London: Academic Press, 1977.

Rose, S. A., Schmidt, K., & Bridger, W. M. Cardiac and behavioral responsivity to tactile stimulation in premature and full-term infants. *Developmental Psychology,* 1976, *12,* 311-320.

Sigman, M., Cohen, S. E., & Forsythe, A. B. The relations of early infant measures to later development. In S. L. Friedman & M. Sigman (Eds.), *Preterm birth and psychological development.* New York: Academic Press, 1981.

Sokolov, E. N. *Perception and the conditional reflex.* New York: MacMillan, 1963.

Sroufe, L. A. & Waters, E. The ontogenesis of smiling and laughter: A perspective in the organization of development in infancy. *Psychological Review,* 1976, *83,* 173-189.

Sroufe, L. A., & Wunsch, J. P. The development of laughter in the first year of life. *Child Development,* 1972, *43,* 1326-1344.

Sroufe, L. A., Waters, E., & Matas, L. Contextual determinants of infant affective response. In M. Lewis & L. Rosenblum (Eds.), *The origins of behavior, Vol. 2: Fear.* New York: Wiley, 1974.

Stern, D. A micro-analysis of mother-infant interactions: Behavior regulating social contact between a mother and her 3½-month-old twins. *Journal of American Academy of Child Psychiatry,* 1971, *10,* 501-517.

Stern, D. N. Mother and infant at play. In M. Lewis & L. Rosenblum (Eds.), *The effect of the infant on its caregiver.* New York: Wiley, 1974.

Stern, D., Beebe, B., Jaffe, J., & Bennett, S. L. The infant's stimulus world during social interaction: A study of caregiver behaviors with particular reference to repetition and timing. In H. R. Schaffer (Eds.), *Studies in mother-infant interaction.* New York: Academic Press, 1977.

Stoller, S., & Field, T. Alteration of mother and infant behaviors and heart rate during a still-face perturbation of face-to-face interaction. In T. Field & A. Fogel (Eds.), *Emotion and early interactions.* Hillsdale, N.J.: Lawrence Erlbaum Associates, 1981.

Trevarthen, C. Conversations with a 2-month-old. *New Scientist,* 1974, *22,* 230-235.

Tronick, E., Als, H., Adamson, L., Wise, S., & Brazelton, T. B. The infant's response to entrapment between contradictory messages in face-to-face interaction. *Journal of Child Psychiatry,* 1978, *17,* 1-13.

Tulkin, S. & Kagan, J. Mother-child interaction in the first few years of life. *Child Dev.,* 1972, *43,* 31–41.

Vaughn, B., & Sroufe, L. A. The temporal relationship between infant heart rate acceleration and crying in an aversive situation. *Child Development,* 1979, *50,* 565-567.

Walker, J. A., & Kershman, S. M. Deaf-blind babies in social interaction: Questions of maternal adaptation. Paper presented at the biennial meeting of the Society for Research in Child Development, Boston, April, 1981.

2 Comments on Field's Chapter

Megan R. Gunnar
*Institute of Child Development
University of Minnesota*

One goal of this symposium was to consider how research on special populations contributes to our understanding of normal development. Although Field's work involves high risk infants, it highlights two current themes in social development as a whole. The first concerns the role of infant temperament in the development of the parent-child relationship. The second concerns the importance of control in early childhood.

The past two decades have seen a resurgence of interest in a very old topic in psychology: that of individual differences in temperament. Interest in infant temperament reflects a reassessment of the role of the child in early parent-child interaction. Socialization is no longer viewed as a unidirectional process in which children are shaped or molded by their parents. Instead, relationships between parents and children are viewed as systems of mutual influence, in which children are seen as active social agents from the very first (Bell, 1968; Lewis & Rosenblum, 1974).

As a result of this reassessment of effects we have become increasingly interested in identifying dimensions of variability in children that may affect the development of the parent-child relationship. Unfortunately, to date, we have not progressed very far in identifying these dimensions. Work with high risk infants holds promise in this area. As Field reported, preterm RDS and post-term, postmature infants possess characteristics that make it difficult for parents to adapt to them. The problems that parents of these high risk infants have may be useful in clarifying contributions that the infant makes to the interaction process. It is important to note that in Field's work, the critical characteristics appear to be ones that involve the infant as the recipient of social stimulation. However, this is not surprising, given that during the early months of life the infant possesses only limited capacities to initiate interaction. The young infant can look, smile, coo, and cry to gain attention from others, but she cannot approach, touch, and otherwise demand attention. During these early months the infant tends to be more of a recipient than an initiator of social interchanges. However, as Field has indicated, the role of recipient is not a passive one, instead, the recipient serves as the regulator of social interaction. That is, by her reactions to stimulation she sets limits on the amount and type of interaction that will occur.

High risk infants apparently set severe limits on the amount of social stimulation that they will accept and respond to positively. This in turn affects the course of interaction between parent and infant. If the parent does not adjust to the infant's limits, the interaction becomes stressful for both parties. And, even if the parent does adjust we should still see a different pattern of interactions as a function of the limits imposed by the infant. Thus, as Field argued, one aspect of infant temperament that may affect interaction is the infant's activation band, or the range of stimuli to which she can accommodate.

Describing high risk infants as possessing a more limited activation band gives us a general model of these infants as recipients of social stimulation. However, the model ultimately needs to be made more specific. For example, does a narrower activation band mean that these high risk infants are equally restricted in the range of stimuli to which they can accommodate across all modalities? This question is relevant to Field's imitation manipulation. When the mothers were asked to imitate their infants, the infants responded more positively. But, what aspects of the mothers' behavior were altered by these instructions? Imitating the infant no doubt altered the intensity and patterning of the mothers' action, but, in addition, imitation also probably altered the modalities in which the mothers were stimulating their babies. Stimulation in some modalities may have dropped out or have been severely restricted by the instruction to imitate the baby's behavior, while stimulation in other modalities may not have been as severely affected. Consider tactile stimulation. When not involved in imitation the mother probably touched her baby a good deal. This might have included reaching out and touching the baby's face, stroking the baby's head, and so on. Because the infant would not engage in these behaviors, these forms of tactile stimulation probably dropped out during imitation. On the other hand, vocal stimulation probably remained fairly constant, or was not so greatly reduced. Knowing which of these variations was crucial in altering the infant's response is necessary if we are to specify the nature of the limits the infant sets as a recipient of social stimulation.

In addition, it is of course important to know why these infants seem to possess a more limited activation band. Indeed, it may be that the band appears limited because of other temperamental characteristics that differentiate high risk infants from normal infants. For example, it was noted that mothers of these high risk infants failed to respond appropriately to the infant's signals to pause during interaction. When the mothers were instructed to pause when their infants looked away from them, these high risk infants did respond more positively to social stimulation. Why weren't the mothers sensitive to the baby's need to take "time-outs" from stimulation? There are at least two possibilities that would involve differences in the temperament of these high risk infants. First, these infants may need to take more or longer time-outs from social interaction than normal infants. That is, they may need more time to recouperate from stimulation. When given this time, they may be able to respond to a much greater range of stimulation. When not given this time, however, they may more easily become distressed, especially with intense stimulation. If this is true, then the need for longer or more frequent "time-outs" may not fit with the mother's own "time-out" needs, making it less likely that she will be sensitive to the infant's rhythms.

A different, but related hypothesis is that high risk infants have difficulty organizing responses to cope with stimulation. As noted in Field's chapter, mothers of high risk infants may not be responding to their infant's signals to pause during interaction, because the infant's signals are hard to read. However, what are we reading when we try to determine the infant's need to pause during interaction? In many cases what we are reading are the infant's own attempts to reduce arousal by turning away, engaging in self-stimulation, and so on. If these risk infants are more difficult to read, then this may imply that their own "arousal-reducing" strategies are less well-developed than are those of normal infants. Perhaps they fail to turn-off stimulation before they become over-aroused. Perhaps they have trouble organizing the kind of rhythmic repetative stimulation that should help them calm down. In short, perhaps their coping processes are less efficient or less effective. If this is true, then it would suggest that these infants not only need their parents to respond to their time-out signals, but they also need their parents to anticipate when to reduce stimulation and when to help the high risk infant organize her own means of regulating arousal. Again, if we are to understand the role of the infant in the development and maintenance of interaction, we will need to specify the precise nature of the infant characteristics that influence the interaction process. However, as Field's work indicates, reseach with high risk infants holds a great deal of promise in this regard.

A second theme in Field's chapter involves the importance of control early in development. The 1970s saw an outpouring of research on the importance of perceived control. Research, both with animals and with human adults, indicated that uncontrollable aversive stimulation could produce subsequent abnormal cognitive and affective responses (Seligman, 1975).

Specifically, individuals who experienced uncontrollable events later acted as if they were helpless even when events were clearly controllable. We are now beginning to examine the effects of control and lack-of-control during infancy. It is striking, however, that in most of our research we have focused on situations where the infant performs some action to *produce* stimulation (e.g., Watson & Ramey, 1972). We have spent much less time considering the importance for the infant of being able to act to reduce or turn off stimulation (Gunnar, 1980).

As the research we have just heard suggests, both types of control are likely to be important for normal development. When the mothers were insensitive to their baby's signals to reduce stimulation, interaction between the mother and baby was disrupted. The babies increasingly attempted to avoid interaction and ultimately became distressed. This response to lack-of-control over *reducing* stimulation is similar to the infant's response to lack-of-control over *producing* stimulation. When an infant is confronted by an adult who refuses to respond to the infant's smiles and coos, the infant also shows gaze aversion and ultimately becomes distressed (Rheingold, Gewirtz, & Ross, 1959). It would seem that in social situations infants are sensitive to their control over both causing the adult to respond and causing the adult to stop responding.

Lack of sensitivity to the baby's need to regulate decreases as well as increases in stimulation may not only disrupt immediate interactions, but may also have long term consequences for the child. In other research, Field has found that mothers who are not sensitive to the infant's needs to pause during interactions early in the first year, have infants who at two years are delayed in language development (Field, 1980). Similarly, Ainsworth and her colleagues have found that maternal sensitivity is related to the development of a secure attachment relationship between the mother and child (Ainsworth, Blehar, Waters, & Wall, 1978). Ainsworth's rating of maternal sensitivity includes a measure of the mother's willingness to let her infant control both when they will and when they will *not* interact. More recently, Martin (1981) has demonstrated that for boys, at least, the mother's willingness to let her infant ignore her at times was related to the boy's later interest in exploring novel events out of the mother's sight and the boy's positive, friendly approach to an adult experimenter. In fact, in the middle-class samples Martin worked with, a boy's control over *not* interacting with his mother was more predictive of later exploratory behavior than was his control over eliciting social responses from his mother.

In sum, these data indicate that the infants' control over reducing and at times avoiding social interaction is an important aspect of early experience. The question we must address is why control over *not* interacting is apparently so important for the child? In developing a sense of efficacy, of being able to control events, the experience of producing stimulation is only one component. The other side of the control coin that should affect the developing infant's sense of efficacy is being able to act to reduce stimulation. Social experiences may be especially important in this regard. We have tended to view parent-infant interaction as the context in which the child learns that she can cause events to occur (Lewis & Goldberg, 1969). Thus we have focused on the importance of parents responding to the child when she looks, smiles, or coos at them, or picking the child up when she cries. But, even very early in infancy the infant should be experiencing a good deal of response-contingent stimulation in dealing with the non-social environment (Yarrow, Rubenstein, & Pederson, 1975). In dealing with both people and inanimate objects the infant has a chance to learn that her actions cause things to happen. However, inanimate objects probably do not provide the infant with the experience of acting to turn-off or reduce stimulation. Inanimate objects rarely act unless the infant acts on them. Therefore, turning off an inanimate object frequently means just *not* acting on it. For example, the infant turns off a rattle by not shaking it, or stops the mobile from shaking by lying still in her crib. People are another matter. People frequently provide stimulation even when not acted upon. They approach, touch, talk to, and otherwise stimulate the infant even when the infant has not "signalled" an interest in being stimulated. In order to turn off people the infant must do more than merely not turning them on. What the infant learns about her control over reducing stimulation may, therefore, come primarily from interacting with other people. If so, then in order to understand the development of individual differences in self-efficacy, we may need to pay special attention to the child's early experiences with being able to "turn-off" as well as "turn-on" social interactions.

Work with high risk infants does hold promise for a better understanding of both normal and atypical children. High risk infants, because of their special needs, place a high demand on their caregivers. This greater demand, in turn, both highlights the types of stimulation that are important in social development and indicates how the infant's characteristics influence social interactions.

REFERENCES

Ainsworth, M. D. S., Blehar, M., Waters, E., & Wall, S. *Patterns of attachment: Observations in the strange situation and at home.* Hillsdale, N.J.: Lawrence Erlbaum Associates, 1978.

Bell, R. Q. A reinterpretation of the direction of effects in studies of socialization. *Psychological Review,* 1968, 75, 81–95.

Field, T. Interactions of preterm and term infants and their lower- and middle-class teenage and adult mothers. In T. Field, S. Goldberg, D. Stern, & A. Sostek (Eds.), *High-risk infants and children: Adult and peer interactions.* New York: Academic Press, 1980.

Gunnar, M. Contingent stimulation: A review of its role in early development. In S. Levine & H. Ursin (Eds.), *Coping and health.* New York: Plenum Press, 1980.

Lewis, M., & Goldberg, S. Perceptual-cognitive development in infancy: A generalized expectancy model as a function of mother-infant interaction. *Merrill-Palmer Quarterly,* 1969, *15,* 81–85.

Lewis, M., & Rosenblum, L. (Eds.). *The effects of the infant on its caregiver.* New York: Wiley, 1974.

Martin, J. Longitudinal study of the consequence of early mother-infant interaction: A microanalytic approach. *Society for Research in Child Development Monographs* (Serial #190), 1981.

Rheingold, H., Gewirtz, J., & Ross, H. Social conditioning of vocalizations in the infant. *Journal of Comparative and Physiological Psychology,* 1959, *52,* 68–72.

Seligman, M. *Learned helplessness: On development, depression, and death.* San Francisco: Freeman & Co., 1975.

Yarrow, L., Rubenstein, J., & Pederson, F. *Infant and environment: Early cognitive and motivational development.* New York: Wiley, 1975.

3　Infant-Caregiver Attachment and Patterns of Adaptation in Preschool: The Roots of Maladaptation and Competence*

L. Alan Sroufe
Institute of Child Development
University of Minnesota

It has long been accepted that effectiveness of work with young children in educational and therapeutic settings is enhanced by an understanding of the individual child. If we can understand a particular child's world view and his/her unique needs and concerns, we can better promote educational growth and healthy development. Such an understanding of the personalities of children is a major goal underlying the preschool research described in this chapter.

The problem of defining meaningful individual differences in young children is indeed a challenging one. To be sure, individual differences are obvious to any teacher. Children differ in countless ways, each child being unique. But which of these differences are vital to the functioning of the child? Which require special note for planning and intervention? Equally important, while each child is unique, groups of children also share similarities. In fact, any two children may be grouped together on some basis. So how do we determine the crucial bases for grouping; that is, which

---

*This paper is dedicated to the memory of Jeanne H. Block, an exemplary developmental psychologist. Her work was both directly and indirectly an inspiration for this project: directly in that her work with Jack Block suggested some of the ties between infancy and early childhood that we sought; indirectly from her contagious attitude that solid developmental psychology was both possible and worth doing. No one approached the study of the developing child more thoughtfully than Jeanne.

The paper was supported by a grant from the National Science Foundation (NSF/BNS 8004572) and, in part, by a program project grant from the National Institute of Child Health and Human Development (5 POI HD 05027) and a grant from Maternal and Child Health (MC-R-270416-02-0).

children require a common approach from the teacher or therapist in contrast to a very different approach for another group of children? Teachers commonly decide to let one child engage in a minor rule infraction for a time, while another child is promptly limited. Such decisions must be based on the idea that these children have different requirements (at least at this point in time). Currently, variations in educational approach and intervention on the part of a given practitioner are largely intuitive. In my opinion these intuitive approaches tend to be remarkably appropriate in the case of good teachers, no doubt because they get to know the children and understand the dynamics of their behavior. But, still, as developmental researchers we should be able to offer more. One objective of the current developmental research is to evolve more powerful ways of comprehending individual differences so that these heretofore intuitive approaches to education and intervention may be sharpened.

Even before introducing formal theoretical considerations, it may be useful to present some common-sense ideas that underlie this research. The first set of ideas has to do with the aspects of behavior to address. The assessment of intelligence, for example, has had a limited place in my research. Essentially, it is a modulator variable, something to be controlled. This is because well functioning children may be relatively high or low on intelligence, and many severely troubled children have adequate intelligence. Weikart (this volume) has shown that children experiencing quality preschool intervention regress to the same IQ as a control group; nonetheless, they show dramatically better adjustment to the school situation and to life. Being bright may well be an advantage in facing the challenges of the preschool classroom, but it is neither necessary nor sufficient to insure healthy functioning. Also, assessments of IQ can always be added to assessments of quality of adaptation for a more complete picture.

Similarly, temperament, as it is usually understood, has received limited emphasis in our work. I believe that temperament is a useful concept, that is, that infants and children differ in terms of preferred tempo and so forth. However, such temperamental differences are encompassed by our interest in quality care, because good quality care involves responding to the particular nature and characteristics of a given child. I believe also that more meaningful individual differences are best captured by other concepts. Well functioning children, at times may be described as energetic, busy, and active, and at other times as calm, easy-going, and unflappable. Emotional health comes in many different forms. Moreover, characteristics such as undue reliance on adults, tendency to withdraw in the face of stress, isolation, good frustration tolerance, empathy, and curiosity are not well captured by temperament concepts, as our research shows. And these are the characteristics we seek to capture. These are the dimensions of behavior that underlie what I am calling *meaningful* individual differences. In contrast to IQ and temperament, this variation is not viewed as largely inborn; it is assumed to derive from the child's developmental history.

The second set of ideas concerns the way we view behavior. It is clear that simple frequency counts cannot do justice to the complexity of the child. The meaning of the behavior, as inferred from the behavioral and situational context, is essential. Two children may engage in an equivalent frequency of aggression. But in one case this may be rather uniformly associated with a flailing out in the face of frustration or disappointment (a tower falls, a toy is stepped on, etc.). The other child, in contrast, may engage in systematic victimization of other children, especially those who are vulnerable or who respond to attack by becoming very upset. Surely, these contextual differences are of equal importance to the sheer frequency of aggressive acts. More generally, children may "act out" in a variety of ways and for a variety of reasons. Determining that a child is an "externalizer" (e.g., Achenbach, 1966) is only the beginning of understanding. The frequency of acting out may indicate a problem, but, in addition, our goal is to understand the particular *nature* of the problem.

Likewise, some children may be frequently engaged with others; other children may engage very little. But a high social participation score is not nearly as meaningful as the quality of the interaction, the degree of reciprocity, the sensitivity to the other's signals, and so forth. Social competence cannot be adequately indexed by frequency of interaction. Even solitary behavior has vastly different meanings, as a function of the situations in which it occurs, what the child does while solitary, and so forth.

Use of molar concepts, such as self-direction, sensitivity, flexible management of impulses, and self-confidence requires that the observer take context into account when recording behavior. And the use of molar constructs is essential in order to deal adequately with the complexity of social/emotional behavior. I prefer such complex, context-dependent variables to more discrete behavioral variables, despite the difficulty of operationalizing them. A suitable solution to the problems involved in operationalizing molar constructs often is to assess both discrete and molar variables and support each set with the other. This was our approach in the Minnesota Preschool Project.

But even molar measures or ratings fall short of the richness we would like to capture. Therefore, in our assessments we attempted to develop profiles of behavioral organization—patterns of adaptation—across contexts and across levels of analysis. That is, what we really wanted to understand was the particular way the child put together his approach to the world, his orientation and style. A child's pattern of adaptation included his expectations, fears and hopes; his beliefs about himself and others; his orientation to adults and peers and his preferred ways of relating; his ways of coping with stressful and emotionally arousing situations, as well as more specific capacities, such as physical abilities. The Blocks' (1979) concepts of ego control and ego-resiliency come very close to what we had in mind when we talked about behavioral profiles, in that they are addressed to the management of impulses and feelings. Two dimensions, of course, cannot capture the entire complexity of individuals, but the Block dimensions do as well as any two might. And their work encouraged the expectation that meaningful and coherent individual differences in personality patterns could be assessed.

HISTORY OF THE PROBLEM

Our developmental approach to individual differences in social and emotional development is tied historically to psychoanalytic theory. From the beginning Freud acknowledged a central role for affect and emphasized the control and expression of impulses and feelings. He argued also that early experiences continued to affect the individual and that maladaptation resulted from ongoing conflict.

The metaphorical language in which Freud originally described his insights is now no longer considered acceptable. The assumption that behavior is motivated primarily by the goal of keeping tension at the lowest possible level (drive reduction) has been thoroughly discredited, and Freud's mechanistic model yielded a passive view of the person and a static view of development. Individuals are not pushed back to earlier stages of functioning, and development does not stop (fixate on a single issue). Rather, individuals evolve and organize (hierarchically) strategies for dealing with crises and opportunities in the environment, and they carry forward earlier strategies to subsequent periods of development.

As Bowlby (1969) and others have pointed out, the basic insights in psychoanalytic theory are not tied to drive reduction or the mechanistic model. Loevinger (1976) traces Freud's own changing metapsychology from an early position based on trauma and repression of affect to an increasing emphasis on the quality of significant early relationships and on how prototypes or characteristic ways of coping with conflict evolve within these. In this evolved position, anxiety, and therefore symptomatology, is not the result of dammed-up drive, but is a signal to the individual that there is a threat of a significant interpersonal loss (and ultimately a threat to the self). In varying degrees such anxiety is common to all individuals, but experiential history determines the degree and circumstances of anxiety, characteristic ways for dealing with anxiety, and vulnerability to disorganization in the face of anxiety. This position is integrated readily with a modern biological perspective.

Many investigators have contributed to the continuing evolution of psychoanalytic theory (e.g., Breger; 1974, Erikson, 1963; Klein, 1976,

Loevinger, 1976; Mahler, Pine & Bergman, 1975; Sander, 1975; Sullivan, 1953). I have discussed this progress elsewhere (Sroufe, 1979). Here, I can present only a brief overview of a current perspective.

Four assumptions are central to this modern perspective, which is actually an integration of psychoanalytic, evolutionary, and organismic theory (cf. Breger, 1974):

1. Individuals are biologically disposed to form intimate (attachment) relationships, and development takes place in the context of these relationships.

2. The earliest relationship(s) are of special significance because they provide the context for the emergence of the self and because they represent prototypes for later relationships.

3. Early prototypes are carried forward through attitudes and expectations the child forms concerning the availability and likely responses of others and the outcome of his/her own efforts to cope with stress.

4. A prototype behavioral organization will be manifest in different, though coherent forms, in different circumstances and at different points in development.

For example, some infants learn early that in times of strong emotional arousal others will *not* be available. Based on these salient experiences (and not sheer frequency of contact) they learn *not* to seek people in these contexts and, in fact, even to avoid emotionally laden situations more generally, including close personal relationships. In general, they may cope with strong arousal by withdrawal, with perhaps occasional outbursts of intense feelings, or they may develop a hostile, guarded stance toward the interpersonal world. But, because it is based in the child's biology, the underlying need for intimacy does not abate. The child's dependency needs will continue to be manifest, though perhaps in distorted ways or in restricted circumstances. For example, given sustained opportunity in a comfortable setting, such a child may show striking dependency. The child did not learn *not* to need people; rather, a certain set of expectations has been learned that shapes his/her patterns of response.

This framework for looking at individual differences is quite distinctive from traditional trait and milestone viewpoints. (Its distinction from an operant perspective will become obvious.) This framework differs from a trait perspective in that the emphasis is not on isolated characteristics of the individual (aggressiveness, dependency), but on behavioral organization—the way the person approaches and copes with changing circumstances. Morever, particular characteristics are not expected to be manifest consistently across situations; neither are they necessarily stable over time. Linear models of development are rejected. In certain developmental circumstances infants who were quite vigorous and active may end up being very passive as preschoolers. In predictable circumstances cuddly babies very well may be among the more independent young children. Individuals are viewed as actively structuring their experience, based on evolving orientations to the environment. Understanding these orientations will enable prediction of how children will handle subsequent developmental issues. In the end, individuals may have characteristic ways of dealing with impulses and feelings, and indeed, this is a major assumption underlying our research. But these styles of coping result in quite different behaviors at different times and in different contexts, though even within this change there is coherence. Behavior is predictable, though not necessarily stable.

In contrast to the milestone/stage view of individual differences, here little emphasis is placed on the age at which some developmental step is achieved. Instead, following Erikson (1963), Sander (1975), and others, development is viewed in terms of a series of issues *faced by each individual*. All infants become attached, all toddlers individuate, all preschool children relate to others and develop concepts of themselves as boys or girls. All children learn to control and express impulses. Of interest is the quality of adaptation with respect to these issues. Stages are not passed or failed. Rather, the behavioral organization evolved with respect to an early developmental issue lays the ground work for subsequent behavioral organizations. A child with a secure attachment relationship (that is, where a flexible balance is achieved between exploration and contact-based security) will later be more confident in autonomous problem solving, as we and others have shown (Main, 1973; Matas, Arend & Sroufe, 1978; Sroufe & Rosenberg, 1980). The nature of the earlier behavioral organization, with attachment promoting exploration, makes the smooth movement to more autonomous functioning virtually inevitable. The age at which first signs of attachment appeared is of much less importance. And whether a flexible, effective organization of attachment behavior or some maladaptive organization was evolved, no child's development is arrested at the attachment phase. Rather, the quality of attachment is carried forward. Each child faces the issues involved in solving problems on its own, learning to control impulses, and developing relations with peers. A healthy pattern of adaptation is one which promotes a flexible, effective behavioral organization with respect to subsequent issues; an unhealthy pattern is one which does not. But development continues and each child in our culture proceeds through the same series of developmental issues.

Research Background

The immediate foundation for this research program is the work of Bowlby (1969, 1973, 1980) and Ainsworth (Ainsworth, Blehar, Waters & Wall,

1978) on attachment. Bowlby provided a theoretical framework and Ainsworth a method for capturing individual differences in early behavioral organization. In contrast to previous views of attachment (dependency), individual differences here were not conceptualized in terms of degree or intensity. All infants will become attached, Bowlby argued, whether abused, haphazardly treated, or nurtured. Our biology guarantees that. All that is required is a regularly-available conspecific who interacts with the infant. What will vary is not the occurrence, but the quality of the attachment, the efficiency of the signaling and contact maintaining systems evolved by infant and caregiver, and their effectiveness in serving the infant's regulation of affect and behavior.

Two important hypotheses were derived from Bowlby's theory: (1) individual differences in the quality of attachment are the result of the quality of early care, in particular the psychological availability and responsiveness of the caregiver. Infants who experience ready access to the caregiver and prompt and reliable responses to their signals of need or distress are secure in their attachment (i.e., will develop confident expectations concerning the caregiver and the environment more generally); (2) the quality of the attachment relationship lays the foundation for the sense of self (efficacy, internal locus of control, curiosity) and, in particular, the way the person deals with intimate relationships. This includes the manner of meeting dependency needs, nurturing others and dealing with loss or separation.

Ainsworth focused primarily on the first hypothesis (Ainsworth, et al., 1978). She found that the caregiver's sensitivity to the infant's signals (prompt, effective response) and their understanding and respect for the infant's autonomy (as manifest by "cooperative" care as opposed to intrusive, interfering care), assessed at each quarter of the first year, predicted the quality of attachment at 12-months. She also found that rejection in the context of the infant wanting to be picked up (but not total amount of time holding) distinguished a particular pattern of attachment characterized by avoidance of the mother following a brief separation. Infant behaviors assessed during the first quarter did not predict later attachment; indeed, they were highly unstable even within that quarter (Blehar, Lieberman & Ainsworth, 1977). Within the longitudinal study begun by Byron Egeland, this relationship between maternal sensitivity at 6-months and quality of attachment at 12-months has been replicated. In the case of avoidant 12-months-olds, an extensive examination of infant temperamental characteristics in and after the newborn period failed to reveal predictive differences.

My own research has been addressed mainly to a broadened version of the second hypothesis; namely, that quality of infant-mother attachment would be related to later personal and interpersonal competence. (We have studied mothers primarily because in the original middle class study all mothers stayed home and all fathers worked, and in the current Egeland, Deinard & Sroufe sample few of the mothers have had stable male partners.)

Waters (1978) first showed that Ainsworth's attachment patterns were stable from 12-to-18-months. We next showed that toddlers (24-months) who had been secure in their attachments as infants showed a more competent pattern of autonomous functioning than did children who had anxious attachments (Matas, Arend & Sroufe, 1978). In particular, when we assessed them in a problem solving situation, designed to take each child beyond his/her own capacities to cope, secure children approached the problems with more enthusiasm and positive affect (less negative affect), were more persistent, and were more effective in using maternal assistance (cooperated more, opposed and ignored less) than anxiously attached children. This pattern was obtained despite the fact that children came to the limits of their abilities and showed normal two-year negativism in other contexts. It was the behavioral organization, the flexible use of the mother when their own goal attainment capacities were exhausted, that distinguished secure from anxious children. All of this was an explicit confirmation of Bowlby's hypothesis and Mahler's (Mahler, et al., 1975) idea that individuation is influenced by the quality of the earlier symbiosis.

In two subsequent studies (Arend, Gove & Sroufe, 1979; Waters, Wippman, & Sroufe, 1979) we were able to predict from attachment at 15-to-18-months to broad measures of functioning in the preschool and kindergarten. Thus, while the quality of adaptation originally resided in the dyad, ultimately it was revealed in assessments of the child apart from the mother. Securely attached infants were later described (via teachers and observer Q-sorts) as more socially competent and more ego-resilient (flexible, self-reliant, curious, involved) than anxiously attached infants. The Blocks' (Block & Block, 1979) laboratory battery (curiousity box, Lowenfeld mosaics, delay of gratification, level of aspiration, etc.) confirmed the Q-sort data.

These studies provided striking demonstrations of the power of attachment assessments to predict later behavior and of the coherence of individual development. One reason for success was that individuals were assessed in terms of salient developmental issues using molar, integrative measures. Another reason is that the Ainsworth laboratory attachment assessments were anchored upon hundreds of hours of home observation.

The early demonstrations, however, leave us far from other goals of the research; namely, providing a sufficiently comprehensive understanding of individual children and groups of children to aid education and intervention efforts. Our molar outcome variables leave out much concerning more specific characteristics of competent children and what they do to achieve their perceived status with peers/teachers. Moreover, in our previously published studies we have found little difference in the subsequent adaptation of Ainsworth's two distinct patterns of maladaptive attachment (Table 3.1). Children in one of these groups (Group C) were overtly anxious (with much crying), resistant to contact upon reunion, and/or angry (C_1) in her strange situation or were strikingly passive (C_2). They had in common great difficulty being settled, even after one brief separation. Children in the other maladaptive group (Group A) showed little explicit distress. They tended to separate readily and were rarely upset when left with a stranger. When left alone they commonly were readily settled by a stranger. Most significant, however, is that following separation they tended to snub or avoid the mother upon her return, and they did this all the more following a second brief separation. Clearly, these are profoundly different patterns (though occasional children mix these behaviors); yet, in our early work we found little in the way of documented differences in the subsequent adaptation of these two groups. At age two neither group showed enthusiasm in problem solving, neither was effective in using maternal assistance, neither was self reliant; at age 3½-5-years neither was viewed by the teachers as socially competent or ego-resilient.

Some initial progress has been made on this problem. In the kindergarten follow-up of the original middle class sample there was a significant (but small in absolute terms) tendency for the avoidant infants to be overcontrolled and the resistant (ambivalent) infants to be undercontrolled on the Block Q-sort measure, an intuitively appealing finding. More recently, Gove, in his dissertation research, has discriminated As' and Cs' behavior patterns at 24-months in the Egeland, Deinard, and Sroufe poverty sample. This research is especially promising because the discriminations were based on profile and cluster analyses. That these profiles discriminated the groups, even though the individual behaviors and ratings upon which they were based generally did not, is an important clue for ongoing research. Both groups of anxiously attached children show maladaptive behavior (dependency, aggression, negative acting out, non-compliance), but the manner and circumstances in which these behaviors are manifest differ. For example, resistant infants directed more of their anger directly at the mother in our tool problem situation, whereas avoidant infants showed it through object directed behaviors and more subtle non-compliance. The resistant children appeared to have the goal of engaging mother in power struggles, whereas the avoidant children seemed to want to stay outside of her influence. The meaning of the anger and negativistic behavior was different.

Our main objective for the Minnesota Preschool Project was to carry this work forward. By observing in detail the daily functioning of a sizeable number of children with known attachment histories, we hoped to trace the individual patterns of adaptation of competent and incompetent children.

TABLE 3.1

Patterns of Attachment
(Adapted from Ainsworth, Blehar, Waters & Wall, 1978)

Secure Attachment
- A. Caregiver is a secure base for exploration
    1. readily separate to explore toys
    2. affective sharing of play
    3. affiliative to stranger in mother's presence
    4. readily comforted when distressed (promoting a return to play)
- B. Active in seeking contact or interaction upon reunion
    1. If distressed
        a) immediately seek and maintain contact
        b) contact is effective in terminating distress
    2. If not distressed
        a) active greeting behavior (happy to see caregiver)
        b) strong initiation of interaction

Anxious/Resistant Attachment
- A. Poverty of exploration
    1. Difficulty separating to explore, may need contact even prior to separation
    2. wary of novel situations and people
- B. Difficulty settling upon reunion
    1. may mix contact seeking with contact resistance (hitting, kicking, squirming, rejecting toys)
    2. may simply continue to cry and fuss
    3. may show striking passivity

Anxious/Avoidant Attachment
- A. Independent exploration
    1. readily separate to explore during preseparation
    2. little affective sharing
    3. affiliative to stranger, even when caregiver absent (little preference)
- B. Active avoidance upon reunion
    1. turning away, looking away, moving away, ignoring
    2. may mix avoidance with proximity
    3. avoidance more extreme on second reunion
    4. no avoidance of stranger

The project, of course, provided a rich opportunity to document fully the way in which secure attachment relationships and anxious attachment relationships are carried forward to the preschool. Domains such as dependency, aggression, prosocial behavior, affective expressiveness, status with peers, and classroom deportment had not been addressed in our previous outcome research in the preschool years. But, in addition, the project provided an opportunity to once again tackle the vexing problem of tracing coherent patterns of maladaptation. Does the particular quality of the early infant-caregiver relationship predict the unique adaptation of the individual child, beyond the general degree of disorder?

The Problem of Prediction: Coherence vs. Stability

In introducing her report on the 15 year follow-up of Shirley's (1931) babies, Neilon (1948) cogently summarized the problem of predicting from infancy to later behavior: "Even assuming continuity of personality patterns, the individual who cries a great deal as an infant would not necessarily be expected to cry a great deal as an adult. The personality characteristic which caused the excessive crying . . . might persist in a different manner . . . The same infant who cries a great deal might be subject to severe temper tantrums at preschool age, and have an inclination to impulsiveness and emotionality in adulthood (p. 175)." Despite this complexity, judges in the Neilson study were able to match, above chance level, infant "sketches" to independently created adolescent "sketches" which presented overviews of the individual's functioning.

A central postulate of our underlying model (Sroufe, 1979) is that continuity in development takes the form of *coherence across transformations.* It is predicted, for example, that some avoidant infants are hostile and/or aggressive later, even though such explicit aggressiveness was not seen in these infants. That such hostile, acting out children may show schizoid or schizophrenic patterns of adaptation in later life is likewise compatible. Indeed, follow-up studies by Robbins (1966) and others find that schizophrenia is not well predicted by shy, withdrawn, internalizing symptoms in children, but rather by acting out, antisocial (externalizing) symptoms. Such transformations in manifest behavior likely are the rule, rather than the exception.

Not only must one predict heterotypic continuity, but one must allow for diverse outcomes as well. Even in Ainsworth's scheme there are eight, not three, specific patterns of attachment behavior. And there are, of course, many more than eight kinds of infant attachment relationships. Moreover, as development proceeds, even more diversity might be expected. No one would predict that all avoidant infants would look alike as preschoolers, even in general terms. However, *a reasonable and testable prediction is that the various patterns of adaptation shown by avoidant infants represent meaningful developmental outcomes and that the set of adaptational patterns shown by avoidant children are distinct (probabilistically) from the set of patterns shown by resistant infants.* This is true despite a relative absence of differences on particular, discrete variables and ratings. For example, As and Cs may be disciplined with equal frequency by teachers, may be equally low in popularity, may be rated equally high on dependency, may as frequently interact with others, and so forth. Some children in both groups will show externalizing symptoms and some will show internalizing symptoms. But the form, quality, and organization of their behavior, will differ.

At the outset, we expected avoidant children to show some combination of the following patterns: (1) hostile/antisocial; (2) socially and emotionally isolated, withdrawing in the face of stress; and (3) disconnected, psychotic-like. All of this follows from the defensive posture developed within a relationship with a rejecting, emotionally unavailable (perhaps depressed) caregiver. There is a fundamental difficulty in relating, and an underlying anger which the child has not learned to express directly at its source. The resistant children, on the other hand, were expected to show one of two patterns: (1) impulsive, overtly anxious or tense, easily over-stimulated and low frustration tolerance or (2) passive, weak, infantile, adult oriented, fragile. These patterns, it was speculated, are the product of over-involved or ambivalent/inconsistent relationships.

It can be seen that withdrawal from other children, high dependency, aggression, and acting out are consistent with both sets of patterns. For example, the impulsive Cs flail out in frustration; and the aggressive As seek to harm another. Both groups show aggression. But the meaning of the behavior varies—an expression of anxiety and tension (undercontrol) vs. a re-direction of underlying hostility. Likewise, the passive Cs appear in ways similar to the isolated/withdrawn As. Both of these groups of internalizing children are low on peer interaction and certainly low on leadership. But they differ in terms of social orientation and, perhaps especially, orientation toward the teacher. And while some As, as well as Cs, are highly active socially, the social behavior of the Cs has a frenetic quality while that of the As is hostile or disconnected (that is, they may be with other children but without reciprocally participating in or understanding the affective give and take of the interaction).

Many of these distinctions are very challenging to assess but they are, we believe, conceptionally clear. If valid, they have important implications for those who work with preschool children and those who treat psychopathology.

DESCRIPTION OF THE PRESCHOOL PROJECT

We were able to include a total of 40 children in two consecutive classes. The first class lasted 12 weeks (15 children) and the second class lasted 20 weeks (24 children plus 1 replacement). Subjects for the larger, second class were actually recruited first, the first class being viewed as a pilot study. Children were selected on the basis of attachment history, and groups were equated in terms of age, IQ, race, and, in the second class, sex.

In the second class there were originally 24 preschool-aged ($\bar{X}$ = 48.7

mo.; $S = 3.9$) children, equally divided among secure (B), avoidant (A), and resistant (C), and equally divided according to gender. Twenty-one of the children had shown stable attachment classifications from 12-to-18-months. In the three cases where attachment changed (A-C, B-C, and C-A), our 24 month assessment (from the tool problem situation) was consistent with the 18 month assessment. One male, C child moved after the 10th week of the class. He was replaced by a B male, partly because no stable C males were available and partly because we had learned that the ratio of disturbed to well functioning children was too extreme (that is, partly this was a pragmatic decision). This subsample is not completely representative of the larger Egeland, Deinard and Sroufe sample. First, more than 50% of the infants from the larger sample were securely attached at 12-or-18 months (vs. the 33% here). Second, only 62% of the larger sample showed stable attachments. Selection was deliberate, however, to reduce error in the predictor, to promote contrasts between the A and C groups, and to increase the likelihood of continuity across this substantial age span. In many ways, this poverty sample, with their dramatically and continually changing life circumstances, was not ideal for testing our hypothesis. Selection of subjects with stable attachments, in part, countered all of these disadvantages.

The first (pilot) class had 15 children, 6 girls and 9 boys, ranging in age from 47-months to 57-months at the start of the session. Seven of the children had shown stable secure attachments, two had been stable As, one changed from A to C and one from C to A,[1] and four were "mixed"; that is, not classified consistently as secure or anxious.

Comment on the Suitability of Competence-Mixed Classrooms

What began as a research convenience—suitable representation of well functioning and poorly functioning children—came to be valued in its own right. In contrast to mainstreaming, where a disabled child is potentially isolated, and in contrast to a "special" class, where developing competence in peer relations may not be possible, our "integrated" classroom had many advantages. Some disturbed children are ready for meaningful peer contact; others can be helped to become ready. Other disturbed children can have growth enhancing experiences at a level short of fully reciprocal exchange; for example, frequently playing with cars and trucks in parallel. Children of similar competence levels and tolerance can, and do, find each other. At the same time such a therapeutic preschool class need not be disadvantageous

---

[1] Where used in A-C comparisons the child was grouped in terms of his 18 month classification.

for relatively healthy children. These children, too, can profit from clinically sensitive teachers. All children have emotional problems. An experience interacting with children with a wide variety of capacities and weaknesses, within a safe and well supervised context, may serve them well in the future.

Classroom Procedures and Routine

None of the parents of our subjects could provide transportation for their children. Therefore, a van and (in the second class) a car were used to transport the children. This service insured excellent attendance, which was maintained throughout the year, but it also created certain problems. In both classes, children arrived and departed at different times. The entire class was together for only about 1 hour each day; children were with their smaller group (or transportation sub-group) more than two additional hours. In both classes, we were able to match early and late arriving groups for attachment, sex, and IQ, but in the second class, we were not able to match within vehicle (car or van). The size of the second class, and the extended contact for children within vehicles, encouraged friendship patterns based heavily on propinquity, and interfered with the formation of a single group structure. This influenced many aspects of our data.

The routine for both classes was similar. The children who arrived first had outdoor (or indoor) later motor play and small group table activity. When the second group arrived there was 50 minutes of free play for all. After snack (and in the first class large circle time), the first group of children departed, and the second group had small groups and finally outdoor play. For the first class there was a single large circle time (songs, games, sharing). For the second class, early and late groups had large circle separately (before small group time). Again, this probably worked against formation of a single group structure in the second class.

A group of very gifted teachers worked with the children. There was a head teacher, another full time teacher, one full time assistant, and three part time assistant teachers. There was generally a ratio of at least one teacher per six children present. Although the teachers differed greatly in terms of style, classroom rules and procedures were clear and coherent. Inevitably, of course, different children became more closely involved with different teachers and vice versa.

ASSESSMENT OF ADAPTATION IN THE PRESCHOOL

In keeping with the broad-band, integrative approach to assessment underlying this research, a wide variety of data at different levels of abstraction was obtained. At the most integrative level, teachers made rankings, ratings, and Q-sorts based on their entire experience with the children throughout the preschool term. At the most discrete level, frequencies of looks and glances, agonistic behaviors, and peer contacts, and so forth were tallied. We also employed more molar behavior categories, and utilized child sampling and scanning, as well as time sampling. For example, in one procedure observers watched a particular child for 5 minutes and then completed a checklist (see Appendix A) which went well beyond discrete behaviors (e.g., made successful bid for leadership, withdrew in the face of stress, etc.). In all, 30 different observers participated in the research.

Teacher Data

The full time teachers had extensive opportunity to observe each child daily in a variety of contexts. In addition, unlike other observers, they directly interacted with the children. Therefore, they were in an ideal position to provide rich data concerning the child's overall behavioral organization, typical mode of coping, and manner of expressing and managing impulses and feelings. The fact that the three independent assessments could be compiled reduced the possibility of biased or idiosyncratic data. Information from teachers was considered our primary data source; behavioral observations were used to corroborate these data. Data obtained from teachers were of several types: Q-sorts, rankings, ratings, checklists, and nominations. Teachers also described each child in a single, written phrase. Teachers were blind to attachment history and to specific hypotheses.

A teacher-based Q-sort index of adequate functioning was the principal outcome measure for the entire project. The three teachers independently sorted the Block California 100-item Q-sort deck for each child following standard procedures.[2] (For 72% of the cases the average intercorrelation among the teacher Q-sorts was above .50.) The composited sorts for each child were then correlated with the Blocks' "ego-resiliency" criterion sort. This criterion was based on a composited sort by three clinical psychologists asked to describe an ego-resilient (flexible in managing feelings and impulses) child. These correlations became scores. A similar criterion is available for the Block's other dimension, ego control. Waters has provided a self-esteem Q-sort criterion (the composited Q-sort for self-esteem of more than a dozen developmental psychologists), which was also used. The

---

[2]The cards were placed in 9 categories following a quasi-normal distribution. The 5-items that were least characteristic of a child were placed in category 1, for example, and the 5 most characteristic items in category 9. There were 18 items in category 5, the neutral category. The following were example items: "uses and responds to reason," "teases other children," "shows recognition of others feelings," "is easily victimized by other children," "tends to become rigidly repetitive under stress," "is persistent, does not give up easily," "is self-reliant, confident," "tries to take advantage of others" "is inhibited and constricted," "enjoys solitary activities," "over reacts to minor frustrations," "makes social contacts slowly," "cries easily," "tends to go to pieces under stress," "is eager to please."

Block Q-sort data also can be used to generate scores on sets of items (category ranks simply being combined). Such a mega-item was available for empathy, and we (Nancy Schaeffer) created our own dependency mega-item.

In addition to Q-sort descriptions, the teachers also rank ordered the children in each class on the following: emotional health/self esteem, self-confidence, social competence, social dominance, dependency, and their liking of the child. Brief paragraphs describing these constructs were provided.

The teachers made ratings of agency, compliance, social skills, ego control, negative affect, and positive affect (7 point scales developed by Don Rahe). Several different ratings of dependency were utilized, one developed by Don Rahe, one developed within the preschool project, and the eight dimensions developed by Beller (1955). The teachers were also asked to list each child's friends. The teachers also filled out a revised and extended version of the child behavior checklist devised by Behar and Stingfield (1974).

Peer Behavior and Peer Group Structure

A variety of measures pertinent to understanding the child's status in the peer group were obtained. An attention structure measure, based on the number of looks received from other children, was obtained both indoors and outdoors (c.f., Vaughn & Waters, 1980). Success in object and position struggles, frequency of social participation, and frequency of agonism were time-sampled. In addition, observers made judgments of friendship pairs, and sociometric status was determined using a combination of standard nomination procedures (c.f. Asher, Singleton, Tinsley, & Hymel, 1979) and forced groupings.

Observations of Child-Teacher and Teacher-Child Behaviors

One group of observers "teacher-sampled". They watched each primary teacher for 3 minutes (5 minutes in the Fall class), and coded the following behaviors for children: seeking nurturance, seeking attention, physical help seeking, cognitive help seeking, and social help seeking. They also coded frequency with which the teacher gave support or guidance or discipline to the children. In addition to these data, maps were made of the children's seating in large group, and physical contact between children and teachers and lapsitting were noted.

Affective Expressiveness, Coping with Stress, Impulse Control, and Negative Behavioral Signs

Many aspects of functioning that were of special interest in this study were either represented by low frequency events or required consideration of context. For example, determining that aggression was unprovoked, that a child *smoothly* joined an ongoing group, or withdrew in the face of stress, generally could not be done on the basis of brief time sampling procedures. The observer had to watch the event unfold. Certain characteristics, such as diffuse behavior or wandering, also involved a time dimension. Other behaviors, such as empathy or bizarre behaviors, were quite rare and required context considerations. Typically, licking the wall would be considered bizarre, but not if for some reason the children had created a game in which this was included. A 5 minute child sampling procedure was used to code 60 such behavioral categories, developed by Edward Schork. The codings included aspects of *positive affect* (affectively positive initiation or response to another, positive affect used to sustain an ongoing activity, shows pride in accomplishment, etc.), *negative affect* (becomes very angry, negative response to approach, whines or cries in absence of injury, etc.) and *impulse control* (falls to pieces in face of stress, throws objects, etc.). The entire check list and the definitions of the categories are appended (Appendix A).

Influence of Classroom Ecology on the Data Obtained

Some aspects of the data obtained were heavily influenced by the classroom ecology. In the first pilot class, which was small and included a substantial proportion (50%) of well functioning children, all of the above data collection procedures yielded meaningful results. For example, the time sampled measure of looks and glances yielded a coherent attention structure that was stable across contexts (indoor and outdoor play) and that correlated with other measures in ways consistent with previous research (e.g., Vaughn & Waters, 1980). The correlation between attention rank and sociometric status was .65, and between attention rank and teacher rankings of social competence it was .69. Likewise, while the data on affect and impulse expression were thin in this pilot class, a crude composite of all positive and all negative items distinguished the attachment groups. In addition, indices of dependency from our observational data correlated with teacher rankings of dependency.

In the second class, however, some of the indoor observational data was made less meaningful by the large class size (24), the high proportion of children with emotional and behavior problems (67% were predicted), and the separation of children into transportation groups. The whole class was together for only 1 hour; transportation groups were together for 3 hours.

One of the more obvious effects of these factors was in the indoor attention structure. An integrated, coherent structure simply did not emerge. As a result, attention structure correlated only modestly with other indices of social competence (.37 with sociometric status and .52 with teacher rankings of social competence). Quite strikingly, the child that was highest on popularity was lowest on indoor attention rank, a most paradoxical finding. We assumed this finding was due to the large class size and chaotic classroom circumstances. This is implied by the fact that findings from class 1 were so coherent, and it is also supported by the subgroups data (outdoor and large motor room) from Class 2. Large motor play groups consisted of only 12 children. Here again, coherent attention structures emerged which had reasonable correlates. The high popularity child mentioned above was ranked number 1 in the attention structure outdoors. In this context she showed the social skill and involvement that underlay her popularity. Unfortunately for our attachment outcome assessments, outdoor attention structure was heavily determined by transportation vehicle.

Similarly, we believed that the indoor affect and impulse control data were affected heavily by classroom ecology. In the second class there was little discrimination of attachment groups by this scale indoors. We reasoned that some competent children were spending more time by themselves in productive, solitary activity. Thus, the positive social exchanges we had expected had fewer opportunities to be manifest. Here, where the assessments were individual-based (in contrast to attention structure), the subgroup data was not contaminated by transportation group (it was not the number of contacts but the quality that was assessed), and provided a test of the classroom ecology interpretation. As presented in the following section, subgroup (outdoor and large motor room) data on affect and impulse expression strongly discriminated children with different attachment histories.

Because of these classroom ecology considerations the presentation of findings presented emphasizes data that cut across contexts (all teacher data, peer sociometric) and observational data from the subgroup settings. The teacher data, for a variety of reasons (3 skilled teachers, daily contact, direct interaction) would be expected to be the most robust and outcome relevant data. Subgroup observation provides ample opportunity to corroborate teacher evaluations and determine the extent of any halo effects.

FINDINGS

Secure vs. Anxious Attachment Groups

Ego resiliency. Three and one half years after our infant assessments, children who had been securely attached were found to be much more flexible in the management of impulses and feelings. The teacher Q-sort, ego-resiliency composite findings represent a replication of previous research (Arend *et al.*, 1979) and our strongest outcome prediction to date. As found previously, children who as infants had been secure in their attachments had significantly more positive correlations with the ego-resiliency criterion than did the anxiously attached children (F (2,33) = 7.73, $p<.01$), with Bs significantly different from both As and Cs and As and Cs not different from each other. In fact, across the two classes the average correlation (of the composited teacher Q-sort with the ego-resiliency criterion) of the securely attached children was +.50, and all 16 correlations were positive (see Table 2). The mean correlation for the avoidant subjects was −.13, with 9 of 11 subjects having a negative correlation (i.e., being ego-brittle). The mean of the nine resistant subjects was a modest .07, with four large positive correlations and three large negative correlations. Some children who were anxiously attached as infants were viewed as doing relatively well based on this assessment, but the majority were doing quite poorly. The clear majority of secure infants were doing quite well as preschool children.

Self-esteem and Emotional Health

Results using Water's self esteem Q-sort criterion were identical. (Indeed the average correlation between these 2 scores was .85.) That is, the securely attached children more closely fit ideal descriptions of children high on ego-resiliency (flexibility and resourcefulness) or high on self-esteem.

TABLE 3.2

Individual Correlations Between Composited Teacher Q-sorts and the Blocks' Ego-resiliency Criterion

CLASS 1			
Secure	*Avoidant*	*Resistant*	*Mixed*
.752	−.219	.089	.290
.702	−.452		.202
.646	−.460		−.030
.472			−.2341
.316			
.211			
.041			
CLASS 2			
Secure	*Avoidant*	*Resistant*	
.741	.729	.647	
.722	.654 (.221)	.466 (−.001)	
.686	−.154	.311 (.087)	
.417	−.167	.283 (−.072)	
.413	−.221	−.131	
.356	−.374	−.373	
.091	−.466	−.384	
.086	−.488	−.402	
.052			

( ) Head teacher's Q-sort, taken alone

The Q-sort data were corroborated by the teachers' rankings and ratings. In class 1, where 7 of the 15 children were securely attached (with 4 anxious and 4 mixed), the six highest rankings on emotional health/self esteem, the most comprehensive assessment of functioning, went to securely attached children. The probability of this occurrence by chance alone is 1 in 1000. The same trend was seen in the second class, though here the most clear result was seen in looking at the bottom of the ranking. The final eight children were all anxiously attached ($p = .012$). Securely attached children were also rated higher on the agency scale ($t = 3.28, p < .002$), which conceptually is closely related to self-esteem.

Although the bulk of the behavior observation data is presented in later sections, certain support for the teacher judgments concerning emotional health is pertinent here. Securely attached children showed fewer problem behaviors and fewer behavior aberrations. For example, only nine children were ever observed to exhibit "bizarre" behavior; all nine were anxiously attached ($p < .01$). Securely attached children less often aimlessly "wandered" ($t = -2.04, p < .05$), and less often were "vacant" ($t = -1.84, p = .079$) or showed specific "mannerisms" ($p > .10$). Taken together these signs strongly discriminated the groups. Other aspects of emotional ill health are presented in the following sections.

Dependency

Both groups of anxiously attached children, whether they had been easily distressed and difficult to settle (resistant) *or avoidant* of mother upon reunion, were highly dependent in the preschool. Only one secure child was in the top eight (of 15) ranks (rank 5) in the first class. In the second class (N = 25) there was only one secure child in the first 13 ranks (rank 10), with 8 of the 9 secure children in the bottom half (i.e., independent)[3]. Both of these results are highly significant and quite notable when taken together.

All three dependency ratings (those developed for this project, those devised by Don Rahe, and the overall Beller (1955) dependency rating), as well as the Q-sort mega item for dependency, favored the securely attached children (all $p < .01$). Rating results for the specific Beller dependency scales were quite noteworthy. Anxious children were significantly higher on the subscales having to do with frequency of seeking help in self-management, social management, and seeking attention in negative ways. They were significantly *lower* on seeking attention in positive ways (i.e., secure children showed more *positive* attention seeking). In addition, there was no significant difference on being near the teacher; that is, *it was not*

---

[3]The exact ranks of Classroom 2 were as follows: C, C, A, A, C, A, C, A, A, B, C, A, C, B, B, C, B, B, A, A, C, B, B, B

the frequency of teacher contact that was most revealing, but the nature of the contact that was of greatest importance. Children who were secure as infants were, of course, involved with the teachers, but they were involved in positive ways, which did not compromise their autonomy or budding peer relations.

Large group seating data. The teacher dependency data was corroborated by observations in subgroup song and story time ("large" group). Three scores were computed to represent contact-seeking in large (song time) group in the second class: (1) the proportion of times a child did *not* sit by a teacher (i.e., sat with other children); (2) the proportion of times the child sat on a teacher's lap, and (3) a weighted score in which 1 point was assigned for sitting next to a teacher, 2 points for making contact with a teacher, and 3 points for sitting on the teacher's lap. All were corrected for attendance and were based on 50 or more observations per child. Nonparametric analyses of all three indices revealed that the securely attached children were less dependent on teachers than anxious children in this context. Only the weighted score was properly distributed for parametric analysis and this analysis yielded a significant difference between secure and anxious groups. The weighted index correlated signficantly with the composited teacher rank ordering on dependency (rho = .62). The weighted scores were .71, .86, and .24 for As, Cs and Bs, respectively. In sum, *both As and Cs were found to be highly dependent based on these measures,* despite their different forms of maladaptive attachment in infancy.

Expression of Affect and Impulses

Having experienced a relationship with an emotionally responsive adult, securely attached children were expected to be affectively positive as preschoolers, to enjoy themselves, and to engage and respond regularly to other children with positive affect. Similarly, having had a history in which their emotional needs were met, they were expected to be less frequently angry, tantrumy, or aggressive, and, in general, less affectively negative. Affect measures have been powerful discriminators of securely attached children at younger ages (e.g., Matas et al., 1978; Waters et al., 1979).

All of the relevant data confirmed these predictions. For both classes the teachers rated the securely attached children as significantly higher on positive affect and lower on negative affect. For the first class a Q-sort mega-item for affect also discriminated the groups. The avoidant and resistant groups were never different from each other.

The affect and impulse expression checklist data supported these teacher assessments. Based on subgroup (outdoor) data in the second class, securely attached children more commonly initiated, responded to, and sustained interactions with others using positive affect. The molar composite of these ("positive social engagement") was significant ($t = 2.84, p < .01$). Moreover, securely attached children showed less whining ($t = -2.30, p = .031$) and negative affect in general ($t = -3.15, p < .005$); less aggression ($t = -1.97, p = .061$), and fewer negative responses to initiation ($t = -1.72, p < 10$). Negative affect distinguished the secure from the anxious group, even based on the indoor (total group) observations ($t = 2.40, p = .025$).

Social Competence

Teacher rankings of social competence favored the secure children in each class, and were significant for the two classes combined. Likewise the rating of social skill for the two classes combined favored the securely attached children ($t = 2.53, p < .02$), and the teachers ranked the secure children higher in terms of number of friends ($X^2 = 7.56, p < .01$). The findings on affect, presented above, are congruent with these teacher assessments of social competence.

In addition, although sociometric status is not a pure measure of social competence, it is an important aspect of preschool adaptation, and it is based on an independent source of information—the children themselves. It also was found to correlate with teacher rankings of social competence .56 and .85 in the first and second classes, respectively. The securely attached children held the majority of the high rank positions on popularity in both classes, and for the two classes combined this was significant ($X^2 = 7.56, p < .01$). Given the positive initiations and responses to peers of the secure children, this result is not surprising.

There were no significant differences on any of these measures between avoidant and resistant groups.

Classroom Department

Securely attached children are expected to pose fewer management problems for teachers given their ability to meet their needs for attention in positive ways and their expectations concerning the availability, dependability, and believeability of adults. They would be expected to engage teachers positively and to accept limits readily.

Overall, the teachers rated the securely attached children as more compliant ($t = 2.24, p < .05$), two classes combined). The behavioral data (teacher–child contacts) suggested that this result was due to a small number of anxiously attached children. In Classroom 2, four children were extremely high in terms of frequency of discipline (3 sds above the mean). No other children were more than 1 SD above the mean. Two of these children were

As and two were Cs. Likewise, the three high discipline children in Class 1 were one A, one C and one mixed child (a B who became a C at 18 months). Thus, not all anxiously attached children later showed acting out, behavior problems, but a young child manifesting such problems in an extreme form is likely to have a history of an avoidant or resistant attachment relationship.

Empathy

Prediction of emphatic behavior in preschool children is of great theoretical importance. Parallel to the prediction of independence for those children who had a close, secure attachment relationship in infancy, the prediction here is that these same children, having experienced responsive (empathic) care, and having developed a sense of trust (c.f. Erikson, 1963), will have a functional capacity for empathic response to others. In stark contrast, children from an avoidant attachment relationship, having experienced unavailability or rejection in time of emotional need, should be unlikely to have functional empathic capacity and, in some cases, should even show pleasure (or taunting) to the distress of others. (This would not necessarily indicate a lack of cognitive role taking skill. In fact, to victimize requires as much role taking skill as to empathize). Resistant children would be expected to show limited empathy because of the extent of their disorganization, anxiety, or need; that is, their own preoccupations would interfere. They would not be *un*empathic.

Results for the Q-sort mega item for empathy came out exactly in accord with these hypotheses. Empathy was "characteristic" for the secure group, "uncharacteristic" for the avoidant group, and the resistant group fell between. The appropriate F test for this prediction was highly significant ($F(1,22) = 8.238, p < .01$).

We have not yet analyzed our video tape records or scanning data for empathy. As is well known, instances of empathy in the natural context are rare. But, during scanning periods (two weeks) and on weekly film days, we focused on children's reactions to any instance of injury or emotional upset. These data should provide a sufficient base for examining the behavioral support for the teacher judgments.

DISTINGUISHING AMONG PATTERNS OF MALADAPTATION

Although the empathy results are intriguing, up to this point the other findings presented have pertained to the differences between children with a history of secure attachment and those with a history of anxious attachment, regardless of the particular pattern. The differences presented have been at times dramatic and they have cut across behavior domains, procedures of data collection, and methods of analysis. In the preschool, children with a history of anxious attachment are less ego-resilient (have lower self-esteem), are more dependent, show more negative affect and negative behavioral signs, show less positive affective engagement with others, and are less popular with peers. In general, they are emotionally less healthy than children with a history of secure attachment. The present data provide the strongest support to date for continuity in competence (or maladaptation) across the early years. Still, it remains for us to address the second, and more challenging, objective of this research: to what extent do children with different histories of early maladaptation show different patterns of maladaptation in the preschool? What differences can be demonstrated *between* the avoidant and resistant groups?

Most of the measures reported to this point really are not suitable for discriminating the avoidant (A) and resistant (C) groups. Neither group A nor group C should be ego-resilient, and both groups would be expected to have low self-esteem and marked dependency problems. Both groups would be expected to be low on popularity, low on social competence, and to be unable to cope with stress, but for different reasons. Both groups should present educational and classroom management problems. But these problems should be manifest in different ways.

Even the Block's (1979) ego-control dimension, based on teacher Q-sorts, failed to distinguish between As and Cs; 3 of 8 Cs and 2 of 8 As were highly undercontrol may be associated with either pattern of anxious attachment. expressions of behavior (seeing the "explosion" and not the immediateness or directness), rather than to the child's attempts to screen out the feelings or impulses prior to the expression. More subtle analyses of our videotape material may yet show the avoidant children to be more controlled in dealing with desires and impulses. It is, of course, possible that the avoidant and resistant patterns, which both are so strongly correlated with ego-brittleness (negatively correlated with resiliency) are orthogonal to the ego-control dimension. Early adaptation may interact with the style of parental socialization of impulses during the toddler period such that over and undercontrol may be associated with either pattern of anxious attachment. The seven children who were highly undercontrolled in our preschool all showed undercontrolled patterns in our problem solving situation at age two, as revealed by high dependency and/or frustration directed at their mothers. It was clear by that point that under some circumstances A children could be highly undercontrolled.

It is also clear that A and C children cannot be distinguished by an internalizing/externalizing dimension. Some internalizing children may be emotionally isolated or disconnected (certainly congruent with an avoidant history), whereas others may be timid, passive, and weak, which would be consistent with a history of resistant attachment if a social orientation were maintained. Likewise, some externalizing children may be hostile and antisocial, while others are better described as easily frustrated and impulsive. There is room for both *A*s and *C*s at the externalizing end of the dimension as well. Probably, no single dimension can capture the differences we seek, and it is unlikely that it would be possible to create a single ideal *A* or *C* Q-sort criterion either. The complexity is too great. There is not one kind of "*A* child" at 5-years, nor one kind of "*C* child." Still, it should be possible to distinguish externalizing and internalizing children, who had shown avoidant or resistant (*A* or *C*) patterns of attachment in infancy.

Early in the preschool project it was clear that histories of avoidant or resistant attachment had differential consequences, but that the outcomes were complex and variable. For example, when teachers commented that one particular child (*ET*) was "just like" another (*RJ*), both had the same history; in this case both had been *A*s. And when they said *RE* was just like *KD*, both had been *C*s. Visitors who were theoretically informed, but naive about the classifications of our subjects,[4] were remarkably able to predict the children's attachment history. Similarly, the children who showed "classic" behaviors, such as repeated indirect (i.e., oblique) approaches to teachers or uncontrolled diffuse scattering of objects, had been *A*s and *C*s, respectively. Despite all of this, differentiating children who had been *A*s and *C*s in "objective" terms proved quite challenging.

The teacher data provided several opportunities for making qualitative distinctions between *A*s and *C*s. First, in addition to all of the other data, each teacher had been asked to write a phrase descriptive of each child in Class 2; that is, the most outstanding impression they had formed of the child. These statements, which are presented for each child in Table 3.3, were read by four independent coders and used to classify the children into five categories (see Table 3.4). The first three categories (hostile, isolated, disconnected) represented the theoretical patterns expected as likely outcomes for children who had been anxious avoidant; the final two (impulsive, helpless, etc.) represent the anxious resistant outcomes. The outcome of this procedure was quite clear: 6 of 8 avoidant children consistently were placed in the avoidant categories, none in categories 4 or 5; 5 of 7 resistant children[5] were placed in the resistant categories; one was placed in category 3. The probability of this outcome is .006.

A similar classification was carried out using the five "most characteristic" items for each child from the Block-Q-sorts made by the

---

[4]For example, Eleanor Maccoby.

[5]Descriptive phrases were not available for the 1 resistant child who moved from the area and was replaced.

TABLE 3.3

Teacher One-Phrase Descriptions of Individual
Children in Classroom Two

Group A (Avoidant)
Subject
1. Mean to other children, kept things which didn't belong to her.
   The most dishonest preschooler I have ever met.
   Mean lying — everything is hers.
2. Very mad, "I hate myself!"
   An unhappy and angry kid. Terrible self-concept.
   Angry, unhappy.
3. So mean — lack of respect for humans.
   Angry, mean, playing with cars.
   Out of control, trying to do better.
4. Sad, depressed and withdrawn child.
   By himself.
   Coy, looks like a baby.
5. "She's not my friend," spaced.
   Affable but mentally slow.
   Inappropriately, highly impulsive and vulnerable good natured.
6. An angry, withdrawn, rigid person.
   Attached to Kate (teacher).
   "I love you, Kate." so frail but gutsy.
7. Dominant, self-reliant.
   Sweet/funny and responsible yet not always fair or kind.
8. A very nice kid — level headed, capable of taking care of himself.
   Warm, responsive.
   Loving, calling for Sarah (child), Jane Love (teacher).

Group B
Subject
1. Ideal kid, good looking, OK.
   Well-coordinated, agile, competent.
   Very solid kid. Vulnerable to life changes positive and negative.
2. Happy, rising star in the group — looked better all of the time.
   Agile, coordinated, jumping around room.
   Shy, but gutsy with car group.
3. Spunky sleeper — more powerful than meets the eye.
   Competent, quiet.
   So funny, cute, elf-like.
4. Very nice kid — sensitive and somewhat moody.
   Quiet, drifted at times, kept to herself.
   Depressed, withdrawn easily hurt.
5. Queen bee, to Lewis (child), "I'm not done yet!"
   Sparkplug. Competent, yet over stimulated other kids at times.
   Dominant, trouble waiting her turn. Excited other kids.
6. Very competent yet unsure of self — over-socialized female.
   Feminine.
   Dressed up, sucking finger, coy.
7. A mystery — looks OK, but never in plays where it was "scarey".
   "I don't feel good. I'm sick".
   Dependent, sad, frail.

TABLE 3.3 (continued)

8. Always up high — attached to Kate.
   Up high — look at me.
   Very confusing to me. A spacey, undersocialized kid.
9. Don't know him. Seemed OK yet rigid and somewhat tight.
   Evasive.
   "Boys can't wear those shirts.

Group C
Subject
1. Play with yellow truck. Trouble dealing with stress.
   Confusing — OK outwardly, yet sad and prone to self recrimination/guilt.
   Falling down in dramatic scene — an actor.
2. Bright but impulsive and tense.
   Frustrated easily in play situations inconsiderate of children.
   Holding "gun" saying it is his.
3. "High"—difficult to settle and difficult to concentrate.
   High (hyper).
   An operator — popular and fast (very illusive).
4. Running around being Batman.
   "Bull shit", angry, Batman, didn't like self.
   A confused and angry kid doing the best he can.
5. Immature and unwilling to take a risk/loves Skye.
   Lacks initiative, looking for Skye, controlled.
   A baby, can't tolerate kids.
6. "Kate (teacher), push me", "Where's Karyn (teacher)?"
   Dependent, liking Solomon.
   Happy/sad — is competent but does not handle disapproval or stress well.
7. Always going part way up and then down the loft ladder.
   Weird mouth, sunken eyes, tiny.
   A sleeper, knows more than her withered appearance lets on.

TABLE 3.4

Hypothetical Profiles

A Groups
- A_a Hostile/mean, aggressive, antisocial (lying, stealing, devious).
- A_b Emotionally insulated, asocial, isolated.
- A_c Disconnected, spaced out, psychotic-like. May be oblivious or bizarre, or just not know what is going on.

C Groups
- C_a Overstimulated (hyper), easily frustrated, tense or anxious, impulsive, flailing out, rather than hostile.
- C_b Dependent, passive, weak, helpless, teacher oriented.

three teachers. Three different coders, blind to the identity of the children, used this procedure. In comparison to the results with the descriptive phrases, this procedure was somewhat less discriminating, but still yielded significant results: 5 As were called As, none were called Cs; 4 Cs were called Cs, 1 an A ($p = .020$).

We also used the teacher responses on the checklists developed by Egeland (adapted from Behar, 1974) for the larger longitudinal study. Checklist items were selected that were thought likely to characterize each of our five patterns (Table 3.5). For each item a child could get a score of 2 ("certainly applies"), 1 ("sometimes"), or 0, and the responses of the three teachers were combined across the set of items. A child was then placed in one of the five categories if his score for the given item was more than 1 SD above the mean. When there was more than one elevation, the total profile was examined. (When there was an even split the child was classed as an A. It was reasoned that Cs should not be hostile, for example, though As may well be impulsive, etc.) Consistent with the other findings just presented, using this procedure 5 As were called A, while 1 A was called a C; and 5 Cs were called Cs, with 1 C called an A ($p = .032$). The same C child was called an A by each procedure. (Using the checklist procedure, 17 children were called Bs across the two classes—being high on none of the lists: 14 of these were Bs, 2 were As and 1 was a C.)

Thus, within the teacher data there was considerable evidence for a distinction between the patterns of adaptation shown by children with different histories of maladaptive attachment. Despite the fact that global ratings and rankings, as well as a host of observational variables, failed to distinguish children with different histories of maladaptation, the dynamics of the behavior, as inferred by the behavioral organization, revealed that these remain qualitatively different patterns of maladaptation.

To date we have been able to marshall some tentative support for the distinctions presented above from our observational data. Very few specific variables showed differences between As and Cs, but when they did they were in theoretically meaningful directions (for example, unprovoked aggression, inept leadership, which characterized As and Cs, respectively). It is in the profiles of behavior, however, where we expected the most meaningful differences to lie. This is a matter for ongoing data analysis.

THE POWER OF THE ATTACHMENT ASSESSMENTS

Although it will take years to analyze all of the data from this project, much has already been learned about the study of individual differences in adaptation. First, these data represent the strongest demonstration of the coherence of individual adaptation to date. After the fact, it is sometimes

TABLE 3.5

Items from the Preschool Behavior Questionnaire
(adapted from Behar, 1974)
Relevant to the Five Patterns of Maladaptation

Pattern A_a
  Tells lies
  Bullies other children
  Blames others
  Inconsiderate of others

Pattern A_b
  Tends to do things on own, rather solitary
  Stares into space
  Fails to play with most other children
  Is shy, bashful
  Has flat affect — rarely expresses positive or negative feelings directly

Pattern A_c
  Has twitches, mannerisms, or tics of the face and body
  Stares into space
  Demonstrates little interest in things and activities in environment
  Daydreams frequently
  Rocks, sways, whirls or does othere repetitive whole body movements

Pattern C_a
  Restless. Runs about or jumps up and down. Doesn't keep still
  Squirmy, fidgety child
  Has poor concentration or short attention span
  Is impulsive, acts without thinking
  Is easily upset by failure
  Is tense or jittery in everyday situations or activities

Pattern C_b
  Tends to be fearful or afraid of new things or new situations
  Gives up easily
  Is hypersensitive, easily hurt
  Stays close or clings to mother or adult
  Acts overly fearful and cautious
  Lacks initiative, is passive and easily led

difficult to fully appreciate the importance of such a demonstration. A brief recapitulation of what has been shown may be useful. Concentrating on the comparison of the *A* and *B* (secure) groups is most instructive.

It is important to recall that these predictions were based on assessments of attachment in Ainsworth's strange situation. In that context, there were many similarities between *A* and *B* babies. Both groups readily moved away from mother and got involved with toys during preseparation. Neither group (with the exception of subgroup *B*4, which had little representation in this study) tended to show much wariness of the stranger, proximity to mother, or crying prior to separation. But there were critical differences. The major distinctions were that, during separation, the Bs were less likely to find the stranger an acceptable substitute and, especially, the Bs were more active in seeking contact or interaction upon reunion with the mother. The As tended to avoid their mothers upon reunion, especially following the second separation when stress was presumed to be greater. These were not differences in proximity seeking per se, because some Bs were content with distance interaction. They were differences in seeking psychological contact or avoiding it when needs were aroused; that is, they were differences concerning expectations about the availability and responsiveness of significant people to emotional needs.

As and Bs may be distinguished by reunion behavior alone, 6 minutes of observation or, given the stability required in this study, 12 minutes. From these observed differences in the manner of dealing with the stress of brief separation in the laboratory, the profound differences in adaptation three years later were predicted. For example, 9 of 11 As showed negative correlations with the resiliency criterion versus none of the 16 Bs. The As were higher on dependency and negative peer behavior, lower on empathy and peer acceptance. They tended to be hostile, disconnected, and/or emotionally insulated. Obviously, the attachment assessments did not represent 12 random minutes of behavior. There is something very powerful in this attachment construct. And we, of course, reaped the harvest from the important theoretical work of Bowlby and Ainsworth and the hundreds upon hundreds of hours of home observation that underlay the strange situation assessment. There is something, also, to the developmental perspective that allows qualitatively similar patterns of adaptation to be inferred from changing behavior in different contexts using different methods. Finally, there is something to the notion of coherence in individual adaptation. Developmental history leaves its mark. Early development and early care are important.

ATTACHMENT AND TEMPERAMENT

At this point I would like to make a clear statement about the issue of an endogenous basis for the observed individual differences. Despite the fact that there is *no* evidence that observed differences at or near birth are stable, or predict later behavior, the idea that behavior and emotional disorders are based on inborn temperament is still widely held (e.g., Buss & Plomin, 1975). It is overlooked that the Thomas, Chess, and Birch (1968) data were based on parental report, uncorroborated by behavioral observation, that stability or developmental outcome was not assessed for Schaffer and Emerson's (1964) "cuddly" and "non-cuddly" babies, and that other studies of individual differences in newborns (reviewed by Korner, 1971) had no follow-up. Early pathognomic signs may predict later disorder (Bergman & Escalona, 1949), but such signs of neurological status should not be confused with normal temperamental variation. Moreover, it should be noted that attempts to find stability in early infant behavior yield negative results (Blehar, Lieberman, & Ainsworth, 1977; see also Emde, Gaensbaerer & Harmon, 1976). In our own longitudinal study (Egeland, Deinard & Sroufe), for example, there were virtually no differences between As and Bs on Apgars, Brazelton neonatal exams at 7 days and 10 days, nurses' ratings in the hospital, behavioral observations 3 months, or Carey temperament questionnaire responses (derived from Thomas, Chess, & Birch, 1968) at 6 months (Egeland & Farber, in preparation; Waters, Vaughn, & Egeland, 1980). Infants probably do differ in temperament, and such differences probably influence certain aspects of behavior. But they do not account for the profound differences in quality of adaptation that we observe. Even when relationships have been found, as in the case of Cs in the Egeland sample (Waters et al., 1980), these are best interpreted as due to the additional challenge presented by a neurologically nonoptimal baby to an already overtaxed and under prepared mother. The inborn difficulties do not create the personality.

From a traditional temperament interpretation it would be held that the avoidant infants were constitutionally uncuddly, unexpressive, or precociously independent. It would be difficult from such a position to predict the range of behavioral problems and low peer status of these children. It would not seem possible to predict their hostility and aggression or their *high dependency* upon the teachers (which included much physical contact under restricted circumstances). Yet, these outcomes follow directly from the Bowlby/Ainsworth theory. The avoidant attachment is a pattern of adaptation within the most significant early relationship. As such, it has profound implications for the child's later adaptation; that is, for the manner of meeting basic needs and coping with stresses and challenges in the environment. But it is not an endogenous characteristic of the child. These children are not "independent by nature."

The dependency (and aggression) of the avoidant children also is somewhat paradoxical from an operant position. These children did not seem to be rewarded for contact seeking behavior. On the contrary, in their histories such efforts were met by non-responsiveness or rejection. And to be sure, their initial tendency to *express* these behaviors in the classroom was not high. Yet, given the opportunity, strong dependency needs became manifest. One cannot extinguish dependency. Likewise, aggressive behaviors may have been reinforced somewhere in the histories of these children, but the possibility of predicting aggression at a time when it has not yet become manifest reveals the limitations of a purely operant position for understanding disordered development. For all of its power in explaining the maintenance and expression of behavior in the repertoire, the operant position requires much supplementing to account for meaningful individual differences in behavioral organization.

THE DIFFICULTY OF PREDICTING SPECIFIC PATTERNS OF MALADAPTATION

The difficulty of predicting specific patterns of maladaptation (let alone competence or incompetence) should be neither surprising nor discouraging. The difficulty arises from many sources.

First, each individual child is making an ongoing adaptation to the unique circumstances in which he or she lives (and in this sense there is no *mal*adaptation). These circumstances may be highly changeable, and this is certainly the case in our sample (Vaughn, Egeland, Waters, & Sroufe, 1979). People move in and move out. Residences are changed. Jobs are lost. Siblings are born. Without doubt, experiences within the three years between infancy and preschool have a powerful influence on development. And given the uniqueness in the twists and turns in individual lives, it is no wonder that each behavioral profile appears unique. There are certainly more than five types of maladaptation in the preschool. (The one C child who was consistently categorized in the psychotic-like A_c group makes it clear that, at the least, provision must be made in any classification scheme for Cs who break down). Likewise, it is no wonder that some As and Cs look better than some Bs and that some As and Cs are difficult to distinguish. There are not invulnerable children, only children who are more resilient than others in the face of stress. And A or C refers to a pattern of adaptation within a relationship, not to a characteristic of the child alone. Moreover, parents change. I would expect that if instead of inconsistent, or ambivalent care, a child received responsive, developmentally appropriate care over a period of time (most likely due to changes in the parent's own circumstances), that child may well be competent in preschool. If inconsistent care changed to chronic rejection I expect the child would move toward the A pattern of adaptation (see Egeland & Sroufe, 1981a).

In addition, the quality of a child's adaptation in the preschool likely is influenced by the ways parents managed the child's impulses and feelings during the transition from infancy to childhood (see also Kopp, Krakow, & Vaughn, this volume). Even when such socialization is consistent with attachment history (e.g., inappropriate means of managing impulses following unhealthy attachment), differences between parents' styles contribute to making each child's pattern of adaptation unique. A parent that was emotionally unavailable in infancy could be either punitive and controlling or lax in dealing with a child's budding autonomy (although emotional distance probably would still be maintained). A parent that was disorganized and inconsistent in early care may be either seductive and over-stimulating with the toddler or simply erratic in maintaining limits. We have even seen emotionally distant, rejecting mothers use seductive behavior as a control technique (Sroufe & Ward, 1980). There is no doubt that such styles of dealing with the toddler's impulses and feelings will impact upon the quality of adaptation in complex ways.

The seven cases with a history of maternal seductiveness during the toddler period are instructive here. This history was revealed in each child's behavior, though, as we would now expect, in a variety of ways. All three children in Class 2 who were placed in category C_a (impulsive, anxious, overstimulated) have mothers who were observed to behave seductively. Another child in Class 1 was characterized by "tension bursts" (rapid hand jiggling during periods of arousal) and also was quite infantile. This infantile pattern (along with poutiness and extensive masturbation) characterized another child. The final two children (boys) were the outstanding "pets" of the female teachers, each of them eliciting a great deal of attention and affection. Likewise, they preferred female teachers in preference to any other person. These seven children (4 *C*s, 1 *A*, and 2 mixed, i.e., *B*s changed to *C*s) all were extreme in their own ways, while in terms of other measures they were in many cases indistinguishable from others in the class.

In addition to such complex influences on the pattern of adaptation, in our preschool research another factor worked against prediction; namely, the intervention of the teachers. Our teachers were both skilled and dedicated, and their interventions were aimed at the specific maladaptations of the most troubled children.

Given these considerations, one may wonder how any coherence could ever be demonstrated. I believe there are three reasons for the demonstrated coherence. First, fortunately and unfortunately, there is often continuity in the quality of care. Parents who are inconsistent in responding to the infant's signals commonly are inconsistent and unclear in setting and maintaining limits for their toddler, and so forth.

Second, since children interact with the environment in terms of their previous adaptation, a self-perpetuating cycle is maintained. The *C* baby, for example, commonly is a tantrumy, difficult toddler who taxes the patience of the parent, and later is a highly dependent or impulsive preschooler who alienates others. The *A* baby learns not to seek the emotional support it needs and later keeps others at a distance through emotional isolation or hostility.

Finally, development is hierarchical; it is not a blackboard to be erased and written upon again. Even when children change rather markedly, the shadows of the earlier adaptation remain and, in times of stress, the prototype itself may be clear. Thus, one child who changed to a behavior pattern we identified as C at 24 months, despite being an A at 12 months and 18 months, looked in many ways like a C in the preschool. He was a severe behavior problem, disruptive, difficult and tantrumy. He even had a high score on crying. Yet, he was different from the Cs in the deviousness of his behavior, in his pleasure at other's distress, and in his systematic victimization of vulnerable children. This organized, antisocial behavior is out of the repertoire of the C child in our experience. Another child who went from a B to a C at 24 months was anxious, and somewhat passive and immature like some Cs, but he was also resilient, popular, and well organized in independent activities, like the Bs.

In many ways we are just beginning the complex task of defining specific patterns of developmental disorder. The results are encouraging in that they suggest that understanding the course of such specific patterns will be possible. There is reason to believe that within the next decade we may go well beyond the externalizing-internalizing dimension which has been of such importance in developmental psychopathology. Understanding in a precise way the course and dynamics of particular patterns of maladaptation will surely have implications for prevention and treatment of childhood and adult disorders. There are different reasons for aggression and social isolation, and, as teachers and therapists know, within these reasons are the clues for effective intervention.

FURTHER RESEARCH

There is much more to examine within our data concerning similarities and differences in patterns of adaptation. The children were seen in ongoing play pairs with a constant partner. It is reasonable to expect that patterns of adaptation are more clear within relationships than within the behavior of a particular child. These data will be analyzed in the future.

Another fruitful approach is to examine critical incidents in our video tapes, made weekly in the classroom. Certain events, although exceedingly rare, are revealing with respect to a child's inner dynamics. I have already mentioned the child who approached teachers through a series of oblique angles (much like one tacks a sailboat into the wind), and ultimately backed his way very near her, to wait for her initiation. Another child, having stood up under our observation booth and cracking her head, crawled off into a corner by herself. And another folded his arms and withdrew from everyone when he was disappointed. Still another hid a contraband toy in his pocket, went to great efforts in trying to elude the teacher, and then denied having the toy when questioned. All of these children were avoidant as infants, in accord with theoretical pedictions. Contrasting examples could be presented for Cs[6]. From such examples, which are present in sufficient numbers over the entire session, observers who are theoretically informed, though blind to developmental histories, should be able to describe and categorize individual children.

In further research on this problem it would be well to emphasize even more qualitative aspects of behavior and the meaning of the behavior as inferred from behavioral and situational context. Unless meaning is attended, it is doubtful that frequently occurring discrete behaviors, however complexly analyzed, will tell us very much about individual adaptation. Thus, I would not advocate sequential analysis as it is often thought of (the conditional probabilities of matrix of commonly occurring behaviors). On the other hand, sequential analysis, in the sense of trying to capture the flow of behavior should be very fruitful. We have to know not only what led up to a situation and its immediately surrounding context, but how the child perceived and experienced the situation and how his/her responses followed from that. We need to know how the child's behaviors are tied together. Characteristic reactions to situations, which in part are what we are after, can only be determined once we understand how the child construes the situation.

Finally, in continuing to look at data from this project, and in future studies, an important area for investigation is the relationships between children and teachers, which must have important implications for intervention. Teachers, of course, having individual personalities, behave differently toward different children. It was quite clear in our class that both teachers and children had special relationships. Different teachers felt especially close to particular children and had more difficulty being close with others. Children tended to select a specific attachment person. (When they did not, or, in some cases when the selected adult was of the opposite sex, this suggested problems.) Teachers knew quite well who was each child's "special person." This is all reasonable. From attachment theory, one would expect children, and even teachers to a lesser extent, to be selective. But it seemed clear to us that the availability of such a special relationship was critical. This means several adults should be in each classroom and, at times, the child's placement should be changed. All children deserve to be in a program where someone cares for them unconditionally. And no teacher should be expected to unconditionally love every child. I think this issue has been avoided too long.

Perhaps even more significant is the hypothesis that children elicit reac-

---

[6]For example, diffuse scattering of objects when upset, panic when unable to sit by a teacher, getting so excited that settling was not possible.

tions from teachers which are congruent with their history of maladaptation. Whenever a child so infuriated a teacher that he or she wanted to isolate the child in another room or in the corner, it was inevitable that this child had a history of chronic unavailability or rejection (and had been a Group A infant). Teacher reactions elicited by children who have experienced seductive maternal behavior have already been mentioned. Such observations should not be surprising. Systems are more powerful than people. It is not that teachers' feelings are wrong or inappropriate. On the contrary, their reactions generally may reflect the child's relational history. When it has been pathogenic, it is this history that must be countered. Our teachers understood this. And the preschool experience of our children was therapeutic.

CONCLUSION: MAY PATTERNS OF MALADAPTATION BE ALTERED?

Perhaps the major implication of this research is to underscore the fact that each child is making a particular and unique adaptation to his or her world. The closer we observed the children and the richer the data we obtained, the more coherent each child appeared. Even children with very disturbed behavior became understandable. Increasingly, disturbance was seen more in terms of pattern, rather than simply in terms of degree.

Even the most disturbed children must be viewed in terms of their particular patterns of adaptation. For example, *RE* was chronically anxious, a "wild eyed man" as one observer put it. He had little or no frustration tolerance, limited coping capacity, and was very immature. His inability to engage in reciprocal give and take, and his impulsive, acting out alientated other children. On the other hand, he "wore his heart on his sleeve." He was so clear about his desire for closeness and care that his behavioral and emotional problems did not alienate the teachers. In fact, they were continually supportive. In contrast, *EL* often irritated the teachers. His acts of hostile aggression toward weaker children, his devious behavior, and his blunt, matter-of-fact noncompliance ("No way, Jose!") infuriated them. But *EL,* unlike *RE*, was well-organized. And while some children disliked him strongly, several others chose him as friend. His social skills advanced far more quickly than did *RE*'s. The point is not new. But it bears repeating that each child should be considered in terms of the particular strengths and weaknesses he or she shows. These strengths and weaknesses will have implications for intervention.

In this context, it should be clear that these children are not beyond intervention, with *very* rare exceptions. It is sometimes concluded that the strong evidence in our research for continuity of individual adaptation (or even a downward spiral of maladaptation; Egeland & Sroufe, 1981b) suggests a pessimism concerning intervention. This is certainly not the case. It does suggest, in contrast to positions assuming relatively complete resiliency (e.g., Kagan, Kearsley, & Zelazo, 1978), that powerful forces—within and outside of the child—operate to perpetuate a pattern of maladaptation once established. But intervention can be aimed to explicitly counter these influences, especially those within the child. For example, if the child does not expect people to be available, the teacher may be available—patiently, inevitably, constantly.

EL is a good example of this reachability of young disturbed children. His malicious, antisocial behavior, his apparent pleasure at others' distress, and his fearless contesting of wills with the teachers had all the marks of incipient sociopathy. His elaborate deviousness and his swaggering style seemed to confirm that he was beyond reach. But in fact, of course, no four year old can genuinely be a sociopath. And beneath the swagger was a desperately needy child (in terms of intensity no less needy than *RE*). The teachers quickly learned to see opportunities for closeness with *EL* and explicitly disconfirmed his feelings of low self worth by not rejecting him. As often as possible, the teachers prevented *EL* from engaging in hostile behavior. And when it was necessary to separate *EL* from other children, which was often the case early in the term, a teacher would stay with him. Having difficulty confirming his image of himself as bad, and being totally unable to confirm the belief that he was unworthy, *EL* had little choice but to change his behavior. He formed a strong attachment to the male teacher and made remarkable progress toward learning to meet his basic needs for closeness, as well as toward learning the rewards that may be found in relationships.

The "veneer of toughness" *EL* was building would have, of course, been much "thicker" in later years. Or, in Bowlby's (1980) more contemporary terms, his conceptual models of himself and others would have been more firmly established. Whether, untouched, children like *EL* can be reached in adolescence is open to question. "Models once established prove very hard to change (Bowlby, 1980, p. 241)." But I have no doubt that in the preschool years the vast majority of these troubled children could be helped in a fundamental way toward healthier development. One unfortunate implication of our data is, however, that without help these children are likely to carry forward patterns of maladaptation into later childhood and even adulthood. From a scientific point of view, this remains a hypothesis to be confirmed by further longitudinal data. From a humanitarian point of view, enough is known to compel programmatic, preventative action.

REFERENCES

Achenbach, T. M. The classification of children's psychiatric symptoms: A factor analytic study. *Psychological Monographs,* 1966, *80.*
Ainsworth, M. D. S., Blehar, M., Waters, E., & Wall, S. *Patterns of attachment.* Hillsdale, N.J.: Lawrence Erlbaum Associates, 1978.
Arend, R., Gove, F., & Sroufe, L. A. Continuity of individual adaptation from infancy to kindergarten. A predictive study of ego-resiliency and curiosity in preschoolers. *Child Development,* 1979, *50,* 950–959.
Asher, S. R., Singleton, L. C., Tinsley, B. R., & Hymel, S. A reliable sociometric measure for preschool children. *Developmental Psychology,* 1979, *15,* 443–444.
Behar, L. B., & Stingfield, S. A behavior rating scale for the preschool child. *Development Psychology,* 1974, *10,* 601–610.
Beller, E. K. Dependency and independence in young children. *Journal of Genetic Psychology,* 1955, *87,* 25–35.
Bergman, P., & Escalona, S. Unusual sensitivities in very young children. In P. Greenacre (Ed.), *The Psycholanalytic Study of the Child.* New York: International Universities Press, 1949.
Blehar, M. C., Lieberman, A. F., & Ainsworth, M. D. S. Early face-to-face interaction and its relation to later infant-mother attachment. *Child Development,* 1977, *48,* 182–194.
Block, J. H., & Block, J. The role of ego-control and ego-resiliency in the organization of behavior. In W. A. Collins (Ed.), *Minnesota symposia on child psychology* (Vol. 13). Hillsdale, N.J.: Lawrence Erlbaum Associates, 1979.
Bowlby, J. *Attachment and Loss,* Vol. I, *Attachment.* New York: Basic Books, Inc., 1969.
Bowlby, J. *Attachment and Loss,* Vol. II, *Separation: Anxiety and Anger.* London: Hogarth, 1973.
Bowlby, J. *Attachment and Loss,* Vol. III, *Loss, Sadness and Depression.* New York: Basic Books, 1980.
Breger, L. *From Instinct to Identity.* Englewood Cliffs, N.J., Prentice-Hall, Inc., 1974.
Buss, A., & Plomin, R. A. *Temperament theory of personality development.* New York: Wiley, 1975.
Egeland, B., Deinard, A., & Sroufe, L. A. Early maladaptation: A prospective-transactional study. Office of Maternal and Child Health, 1977.
Egeland, B., & Sroufe, L. A. Attachment and early maltreatment. *Child Development,* 1981, *52,* 44–52. (a)
Egeland, B., & Sroufe, L. A. Developmental sequelae of maltreatment in infancy. In R. Rizley & D. Cicchetti (Eds.), *Developmental perspectives in child maltreatment.* San Francisco: Jossey-Bass, 1981. (b)
Emde, R., Gaensbauer, T., & Harmon, R. Emotional expression in infancy. *Psychological Issues Monograph Series,* 1976, *10,* (No. 37).
Erikson, E. H. *Childhood and society.* New York: Norton, 1963.
Gove, F. Patterns and organizations of behavior and affect expression during the second year of life. Unpublished doctoral dissertation, University of Minnesota, 1982.
Klein, G. S. *Psychoanalytic theory, an exploration of essentials.* New York: International Universities Press, Inc., 1976.
Kopp, C., Krakow, J., & Vaughn, B. Patterns of self-control in young handicapped children. In M. Perlmutter (Ed.), *Minnesota symposium on child psychology,* Vol. 16. Hillsdale, N.J.: Lawrence Erlbaum Associates, 1983.
Korner, A. Individual differences at birth: Implications for early experience and later development. *American Journal of Orthopsychiatry,* 1971, *41,* 608–619.
Loevinger, J. *Ego development.* San Francisco: Jossey-Bass, 1976.

Mahler, M., Pine, F., & Bergman, A. *The psychological birth of the human infant.* New York: Basic Books, 1975.

Main, M. Play, exploration and competence as related to child-adult attachment. Unpublished doctoral dissertation, The Johns Hopkins University, 1973.

Main, M. Analysis of a peculiar form of reunion behavior seen in some daycare children: Its history and sequelae in children who are home-reared. In R. Webb (Ed.), *Social development in daycare.* Baltimore: Johns Hopkins University Press, 1977.

Matas, L., Arend, R., & Sroufe, L. A. Continuity of adaptation in the second year: the relationship between quality of attachment and later competence. *Child Development,* 1978, *49,* 547-556.

Neilon, P. Shirley's babies after 15 years: a personality study. *Journal of Genetic Psychology,* 1948, *73,* 175-186.

Robbins, L. *Deviant children grow up.* Baltimore: Williams and Wilkins, 1966.

Sander, L. Infant and caretaking environment. In E. J. Anthony (Ed.), *Explorations in child psychiatry.* New York: Plenum, 1975.

Schaffer, H., & Emerson, P. Patterns of response to physical contact in early human development. *Journal of Child Psychology and Psychiatry,* 1964, *5,* 1-13.

Shirley, M. *The first two years: A study of 25 babies.* Minneapolis: University of Minnesota Press, 1931.

Sroufe, L. A. The coherence of individual development. *American Psychologist,* 1979, *34,* 834-841.

Sroufe, L. A., & Rosenberg, D. Coherence of individual adaptation in lower class infants and toddlers. Paper presented at the International Conference on Infant Studies. Providence, RI, 1980.

Sroufe, L. A., & Ward, M. Seductive behavior of mothers of toddlers: Occurrence, correlates and consequences. *Child Development,* 1980, *51,* 1222-1229.

Sullivan, H. S. *The interpersonal theory of psychiatry.* New York: W. W. Norton, 1953.

Thomas, A., Chess, S., and Birch, H. G. *Temperament and Behavior Disorders in Children.* New York, New York: University Press, 1968.

Vaughn, B. E., Egeland, B., Sroufe, L. A., & Waters, E. Individual differences in infant-mother attachment at 12 and 18 months: stability and change in families under stress. *Child Development.* 1979, *50,* 971-975.

Vaughn, B., Taraldson, B., Crichton, L., & Egeland, B. The assessment of infant temperament: a critique of the Carey Temperament Questionnaire. *Infant Behavior & Development,* 1981, *4,* 1-17.

Vaughn, B. E., & Waters, E. Social organization among preschool peers: Dominance, attention and sociometric correlates. In D. Omark, F. Strayer, & D. Freedman (Eds.), *Dominance relations: An ethological view of human conflict and social interaction.* New York: Garland, 1980.

Waters, E. The reliability and stability of individual differences in infant-mother attachment. *Child Development,* 1978, *49,* 483-494.

Waters, E., Vaughn, B., & Egeland, B. Individual differences in mother-infant attachment relationships at age one: Antecedents in neonatal behavior in an urban, economically disadvantaged sample. *Child Development,* 1980, *51,* 208-216.

Waters, E., Wippman, J., & Sroufe, L. A. Attachment, positive affect and competence in the peer group: two studies in construct validation. *Child Development,* 1979, *50,* 821-829.

Weikart, D. Intervention programming for preschool children. In M. Perlmutter (Ed.), *Minnesota symposium in child psychology,* Vol. 16. New Jersey, Lawrence Erlbaum Associates, 1983.

Appendix

MINNESOTA PRESCHOOL AFFECT CHECKLIST

Edward J. Schork and L. Alan Sroufe
Institute of Child Development, University of Minnesota

CHILD:_____ Time:_____ Activity:
Date:_____ Observer:_____ FPW FPH
Period: I II III   C   SG
                                                     LMO LMI

Positive Affect
1. ____ displays positive affect in *any* manner (baseline)
2. ____ uses positive affect to initiate contact, to engage another (must begin, or restart interaction after a substantial break)
3. ____ when *already in interaction with someone,* directs positive affect at them (affect is *directed at a specific person)*
4. ____ when in a social situation, displays positive affect but *does not direct it to any one in particular.*
5. ____ shows *very positive affect:* exuberance, "lights up"
6. ____ shows *ongoing high enjoyment,* "has a lot of fun" (sustained continuously for 30 sec. or more)
7. ____ *uses face very expressively* to show *positive* affect *in communicating directly with another.*
8. ____ uses positive affect in a way that makes a significant contribution to keeping a social interaction going (with one or more others)
9. ____ shows pride in accomplishment (usually verbal statement)

Negative Affect
10. ____ displays negative affect in *any* manner (baseline).
11. ____ uses negative affect *to initiate contact, to begin a social interaction* with someone.
12. ____ directs negative affect specifically *at a particular other person* when *already in interaction with them.*
13. ____ *uses face very expressively* to show negative affect in *communicating directly* with another.
14. ____ facial expression *looks depressed* (can be brief).
15. ____ shows *very negative* affect: anger, distress, protest, crying vigorously, etc.

Inappropriate Affect
16. ____ expresses *negative affect* to another *CHILD* in *response to the other's neutral or positive overture* (appears inappropriate in context)
17. ____ *fails to show positive affect when appropriate* (as defined by context) (e.g., in a group when others are all laughing)
18. ____ *fails to show negative affect when appropriate* (e.g., after being hit)
19. ____ takes *pleasure in another's distress.*
20. ____ *does not respond* when approached affectively by another.
21. ____ *cries* in the *absence of physical injury.*
22. ____ *whines* in the *absence of physical injury.*

Involvement: Productive, Focused Use of Personal Energy
23. ____ *engrossed, absorbed, intensely involved* in an activity: *emotionally invested* in *creative, productive, thematically organized,* or *other* activity that has a positive emotional function (does *not* include intensive but unfocused activity, e.g., running around the room)
24. ____ *independence:* involvement in an activity that the child *organizes for himself.*

Involvement: Unproductive, Unfocused use of Personal Energy
25. ____ *wandering: moves around the room* with *no/little involvement* in social interaction or activities.
26. ____ *listless:* looks fidgety and *emotionally uninvested but still emotionally "present"; stays in one area,* but shows *little/no involvement* in activities or social interaction.
27. ____ *vacant: very flat,* unexpressive, *detached face,* no involvement, *looks "emotionally absent."*
28. ____ *tension bursts:* undirected motor release (one or several) (usually brief).
29. ____ *extremely high activity* in comparison to context (outdoors: risk of harm to self/others also involved).
30. ____ *diffuse:* looks *somewhat emotionally invested but unable to sustain it* for long in any one activity, i.e., "jumps from one thing to another" (gets slightly *involved in one thing, then soon moves on, repeatedly).*

Lapses in Impulse Control and Negative Responses to Frustration, Conflict, and Other Emotionally Arousing Problem Situations (e.g., object struggle, teasing, rejection, inability to solve puzzle, encountering obstacle to goal attainment)

(check *left* if behavior is *response to emotionally arousing event,* check *right* if *no emotionally arousing "precipitating event" is observed,* including when already displaying behavior at beginning of observation) (*except:* note special rules for #31 and 36)

31. ____ *context-related, physical, interpersonal aggression* (someone does something to which the child responds with aggression—an emotionally arousing preceding event *must* be observed, usually but not necessarily provocation by another) (when no provocation is observed, check #45a) (see also #10-15, 21, 22)
32. ____ *hits,* kicks, shoves, knocks over, or throws *objects* (see also #10-15, 21, 22)
33. ____ *tantrum* (pronounced upset *and* loss of control) crf. #10-15, 21, 22)
34. ____ *very angry* (vs. tantrum: not as sustained, loss of control not as great and may be limited) (crf. #10-15, 21, 22)
35. ____ *inability to stop* ongoing behavior
36. ____ *withdrawal* (= *becomes withdrawn), "shuts down"* (whether leaves area or not) (NB: must see the withdrawal occur) (check *left* if withdrawal is response to emotionally arousing event, *right* if no precipitating arousing event is observed, and *neither* if already withdrawn at beginning—and in all cases consider also #14 and #27)
37. ____ *disorganized, non-goal-directed activity (left,* response to emo. arous.; *right,* no arousing event, including already this way at beginning.
38. ____ *pouty, sullen (left,* response to emo. arous.,; *right,* no arous. event, including already this way at beginning of interval)
(describe behavior, emotionally arousing events, responses of others:)

_____
_____
_____

Positive Reactions to Frustration, Conflict, and Emotionally Arousing Problem Situations (e.g., object struggle, teasing, rejection, inability to solve puzzle, encountering obstacle to goal attainment)

39. ____ *promptly expresses, in words, feelings arising from problem* situation *then moves on* to same or new activity (vs. withdrawing, displacing the affect to others or to objects, staying upset)
39a. ____ *shows* primarily *neutral or positive affect*
39b. ____ *shows primarily negative affect*
40. ____ shows ability to *tolerate well* (although *does not promptly verbalize feelings to others)*
(describe emotionally arousing event and behavior:_____

_____

Unusual Behavior
41. ____ *bizarre* bahavior (e.g., licking the wall)
42. ____ *mannerisms,* stereotypes (e.g., rolling the tongue around the mouth, characteristic facial distortions, characteristic nonverbal vocalizations) ("quirky gestures")

43. ____ *ritualistic, repetitive behaviors* (more complex, organized, and larger-scale than mannerisms, more normal than bizarre behaviors)

Social Isolation
44. ____ *no social interaction continuously* for *3 min.* or more.

Hostility
45a. ____ *unprovoked,* physical, interpersonal *aggression (no preceding provocative behavior by the victim)* (describe aggression and subsequent behavior by all involved):_____

_____

45b. ____ hazing, teasing, or other verbal or nonverbal provocation or threat

Skills in Leading and Joining
46a. ____ *successful leadership:* plays an organizing role in an activity in which other children "follow the lead" and participate
46b. ____ *inept attempts at leadership:* attempts to exert an organizing, directive, or leadership influence on others, but they do not comply (check on basis of others' noncompliance) (often includes self-defeating use of affect, e.g., bossiness)
47a. ____ *smoothly approaches* an already ongoing activity (does not disrupt or antagonize) and GETS ACTIVELY INVOLVED.
47b. ____ *smoothly approaches* an already ongoing activity (does not disrupt or antagonize) but DOES NOT GET ACTIVELY INVOLVED.

Empathy and Prosocial Behavior
48. ____ *interpersonal awareness:* behavior reflecting *knowledge or awareness about another person.*
(describe):_____

_____

49. ____ *empathy: concern* or other empathic response to another person's *emotional display* (usually when another is distressed)
(describe): _____

_____

50. ____ *helping* behavior (unsolicited) directed *to other child.*
51. ____ *helping* behavior (unsolicited) directed *to teacher.*

4 Comments on Sroufe's Chapter

William D. Erickson
Department of Child and Adolescent Psychiatry
University of Minnesota

CLINICAL IMPLICATIONS OF INDIVIDUAL PATTERNS OF ADAPTATION IN EARLY CHILDHOOD

Child psychiatrists have an obvious proprietary interest in the psychosocial development of young children. It is in the nature of our art that we spend much time and energy trying to correct the consequences of developmental failure, and salvaging the children of earlier disordered generations. Clinicians have known for some time that it is well to have a good relationship with one's mother, and that the benefits therefrom may be reaped for years to come. Mrs. Freud was enormously proud of her eldest son, whom she referred to as her "goldener Sigi," and Sigmund, the son, wrote "A man who has been the indisputable favorite of his mother keeps for life the feeling of a conqueror, that confidence of success that often induces real success" (Trilling & Marcus, 1961). But Sroufe's findings shake some other basic clinical assumptions, and he puts forward a challenge for intervention which can only be described as onerous.

Most intervention strategies used in child care are predicated on nature-nurture interaction models and assume that, while there are obvious individual differences between children, they are all possessed of intrinsic characteristics which might be used to correct problem behaviors. One of these supposedly innate qualities has been called the ortho reflex, the innate drive to right the ship of self in the face of adversity. It implies that children will naturally seek relationships with nurturing available adults, that emotional wounds may be healed and bonds reestablished with variable ease, but always by eventually "reaching" that inner core of health which is assumed to be present. But if the abilities of children to make efficient use of environments for the satisfaction of their needs depend so heavily on the outcome of early transactions, of being able to make such demands easily and successfully with their mothers, then children with other patterns of less fruitful early interaction will logically have different ways of organizing their behavior. They may have conceptual worlds and psychological tools sufficiently different from those clinicians assume to be present in all children that many intervention efforts may be foiled.

It was simpler to think that the line of development which characterizes securely attached children was not just the optimal line, but the only one, and that the behavior of avoidant and resistant children simply reflected more primitive stages or hopefully transient disorganization (Escalona & Heider, 1959), with the task of therapy and education being to tap the inherent abilities of the child and bring them up to criterion. A recent essay by two eminent child psychiatrists, Stanley Greenspan and Reginald Lourie (1981), though entitled *"Developmental Structuralist Approach to the Classification of Adaptive and Pathological Personality Organizations,"* still refers to "baseline" characteristics of the child's personality, and the authors clearly imply that adaptive structures are the child's own intrinsic tools for dealing with an external environment. If we are obliged to consider that transactions with the environment in fact shape those tools in deep and enduring ways, then we must consider that less well adapted children are not just further back on the common developmental road but on a different route, and we must quickly realize that these children risk becoming more firmly established in inefficient or frankly destructive patterns with each passing year. Such a downward spiral of maladaption is not inevitable, of course. In a random world there would be as much likelihood of healing revisions as there would be of destructive exploitation of earlier vulnerability. But the world is not random, and experience suggests that there is in fact a differential probability of change for different patterns of development. This differential likelihood of change and growth has special significance for clinicians, since it contributes significantly to determining who we are asked to care for and how we go about it.

Two aspects of these different patterns of development have particular importance for clinical work. One is the internalizing or externalizing of behavioral controls, and the other is the concept of anticipatory behavior. Aggressive externalizing patterns have far more potential for destructive outcomes than do other modes, and they are likely to bring out the worst in others as well. Followup studies of childhood behavior disorders are quite uniform in their findings that aggressive behaviors, especially if associated with other disorders of interpersonal relations, are most likely to continue into adult life and are often associated with antisocial patterns of adult behavior (Cantwell, 1978). Experienced clinicians know the difficulty associated with attempting to help such aggressive children well, though we have not thought clearly about implicating their early experience with their mothers as a cause of our trouble. High behavioral activity levels or other temperamental variables do not by themselves account for poor outcomes. Followups of hyperkinetic children indicate that antisocial outcomes are associated more with histories of physical abuse by parents than with hyperactivity alone (Milich & Loney, 1979). Hyperkinetic children are known to elicit such abuse, and the sort of troubled parent who might well have provided only an anxious mode of attachment to their infant would also be vulnerable to becoming abusive of a hyperkinetic child. Internalizing children, on the other hand, appear to have a better overall prognosis. Robins' (1966) study found that only about 25% of children referred to a clinic for withdrawn behaviors had clinical difficulties in adult life, a much lower percentage than for aggressive behavior disorders.

Clinicians and theorists alike have tended to attribute the characteristics of both the internalizing and externalizing children to themselves, and to take as given that there is one assumptive world in which we all live and on the premises of which we may all depend. But the different patterns of behavior of the different attachment groups lead to the logical speculation that these children are behaving differently in part because of their anticipation of response by others. The securely attached child is likely to assume that he or she is able to elicit satisfying responses, and proceeds on the basis of that confident expectation of success which often predicts success. Less well attached children develop repertoires of behavior which anticipate different responses from the environment, and these anticipatory behaviors have considerable power to elicit some variant of the expected response from persons often far different than the original caretaker. Hostile aggressive acts by a child, acts made in light of the memory of neglect and abuse, and in anticipation of more of the same, often elicit just the sort of angry rejecting response which was anticipated, and a downward spiral of maladjustment is perpetuated. Isolation and withdrawal do not have quite such off-putting force, and leave the child with a pattern of adjustment somewhat more available for professional intervention. These children make little use of peer interactions though, and they require an active interest on the part of workers to overcome the barrier of social isolation.

The concept of borderline personality organization also shares the notion of the importance of anticipatory behavior to interpersonal relationships and personality development. There are several different applications of this concept in children and adolescents, taken from various perspectives. The work of Masterson (1972), though, anticipates Sroufe's findings by describing the conceptual world of individuals with borderline personalities in terms of their expectation that others are likely to be punitive or rejecting or, conversely, that they might possibly satisfy unmet needs in some omnipotent and unmodulated fashion. These youths (and adults) then behave toward others on the basis of these expectations in a predictable, persistent and self-destructive fashion, quite often succeeding in eliciting just the sort of rejection they expect. Because their demands for need gratification are endless and ravenous, they are often disappointed in any help which they do get, and their disappointment and rage is fueled further. There is little that appears operant in this pattern of behavior, but it is understandable in light of particular sorts of relationships with early caretakers which shaped their personalities in enduring ways. Redl's (1957) examinations of the personality structures of delinquent children also make an unconscious acknowledgement of the influence of early relationships on personality development, and on the need for developing specific therapeutic approaches in order to change the behaviors which reflect that inner structure.

In the transactional model which appears to be evolving from Sroufe's findings, the characteristics of parents have equal importance in the shaping of children's development. Offer and Offer's (1976) *"Three Pathways Through Normal Male Adolescence"* describes the different relationships between normal children and their competent parents which allowed for optimal ease of development through the adolescent years. The three types of relationships were characterized by variation in the amount of family loss, stress and change, but most importantly by the sensitivity of the parents to the individual needs of their child, and how those needs changed over the course of childhood and adolescence. The smoothest courses and the most optimal outcomes were found in families where the parents did not attempt to impose on their sons their own hopes for them, realizing the need of each individual to construct their own life. Similarly, in a 15-year followup, Thomas, Chess and Birch (1968) found that those children who showed behavior disorders in later years were characterized not only by their own temperament, but also by the fact that they were a bad match with their mother's characteristics, with enduring troubled relationships which had considerable influence on later behavior patterns. Masterson insists that it is highly improbable that a child will develop a borderline personality without having had a mother who was herself one, and who treated the child in a way very similar to the pattern shown by the child later on. On the other hand, psychological characteristics of mothers which might logically be expected to influence their ability to care for their children, such as schizophrenia, appear to have less influence in many cases than their simple availability to the child (Samaroff & Chandler, 1975). The finding that abusive parents are likely to have been abused themselves as children is more clearly understandable in this context of the seminal influence of early relationships on later personality development. The same holds for incestuous sexual abuse, since it occurs in families marked by frequent childhood histories of abuse of both parents, and showing other evidence of assumptions and relationships which have grown therefrom (Meiselman, 1978). These studies illustrate the ways in which parents pass on characteristics to their children, not through the teaching of a repertoire of behavior, but through their interaction. Competent parents show a sensitive awareness of the capabilities and needs of the children, and pass on their own competency by a carefully monitored performance which optimizes the children's instrumental competence. Many more examples could be given, but enough has been mentioned to emphasize the dyadic aspects of early learning, and its importance for competence, affect management, and the development of expectations both of the nature of others and of one's likelihood of being able to influence them to one's own benefit.

Concerned as they are with seriously disturbed children and with the prevention of further destructive influences, clinicians have a vital interest in the next obvious question, which is, when is it likely to be too late to make meaningful changes in these basic constructs, realizing that early social experiences have such importance for later personality organization. I suspect that two rules apply, one for the securely attached youngster with a satisfying relationship with others, and another much more draconian rule for children who were insecurely attached. Securely attached children are imbued with the tools to master their world in efficient fashion and are thereby best equipped to resist trauma, repair emotional damage quickly, and to approach subsequent developmental tasks confidently. Therefore, they would logically remain sensitive to helping hands and make good use of intervention throughout their development. Insecurely attached children show patterns of maladaptation which identify them both as less efficient in the use of their environment and less apt to mold their psychological tools for future use in the best possible fashion. These children are at risk of becoming unavailable for corrective experiences relatively early on. Their earliest adaptive modes are shaped by unresponsive or provocative mothers, and they bring maladaptive patterns of behavior to subsequent encounters. As development progresses to stages characterized by greater and greater reliance on symbolic interaction and on introjection, they may not elaborate skills necessary to adapt to the growing complexity of interaction. These handicaps may, of course, be corrected naturally by changes in the quality of care, the amount of ambient stress, or by other happy circumstances which allow for the elaboration of better coping skills. While change by parents can account for a good deal of remediation of old patterns of relating, it seems to me more parsimonious and more consistent with developmental theory to say that circumstances, the amount of stress and the percent of parenting skills available to the child change, while the essential personality and degree of relatedness of the parent remains basically the same.

Intervention plans which take into account the evidence for different basic patterns of adaptation must attend to three critical needs. The first, already discussed by Sroufe, is that of providing sensitive child care workers with good intuitive skills to understand the oblique and often seemingly contradictory ways in which these children seek contact. Intuition and warmth are not enough, though, when dealing with more severely disordered children, and the second critical need is to educate these workers to recognize anticipatory behavior, and especially to understand the power of certain such behaviors to elicit just the sort of withdrawal or angry response which shaped the behavior in the first place. Highly intuitive workers often sense this phenomenon in some children, but invariably they have blind spots, limitations on their skills which originate in their own personal makeup. Workers who are able to discern that their own behavior is being shaped by the anticipatory initiations of the children will be better equipped to respond to them in corrective ways and less likely to perpetuate maladaptive patterns. The ability of an appealing and socially skillful child to elicit cooperative and attentive responses from workers is often noticed and chuckled over, but the equally common ability of disturbed children to elicit withdrawal or anger is rarely recognized as such, and rejecting responses are attributed simply to logical consequences of the child's behavior. These natural social tendencies must be overcome through training and experience before remediation of more difficult cases can begin.

The third, and perhaps most challenging issue in remediation is that of controlling aggressive behaviors. Practically speaking, these behaviors present two difficulties. They are very efficient ways of discharging emotional energy, so efficient that other means of engagement are blocked as long as the aggressive behaviors continue. They are also unappealing behaviors which do little to enlist the desire of a therapist to engage with these children. Followup studies tell us again and again that children with seriously aggressive patterns of behavior tend to have unsatisfying and often antisocial adult lives (Robins, 1979, 1981). The immutability of aggressive behavior disorders appears to lie with the meaning of the behaviors within the conceptual world of the child, with the difficulty in overcoming their anticipatory behaviors, and with the therapist's natural antipathy to other aspects of their personality. Successful efforts to change them must begin early and incorporate strategies to deal with each of these factors.

Intervention strategies which recognize the influence of early patterns of adaptation and the phenomenon of anticipatory behavior must necessarily include, then, workers who are warm, available, and skilled at understanding both the apparent contradictions and the ineptness of their charges' behavior, and who can maintain a steady monitoring of their own feeling responses. It requires a high degree of skill to be able to interpret the behavior of troubled children in the context of their own world rather than the assumptive world of the warm, well-meaning and helpful child care worker. A durability beyond all reasonable expectation is needed to survive the efforts many of these children make to force the worker into the punitive and rejecting molds of their mothers.

Garmezy (1974) has wondered what transactional analysis might add to predictions of outcome for children at risk that are based on nature-nurture interaction models. The answer may possibly be given only in a transactional way. Outcome of interventions which acknowledge the shaping influence of interaction not solely to optimize opportunities to right the ship of self, but to shape the very perceptions of the world and the tools with which to grow in it, should tell us. Clinicians have been dimly aware of the need to do just this, and the careful, precise and skillful observations of Sroufe and his colleagues have begun to show us how. For this we are truly grateful.

REFERENCES

Cantwell, D. Hyperactivity and antisocial behavior. *Journal of the American Academy of Child Psychiatry,* 1978, *17,* 277-288.

Escalona, S., & Heider, G. *Prediction and outcome: A study in child development.* New York: Basic Books, 1959.

Garmezy, N. Children at risk: The search for the antecedents of schizophrenia. Part 1. Conceptual models and research methods. *Schizophrenia Bulletin,* 1974, *8,* 14-90.

Greenspan, S., & Lourie, R. Developmental structuralist approach to the classification of adaptive and pathological personality organizations: Infancy and childhood. *American Journal of Psychiatry,* 1981, *138,* 725-735.

Masterson, J. *Treatment of the borderline adolescent: A developmental approach.* New York: Wiley-Interscience, 1972.

Meiselman, K. *Incest.* New York: Jossey-Bass, 1978.

Milich, R., & Loney, J. The role of hyperactive and aggressive symptomatology in predicting adolescent outcome among hyperactive children. *Journal of Pediatric Psychology,* 1979, *20,* 61-72.

Offer, D., & Offer, J. Three developmental routes through normal male adolescence. In S. Feinstein & P. Giovacchini (Eds.), *Adolescent psychiatry, Volume IV.* New York: Jason Aronson, 1976.

Redl, F., & Wineman, D. *The aggressive child.* Glencoe, Illinois: The Free Press, 1957.

Robins, L. *Deviant children grown up.* Baltimore: Williams and Wilkins, 1966.

Robins, L. Follow-up studies. In H. Quay & J. Werry (Eds.), *Psychopathological disorders of children.* New York: Wiley, 1979, pp. 483-513.

Robins, L. Epidemiological approaches to natural history research. Antisocial disorders in children. *Journal of the American Academy of Child Psychiatry,* 1981, *20,* 556-580.

Sameroff, A., & Chandler, M. Reproductive risk and the continuum of caretaking casualty. In F. Horowitz (Ed.), *Review of child development research.* Chicago: University of Chicago Press, 1975, pp. 187-244.

Thomas, A., Chess, S. & Birch, H. *Temperament and behavior disorders in children.* New York: New York University Press, 1968.

Trilling, L., & Marcus, S. (Eds.) *The life and work of Sigmund Freud* by Ernest Jones. Edited and abridged in one volume. New York: Basic Books, 1961, p. 6.

5 Patterns of Self-Control in Young Handicapped Children

Claire B. Kopp
Joanne B. Krakow
Brian Vaughn
University of California, Los Angeles

The socialization of young children demands the transmission of adult values, expectations, and norms. Although social influences begin almost as soon as the infant is born, the most direct and forceful socializing acts of caregivers occur when infants start to use the language of their culture and to ambulate freely. The talking, walking year old child's behavior, reflecting more action than thought, is a cue that socialization must begin in earnest. Many caregivers respond by adopting a variety of "new" rearing techniques with the aim of showing the child that expectations exist about behavior. At first, children's responsiveness is limited to simple forms of compliance, but in a matter of weeks the ability to begin to monitor their own behavior appears. Compliance and self-monitoring also indicate that substantial changes have occurred in the child's cognitive abilities and reciprocal interactions; rudimentary manifestations of self-regulation are emerging.

Despite the significant ramifications of this form of growth, this age period has not been adequately researched. Neither child nor parent has been studied to the degree and with the intensity directed toward the younger aged infant. Further, in the second year, major individual differences in capability appear and remain relatively stable (Honzik, MacFarlane, & Allen, 1948; McCall, 1979). Although this variability is well documented, detailed discussions of child and caregiver contributions to it are notably sparse.

A scenario reflecting a "first year emphasis" occurred in the Infant Studies Project, a major research effort devoted to the study of infants who were at risk for cognitive impairments (Parmelee, Kopp, & Sigman, 1976). Those of us involved in the design phase (Parmelee, Kopp and Sigman, 1976) planned frequent and detailed observations of infants in the first eight to nine months of life, whereas in the second year, the children were to be seen twice. As the project progressed, we began to observe subtle signs of caregiver and child variability at eight and nine months testing sessions. By two years, these had been translated into major differences, with some children showing clear evidence of problematic behavioral and cognitive development. (In some instances, behavioral problems centered around the child's difficulty in monitoring his/her own behavior.) The question of what had happened in the second year of life that amplified individual differences was a vexing one, and one that we had little information about.

Later, in the mid 170s, the Bureau for the Education of the Handicapped (now Office of Special Education) funded large scale research programs centered around young at-risk and handicapped children. This thrust stemmed, in part, from the fact that many infants and pre-schoolers were being enrolled in intervention programs, but few specifics were available about the cognitive, social, and emotional capabilities of these children. One aspect of the Bureau's mandate required investigators to focus on these characteristics. UCLA was selected as the site for one program known as Project REACH.

Kopp's (1978) plans called for a focus upon the second and third years of life in an attempt to elucidate some of the origins and contributors to developmental problems. One of the domains selected for study included early forms of self-regulation, a decision prompted in part by the Infant Studies Project observations. The decision was reinforced by the knowledge that problems with self-monitoring behavior have been reported for many groups of children who are at-risk or have known handicapping conditions.

Over the years, we have come to realize that the evolution of self-regulation parallels the child's transition from a sensorimotor organism to one who begins to engage in reflective thought. As thought increasingly guides behavior, the child grows to understand that one's self controls one's actions, and that the self must initiate, maintain, or inhibit behaviors in accordance with family and social conventions.

Evolving slowly at first, self-regulation will, by the pre-school years, reflect the child's ability to comply with caregiver requests, to delay gratification when appropriate, to monitor one's own behavior in the absence of socializers, and to modulate the intensity, frequency, and duration of verbal and motor acts in social and educational settings. The acquisition and expansion of these regulatory skills will have important ramifications for the child's success in educational settings and the widening social world.

We believe that self-regulation is a product not only of child cognition, but also of the child's environment. It is caregivers who first expose the child to family conventions and social norms, and provide a milieu in which the child learns. If conditions internal to the child impede or distort the transition and growth of reflective thought, the ontogeny of self-regulation will be distorted; likewise, external conditions exemplified by disorganized home settings will exert negative influences.

Ample justification for our position can be found in the literature focused upon children who have educational, behavioral, and social problems. As an illustration, self-regulation is often problematic for mentally retarded children and others who are hyperactive, or learning disabled (e.g., Douglas, 1980). But problems with self-regulation also arise, sometimes as early as the preschool years, among children who are reared by neglectful parents (e.g., Malone, 1978).

The early onset of these difficulties, and the dearth of specific information about initial forms of self-regulation among children who had few or no developmental problems, prompted several questions: What do emerging components of self-regulation look like? Do these forms look similar for most children? If not, what factors are related to individual differences? Are emerging components of self-regulation similar for handicapped children? If not, why not? What specific roles do caregivers assume?

With these questions in mind, Kopp's initial goal was to conceptualize a developmental sequence for the emergence of self-regulation, and then use this framework as the basis for developmentally oriented research. The plan called for studying normally developing two and three year olds, and then turn to young handicapped children. Using this age group and approach, emergent of forms of self-regulation would be examined, and early problems identified. The products of these research efforts comprise a primary part of this chapter.

The first part of the paper is an overview. In order to acquaint the reader with our developmental perspective and to clarify terminology, we begin with a discussion of Kopp's (1982) conceptual framework. Following, we briefly turn to the clinical and educational literature in which problems related to self-regulation have been identified. The goal is to highlight conditions that are associated with or influence the growth of self-regulation among these samples.

The second part of the paper is data based. We describe the focus of some of the studies, characterize the samples that have been employed, and the nature of our findings, with an emphasis on child data. Findings from two handicapped groups (Down Syndrome and Developmental Delay of Uncertain Etiology) are presented. The data presentation includes analysis of: (1) the comparability or difference in performance found between handicapped samples and normally developing children of similar developmental age, (2) performance in relation to developmental age, (3) the relationship between performance on various tasks, and (4) performance in relation to cognitive processing abilities.

THE LITERATURE

The Ontogeny of Self-Regulation

The topic of self-regulation and the control of one's own behavior has interested students of behavior for many years. Theorists as diverse as Skinner, Mischel, Greenacre, Bowlby, Bandura, Kanfer, and Vygotsky have written about the topic; each has described self-regulation from a particular perspective. The literature is large and diverse, and the terminology is often confusing. In particular, sometimes the terms self-control, self-regulation, and self-initiated monitoring are used interchangeably, other times they are not. Even those who use the same terminology may refer to different behavior or responses.

In addition, the frame-of-reference for those of us who are developmentalists can be very different from that espoused by the behaviorists (see Harter, in press), or psychoanalysts. In order to reflect the implications of growth and change in the child, Harter suggested it is often necessary to generate constructs from a developmental perspective and to adopt very specific terminology.

Kopp employed these tactics in organizing her framework. That is, a developmental structure forms the foundation; and, specific terms are used to signify each new acquisition in the development of self-regulation. Each term is meant to provide a short-hand notation for (1) the level of cognitive development the child has reached, (2) the degree of the child's self-understanding, and (3) the kinds of control the child can exercise. These terms, associated with five, slightly overlapping phases, are neurophysiological modulation, sensorimotor modulation, control, self-control, and self-regulation (see Table 5.1), and each is described more fully below.

The first phase in the sequence is labeled *neurophysiological modulation* (birth to 2-3 months). The term modulation is used to signify a very limited cognitive repertoire and awareness of self. However, the infant does have the ability to handle incoming stimuli, to shut out input that is too intrusive, and to self-soothe. We view neurophysiological modulation as a protective mechanism of early life when the infant is primarily a reflexive organism, and has few psychologic resources to guard itself from discomfort. Although biological phenomena largely govern neurophysiological modulation, data from Als (1978) and Sander (1969) suggest caregiver practices facilitate its refinement.

The second phase is called *sensorimotor modulation* (3 to 9 months). Modulation again refers to limited cognitive mechanisms and self-awareness. Nonetheless, infants can use component parts of their newly acquired sensorimotor repertoire (e.g., grasp, rolling over) and change acts in

TABLE 5.1
Phases of Control

Phases	Approximate Ages	Features	Cognitive Requisites
Neurophysiological Modulation	Birth to 2, 3 mo.	modulation of arousal, activation of organized patterns of behavior	
Sensorimotor Modulation	3 mo. to 9 mo. +	change ongoing behavior in response to events and stimuli in environment	
Control	12 mo. to 18 mo. +	awareness of social demands of situation and initiate, maintain, cease physical acts, communication, etc. accordingly; compliance; self-initiated monitoring	intentionality, goal-directed behavior, conscious awareness of action, memory of existential self
Self-Control	24 mo. +	as above; delay upon request; behave according to social expectations in the absence of external monitors	representational thinking and recall memory, symbolic thinking, continuing sense of identity
Self-Regulation	36 mo. +	as above; flexiblity of control processes that meet changing situational demands	strategy production, conscious introspection, etc.

(From Kopp, 1982)

response to events that arise. Frequently these acts are reflected in simple manipulations of objects or visual-vocal exchanges with caregivers, and do not involve conscious prior intention, or awareness of the meaning of an act. Kopp has suggested that the principle organizer for most of these early sensorimotor activities stems from pleasure, interest, and desire on the part of the infant, rather than from a cognitively based intention. Although infants at this age demonstrate a limited form of appraisal of situational contexts, the appraisal is not based on understanding but instead is a response to salient signals.

In sum, the term modulation, as used above, calls attention to the fact that modification of one's behavior exists in early life. But modulation is accomplished without an understanding of the self, others, or events. The infant has neither the cognitive resources to think about controlling its own repertoire, nor the ability to consider the implications of using the repertoire.

The third phase, labeled *control* (9 to 18 months), signifies that cognitive growth has occurred to the extent that the child shows intentionality, goal seeking behavior, and awareness of an existential self separate from others. Control characterizes the emerging ability of children to show awareness of social and task demands of a situation that has been defined by caregivers, and to initiate, maintain, modulate, or cease physical acts, communication, and emotional signals accordingly. Control represents an important transition along the path to self-regulation.

The term control, rather than regulate, is used to describe this phase of monitoring. This terminology follows dictionary definitions of control and regulate in which the former is defined as "to hold in check," whereas the latter is characterized both as "control by rule" and "adapt to requirements." In this sense, we view control as less flexible and adaptive than regulation.

The first manifestations of behaviors that bear resemblance to mature acts of monitoring appear early in this phase. They are compliance to commands and infant-initiated monitoring of behavior. Compliance indicates that the child has, at least, appraised differential features of the environment, has some understanding of what is acceptable and non-acceptable to caregivers, and responds appropriately to the caregiver's request. Infant-initiated monitoring demands more complex cognitive processing than compliance. In addition to the features noted above, it requires a more elaborate sequence of behaviors: approach to a desired object, recognition (memory) that the object was previously associated with a prohibition, and finally inhibition of the prohibited act even when the request is not explicitly restated.

Infant-initiated monitoring is highly dependent on the presence of key signals, which have become associated with prohibition (e.g., an electric cord with a sharp rebuke or a slap on the hand). The signal serves as a necessary prohibition cue because the child does not have the ability to ideate and remember a string of "you may . . ." or "you may not . . ." Further, the child does not have the ability to reflect, and can not reason why one type of behavior (e.g., approach) is more appropriate than another (e.g., avoidance) for a particular situation.

Because of memory and reasoning constraints, control is a fragile behavior often prone to competition from external or internal stimuli. Locomotion is a good example of an internal pressure. At this age, children are often so mesmerized by their own motor skills, and the pleasure in exercising these skills, that they do not heed cues signifying the need for control. They whirl and twirl oblivious of danger, they climb seemingly unafraid of heights, they chase after rolling objects. These motor activities often cease because of parent intervention or child fatigue, but not because the child has applied "cognitive brakes."

The theme of self, reflected by the child's awareness of a continuing sense of identity, is not intrinsic to the control phase. Children do not understand "identity" until they symbolize the meaning of an independent existence and the relationship between the self and action. This is the focus of the next phase.

The phase immediately preceding self-regulation is defined as *self-control* (18 months to 3 years). Self-control differs from control by virtue of the appearance of representational thinking and recall memory. In the former, the child uses a symbol to stand for an object, whereas in the latter the child is able to evoke and sustain a memory for an absent object or event (at least for a short time). These cognitive mechanisms allow children to begin to understand two essential aspects of control: (1) that they have a continuing and independent identity, and therefore they can begin to associate their own behavioral sequences with events, and (2) that they can remember caregivers' dictums about acceptable and unacceptable behaviors. In essence, self-control means self-initiated modification of behavior because of remembered information. The distinguishing features of self-control include compliance, an emergent ability to delay an act, and to behave according to caregiver expectations in the absence of social monitors. Self-control is not as vulnerable to competing demands as control; nonetheless self-control is limited. The child's capacity to delay is often short, compliance is occasional, there is limited flexibility in adapting new acts to meet changing situational demands.

These constraints are offset by significant changes in the child's awareness of the self, and the role that "self" plays in control. A developing sense of identity can be inferred in a child's pride when a caregiver's request has been obeyed, or in shame and tears when a transgression has occurred. Self also appears to be operating when children use their bodies to erect invisible barriers. For example, two year olds who want to ignore maternal requests often turn away from their mothers, suggesting out-of-sight is out-of-mind. This use of the body can only occur when the child has a fairly well formulated sense of physical being and identity.

The final phase in the developmental perspective is labeled *self-regulation* (3 + yrs.). The transition from self-control to self-regulation reflects a shift to an adaptive, more flexible form of self monitoring. However, adaptiveness to changing demands and situations is dependent on the child being able to quickly encode a changing situation and generate ideas about what should or should not be done. Self-regulation, therefore, is tied to ongoing use of cognitive strategies (see Mischel & Patterson, 1978).

The shift from self-control to self-regulation accordingly parallels the growth of cognitive skills. To the extent that cognitive skills are limited, then self-regulation will be limited. Under ordinary circumstances, it is expected that the emergence of self-regulation is followed by its continued growth and refinement throughout childhood.

THE CLINICAL LITERATURE

The conceptual framework described above was designed primarily as a tool to help us study early forms of self-regulation among normally developing children. By design, the perspective focused primarily on developmental issues and less on concerns about group or individual differences. In Kopp (1982), the few comments made about individual differences centered on external contributors such as caregiver sensitivity to child, or within-child characteristics such as precocious language development.

The conceptual framework met our initial research needs, and in time a reasonable amount of descriptive data was accumulated about the developmental course of the phase labeled self-control. In addition, the role of some of the most obvious and accessible mediators of individual differences in self-control performance (e.g., developmental quotients, caregiver behaviors, etc.) was examined. Later, turning our attention to the handicapped samples, it became apparent that the issue of group and individual differences had to be approached systematically. A first step involved review of the clinical literature where difficulties with monitoring behavior had been identified and associated with impaired or distorted cognitive processing skills. Problem domains were found in relation to performance on sustained attention tasks, use of cognitive stategies, and verbal production. These categories are listed in Table 5.2 along with the clinical group that was noted to have the difficulty.

The clinical reports intrigued us as we began to discern possible developmental ramifications. Consider the fact that each of the processes

TABLE 5.2
Clinical Literature: Examples of Cognitive Processes
Associated with Problems of Self-Regulation

Process	Clinical group	Description
Sustained Attention	acting-out children, depressed, neglected Malone, 1978	diminished capacity to sustain interest
	deaf children Lesser & Easser, 1972	inability to sustain attention
	hyperactive children Douglas, 1980	fail to process subtle aspects of situations, failure to sustain attention
Strategies	hyperactive children Douglas, 1980	do not use organizational, rehearsal strategies
		require help in using cue-producing verbal reminders
Language	acting out children Greenacre, 1950; Lidz, 1978	distortion in relationship between action and speech; may not have words that can categorize experiences so that events have temporal relationships
	deaf children Harris, 1978; Lesser & Easser, 1972	experience inadequate communication modalities to test environment and to interact with others; manual communication may attenuate impaired verbal ability

listed above comes into prominence during the second year of life. Moreover, it is during this time that the ability to monitor one's own behavior also emerges. Therefore, in the capsule summaries of the clinical literature, we also briefly discuss developmental issues that appear to have relevance.

Sustained attention. Sustained attention has been defined as the ability to remain involved in a play or task situation (Douglas, 1980; Kopp & Vaughn, 1982; Krakow, Kopp, Vaughn, unpublished). At least three groups of children have been identified as having problems with sustained attention and the ability to monitor their own behavior. These include children who are deaf, those labeled as "acting-out," and those diagnosed as hyperactive. Sometimes, descriptors used to characterize these children include the term impulsive. "Acting-out" is a term used in the psychoanalytic literature to designate children who are aggressive, impulsive, or predelinquent (see Rexford, 1978). As an example, in describing a group of young children who came from very disorganized and chaotic homes, Malone (1978) mentioned impulsivity, attenuated investment in themselves, "markedly diminished capacity" to sustain interest in things or people, and remarkable caregiving precociousness (e.g., a four year old doing the family shopping, etc.).

Children who have major hearing impairments are also identified as having secondary problems with attention, and with impulse control (see reviews, Harris, 1978; Meadow, 1980). In general, deaf children are characterized as impulsive, prone to acting out, and showing a need for immediate gratification (Altshuler, 1974; Levine, 1956). Impulsive qualities in behavior have been identified as early as the second year of life (Freedman, Cannady, & Robinson, 1971). Parenthetically, some very young deaf children also demonstrate precocious self-care behavior (e.g., a two year old deciding to cook at the stove). Problems with attention have been described by Lesser and Easser (1972) in this way: ". . . The deaf child is not free to take for granted his consistent environmental background in order to concentrate on the stimulus at hand. This interferes with his ability . . . to sustain focused attention . . ." (p. 462).

The final clinical group mentioned here are children who are called hyperactive. In recent years documentation of the problems of these children has been well systematized (see Whalen & Henker, 1980); as a result discussions of the relationship between sustained attention and impulsive behavior often stem from formalized observations (tests, paper and pencil tasks, etc.). On the basis of carefully obtained evidence, Douglas (Douglas, 1980; Douglas & Peters, 1979) and her colleagues noted their hyperactive subjects had problems with sustaining attention, inhibition of impulsive responding, and inadequate production of strategies. These processes, Douglas emphasizes, are intricately interrelated, and the relationship seems most potent in certain situations. She further states that most vigilance type tasks and social situations require only minimal conformity, thus they do not pose difficult challenges for the hyperactive child, whereas complex, perceptual, logical, and social situations that require organized and reflective effort are extremely difficult. Problems arise because the children have to generate enough self-discipline to turn to the task at hand and to remain involved over a period of time. This, they can not seem to do on their own.

Despite the vast difference in the primary problems of these clinical groups, the similarity they demonstrate in the relationship between sustained attention and the ability to monitor behavior is intuitively sensible. Elsewhere (Krakow et al., unpublished), it is argued that the attentive, engaged child may be in the most advantageous position to extract social cues from the environment. However, each of the groups described above appears to have difficulty in "defining" the demands of social (and educational settings), as a result their behaviors tend to be inappropriate.

When does the young child begin to appreciate the nuances of particular situations? Most likely this occurs when children begin to voluntarily control and sustain their own attention (for discussion see Gibson & Rader, 1979). Although maintenance of attention occurs as early as the first months of life, Kagan and Kogan (1970) suggest sustained attention begins to assume importance during the last part of the first year. The phenomenon seems to rest on the infant's ability to distance himself from objects (Werner & Kaplan, 1963); in doing so, he begins to be aware of objects (Collins & Hagen, 1979), and to study them for their own characteristics (Uzgiris, 1967). This type of exploration is controlled, maintained, and directed to the less obvious features of objects (e.g., the wheels of a toy truck that fascinate a ten month old). This attention stands in marked contrast to that observed earlier, where responsiveness occurs because highly salient features capture the infant (e.g., brightness, contrast, etc.).

Developmental changes in sustained attention are followed by the appearance of individual differences. Kagan (1971) reported variability in visual attention to two-dimensional stimuli among thirteen month olds. More recently, Kopp and Vaughn (1982) and Krakow, Kopp, and Vaughn (unpublished) found differences in sustained attention around visual-manipulative play of infants. In the first study, differences were measured when the sample was eight months of age, and later (age two years) were related to developmental test scores. Of interest, this relationship only held for preterm males. In the second study, Krakow et al. (unpublished) found that decreased levels of sustained attention during play among 12 month olds were stable to 30 months, and were also related to poorer self control as measured by performance on a delay task at 24 months. The extent to which these differences herald longer-term stability is unknown. And the extent to which we can link developmental findings with descriptions from the clinical literature is also unknown. With this caveat in mind, we turn to another cognitive process identified in the clinical literature.

Use of strategies. Research with hyperactive children (noted above) indicates they have difficulty producing and using strategies as effectively as do normal children when task demands are not highly structured (Douglas 1980). In one dissertation study, Tant (1978, cited in Douglas, 1980) used a matrix task that demanded production of efficient solutions including ex-animation of clues, consideration of all possible solutions, and evaluation of same. In general, the controlled effort needed to produce strategies was not demonstrated by these children; however, in the few instances where they were, the children did not know how to use them effectively. Findings from this study were mirrored in another dissertation also described by

Douglas (Benezra, 1978, cited in Douglas, 1980). She commented, ". . . the children do not use sound strategies because their defective attentional, inhibitory, and arousal mechanisms have interfered with their learning them; and even when strategies have been learned, the same deficits interfere with the children employing them in a consistent manner" (p. 297).

Douglas' comment about learning strategies is interesting from a developmental vantage point because recent research suggests that rudimentary forms of strategy production can be found as early as the second year of life. By way of background, it seems that intentionality and awareness are requisites for the development of cognitive strategies (Wellman, 1977). Intention involves the production of *means-ends* behaviors (Piaget, 1952; also discussion in Wellman, 1977), whereas awareness requires that actions are appropriate and adopted to a goal, and that the goal is anticipated (Wellman, 1977). The beginnings of intentional acts and awareness can be inferred on the basis of behaviors of children approaching the end of the first year of life (e.g., intention—a 12 month old systematically using a cord to pull a toy closer to herself; awareness—a 14 month old reaching for a prohibited object and withdrawing her hand upon hearing footsteps).

Given these requisites, empirical evidence suggests that rudimentary strategies emerge between 12 and 24 months. Greenfield, Nelson, and Saltzman (1972) demonstrated that the manipulation of stacking-cups by toddlers undergoes a developmental progression linked to the successful production of simple strategies. In addition, Ricciuti (1965) found that 12 to 24 month old infants, when presented with a collection of eight objects, four from each of two classes, were increasingly likely to manipulate successively members from the same class. He suggested that this type of temporal clustering represented cognitively guided organization of objects. Finally, Krakow, Johnson and Kopp (unpublished) examined temporal and spatial clustering, and overall organization of objects in 12 and 18 month olds. They found developmental differences in temporal clustering and overall organization with the older infants showing the more advanced strategies.

With respect to the slightly older child, Johnson and Kopp (1981) observed 24 month olds in a delay situation and found the children were capable of producing motor and verbal acts that were directed *away* from a desired object and toward other objects. The number of these strategy-like acts produced was positively and significantly related to the amount of time that was delayed. Recent studies of memory suggest that three year olds engage in strategic behaviors to aid their memories (see Wellman, 1977). However, Wellman notes that only certain strategic behaviors are used, and only limited intentionality and awareness are demonstrated by the child for these acts.

Again, we have delved into the topic of developmental issues; however, the question of origins of problems awaits empiric investigation.

Language. The fact that language has been associated with self-regulation is not surprising to those familiar with views of Vygotsky (1962) and Luria (1960), and the writings of psychoanalytically oriented theorists such as Greenacre (1950). The former explicitly tied the development of speech to the development of self-regulation, whereas the latter emphasized that differences in verbal ability that appeared in the second year of life might cause differences in impulse control. In particular, Greenacre (1950) suggested that an imbalance between the development of speech and the development of motor abilities led to impulsive behaviors because the child did not have speech to use as a means to inhibit movement. More recently, Lidz (1978)[1] suggested that impulsive or acting-out behaviors occur when children do not use words to categorize events. Without the ability to organize incoming stimuli, Lidz continued, each event remains an isolated, non-recurring experience. As a result, the child meets every situation as if it were a novel one, and thus demonstrates the fumblings and inappropriate acts that go along with inexperience.

The question about the role of early language bears directly on deaf children who have difficulty with spoken language, and are often labeled as impulsive (see Harris, 1978). The deaf child, noted Harris (1978), does not use or learn language during the early years, thus linguistic and symbolic development is limited. In addition, vocal and verbal limitations impede communication between child and parent. Quoting Harris (1978).

> . . . because of inadequate communication between parents and children, deaf children's outlets for venting frustrations, disappointments, and anger are narrowed, and their emotions are often expressed in an impulsive and immature manner. In turn, their impulsive disposition has an adverse effect upon later cognitive development and learning . . . [p. 140].

One wonders if impaired communication modes *per se* are associated with problems in self-monitoring. Do non-verbal children who are not deaf also reflect problems in monitoring their own behaviors? Here the question refers to children whose language development lags considerably behind growth in other domains of functioning. If the child has some means of symbolizing what is being experienced than actual verbal production should not be crucial to the developing of self-monitoring. Indeed, it has been argued that it is limitations in thought that are associated with problems in self-regulation (e.g. Kopp, 1982).

---

[1]There are some interesting parallels between Lidz' and Greenacre's views and some observations reported by Escalona (1973). In addressing the question of early individual differences and prediction to later styles of behavior, she suggested that predisposing characteristics such as high activity level would interfere with ". . . delay and inhibition of movement impulse required for fine motor coordination . . ." (p. 147). Similarly, she predicted that high activity levels were obstacles to learning verbal symbols, early abstraction, and early concept formation. A majority of Escalona's predictions were borne out.

Summary

In the preceding paragraphs we briefly discussed cognitive processes that have been implicated, in the clinical literature, with problems related to children controlling their own behavior. Developmental considerations were also noted, since these processes come into prominence during the second and third years of life, paralleling the emergence of self-control.

THE PRESENT STUDY

The developmental perspective and ideas from the clinical literature presented in the previous section guided the examination of self-control among handicapped children. The information that we hoped to obtain can be summarized in a series of questions. The questions and additional background considerations are outlined below.

(1) Is the development of self-control similar for handicapped and normally developing children of similar developmental age? Answers to this question can help us determine if differences can be detected in self-monitoring behaviors as early as the second year of life among a group of children who are known to have cognitive problems.

The question is also related to the developmental versus difference controversy that has long sparked the field of mental retardation (see Zigler, 1968). The argument centered around the model which best described the abilities of individuals classified as familial retarded. In this study, the developmental hypothesis would be as follows: If self-regulation represents a developmental phenomenon, and if children are equated on developmental age, then there should be few differences in performance irrespective of child diagnosis. As adherents of developmental perspectives, we consider this hypothesis to be important.

(2) Given equivalent developmental ages, does one handicapped group differ from another on self-control performance? This question stems from reconsiderations about the need to use diagnostic categories in research. In the past, investigators grouped children into superordinate categories, for instance, preterm, mentally retarded, visually impaired, and so forth. This practice had the effect of obscuring important within group variability. For example, preterms vary on the appropriateness of birth weight to gestational age, and this variability is associated with differential outcome (see summary in Kopp, in press). Similarly, it has been found that mentally retarded individuals who have varying diagnoses differ on several characteristics (Clausen, Udsky, & Sersen, 1976; Sackett, 1967). Karrer, Nelson, and Galbraith (1979) have called for renewed efforts in studying subgroups of mentally retarded individuals, and suggested that past failure

to find differences related to etiologies may have been due to methodological problems.

In this study, the handicapped samples differed in one fundamental way. Some had chromosomal anomalies, which inevitably are associated with mental retardation; the origins of the developmental delay and the course of development for the other group was unclear.

(3) What can be determined about the mediators of individual differences in self-control? We were interested in learning if some of the factors associated with individual differences in the normally developing sample were similar for handicapped children. In addition, we hoped to explore the association between self-control and attention, and self control and language.

The two handicapped groups were constituted using developmental age (*DA*) and chronological age (*CA*) guidelines. Those children who were less than 60 months *CA* and who had attained a developmental age of 22 months or more were entered into the appropriate handicapped sample, Down syndrome (*DS*) or Developmentally Delayed (*DD*). The criteria by which the *DS* and *DD* children were accepted into the sample included: (1) the children had completed most of the laboratory procedures (4 children were eliminated for failure to do so), (2) their developmental age was 22 months or more, (3) their *DQ* was below 85 and above 50. Then, all the *DS* and *DD* subjects were listed side-by-side in developmental age order. We found that the range and distributions of *CA, DA,* and *DQ* were fairly similar.

We then added a normally developing (*ND*) sample by searching our files for 24 month old children who had developmental quotients between 100 and 115. After our first run through with this procedure, we still did not have a large enough sample size, therefore, other subjects were added who had developmental ages similar to children in the two handicapped groups. This meant that the 24 month range and the limits placed on developmental quotients were exceeded. However, we tried to keep developmental quotients below 120 and to include 18 month olds only if necessary.

ND. Seventeen *ND* children (10M, 7F) between the age of 18 months and 31 months consitituted this sample, some of whom were participating in a short-term longitudinal study. The children and their mothers had been recruited from local YMCA and community center mother-toddler programs. For the purpose of this study, all children, with the exception of one male who was seen at 24 and 30 months, contributed data only once. Details about the background characteristics of the sample are given in Table 5.3.

DS. Fifteen children (9M, 6F) with confirmed diagnosis of DS, (all but one Trisomy 21) and between the age of 31 and 60 months constituted the

TABLE 5.3
Characteristics of Samples

	ND	DS	DD
Chronological age	25.4 (3.8)	46.8 (8.3)	41.3 (5.0)
Developmental age (overall)	29.3 (5.0)	29.6 (4.8)	27.29 (5.0)
gross motor	29.8 (4.6)	30.0 (4.5)	27.2 (7.2)
fine motor	26.9 (6.2)	27.5 (4.3)	27.6 (6.2)
adaptive	29.3 (5.3)	29.4 (6.0)	28.2 (4.2)
language	30.1 (5.8)	27.9 (6.8)	26.2 (6.8)
personal-social	30.3 (5.9)	33.9 (6.9)	29.8 (5.8)
Developmental quotient	115.5 (12.1)	63.9 (7.6)	70.0 (9.6)
Males, females	10, 7	9, 6	13, 4
Birth weight (lbs.), $\bar{X}$	7.6 (1.2)	7.6 (1.7)	5.8 (2.6)
Full term birth, %	100%	100%	62.5%
Past/Recurrent medical problems, %			
minor (ear infections,	35%	33%	35%
major (seizures, repeated hospitalizations, etc.)	0%	14%	59%
Suspected hearing problems %	12%	29%	29%
Visual problems (treated), %	0	40.%	24%
Maternal age, $\bar{X}$	32.1 yrs.	33.6	29.2
Maternal education (% college graduate)	76.5%	16.7%	29.4%
Paternal age, $\bar{X}$	35.6 yrs.	34.7	31.8
Paternal education (% college graduate)	88.2%	50%	33.3%
Paternal occupation (% professional)	82%	33%	67%
Ethnicity	primarily Caucasian	primarily Caucasian	all Caucasian

DS sample. The children and their parents had been recruited from local intervention programs and from DS parent groups. Some of the children had been seen in our laboratory when they were younger; no child contributed data at more than one age point. Additional information about the children's background is provided in Table 5.3.

DD. Seventeen children (13M, 4F) who had diagnoses of mild to moderate developmental delay (DQ range 50–85), selected from a larger pool of *DD* children, consituted the *DD* sample. Chronological ages ranged from 32 to 53 months. Half of the children had experienced stressful perinatal periods and/or were very low birth weight, the other half were delayed but with unknown etiologies. Corrected ages were used for preterm infants for developmental testing and laboratory tests. The children had been recruited from local intervention centers, and most were participating in a two year longitudinal study that was allied with our research project. Some of the children were seen in the infant laboratory more than one time, however, no child contributed data at more than one age point. Additional information about the children's background is provided in Table 5.3.

Several points need emphasis. Although the samples had equivalent developmental ages, the children differed in other ways that were unanticipated. All of the children were healthy when they came to the laboratory, however, a sizable number of handicapped children had experienced far more illnesses than did the normally developing children. In fact, Chi 2 analyses performed on the percentage of children in each group who had health problems was highly significant ($X^2 = 18.86$, $p < .01$). How this health dimension affects performance on tasks was not determined, but surely it had an influence. Further, selection techniques for recruitment of the handicapped samples were not random, a fact that needs to be taken into account when findings are considered. Lastly, discrepant male representation was found in the Developmentally Delayed sample. This may have occurred because of biological factors (e.g. male vulnerability) or other considerations (e.g. parents' likelihood of seeking help for delayed boys earlier than for delayed girls). In any event, discrepancies in sex representation limit attempts to examine for sex differences. Both this situation and the ones noted above restrict the generalizability of findings.

In our laboratory, self-control was operationalized in two ways, both taking into account the relatively limited language ability of most of the children. One was a measure of compliance to a maternal request, and the other was a measure of delay, that is, the child was requested not to touch an object until given permission. Both of these tasks are analogous to everyday experiences of young children, but of course do not reflect the sum total of the child's self-control repertoire.

Delay Tasks

Two different tasks were used to assess children's inhibition and delay behaviors. For *ND* children, one of the tasks was presented during the first testing session and the other during the second visit. In all cases, the experimenter was different across the two sessions. Some of the handicapped children received both tasks in one visit, and with the same experimenter, others had two visits. Mothers of the children were present in the testing room during all procedures. All procedures were videotaped and data were coded at a later time.

Telephone task.[2] The experimenter seated the child and the mother at a low, childsized table. The mother was given a magazine and asked to pretend to read it during the task. She was instructed not to repeat any of the instructions the experimenter would give to the child concerning the telephone, however, in the event that the child attempted to leave the chair, the mothers were asked to tell her/him to remain seated. At that point, the experimenter brought an unusually shaped red telephone into the testing room and told the child that the phone was to be used in the next game. After pointing out some of the features of the telephone, the experimenter told the child that s(he) would have to leave the room to get some additional toys. The experimenter then instructed the child to "sit right there and *don't touch* the phone while I am gone!" In those cases where it was not clear to the experimenter that the child had been paying close attention to the instructions regarding the phone, the instructions were repeated with emphasis on not touching the phone. The experimenter then placed the telephone well within reach of the child, left the room and waited for 2½ minutes or until the child touched/manipulated the phone, whichever came first. The measure used in this task was the number of seconds that elapsed prior to the child's actually touching the telephone.

Raisin game.[3] This task was broken into two segments. First, a series of six short trials were administered (mean length of trial 25 sec. range 20-30-sec.). The experimenter seated the child at a low table and explained that they were going to play a game that involved the child finding raisins (or cookies) that would be hidden, one at a time, under an array of three cups. The experimenter explained to the child that the object of the game was to wait until being told, and then to find the raisin. The experimenter then gave the child a raisin (or cookie) to eat. All children indicated that they liked to eat the food reward, and continued to behave consistently with their reports throughout the trials. After the child had finished eating the preliminary food item, the experimenter called the child's attention to the array of cups and hid the first raisin, making sure that the child watched while the raisin was hidden. The experimenter then said, "Wait until I tell you before you find the raisin." The experimenter then started a stopwatch and after a brief period informed the child that the raisin could now be

---

[2]This task was adapted from Rebelsky, Beavey, Blotner, 1971.
[3]This task was adapted from Golden, Montare, & Bridger, 1977.

found. If the child found and ate the raisin prior to the experimenter's instruction, the experimenter waited the prescribed time, reminded the child of the rule to wait, and proceeded to initiate the next trial (after waiting long enough for the child to finish eating the food item). Each trial was initiated and completed in the same manner, with the instruction to wait until told being given at the start of each trial. No negative sanctions were imposed for failure to wait until the experimenter's instruction before finding food item, nor were positive comments made about waiting. A total of six trials were administered to each child. The mother was present in the room at all times, but was not occupied with a magazine as she had been in the telephone task. The mother was asked not to initiate any contact with the child, however, in the event that the child left, or attempted to leave the chair during a trial or between trials, she was instructed to return her/him to the chair. Two separate scores were derived from this segment of the task: (1) the number of trials in which the raisin was not picked up; (2) the number of trials in which the raisin was not eaten.

After completing the series of six short trials, the child was told that one more trial remained. The experimenter called the child's attention to one of the cups in the array, hid a food reward, and told the child to "wait until I tell you before you find the raisin." The experimenter started the stopwatch and waited for a total of 120 seconds or until the child found and ate the raisin, whichever occurred first. Two scores were derived for this trial: (1) the time until a cup was touched; (2) time until the raisin was consumed.

Compliance Task

The compliance task involved the interaction of the child and mother; specifically, at a signal from the experimenter, the mother was instructed to have her child put away toys with which he/she had been playing for 10 minutes. The instructions were purposely vague unless the mother requested additional information. If so, we suggested that she use whatever procedures she employed at home. The experimenter was not in the setting.

Child actions were coded for (1) time to the child's first clean-up act, (2) three two minute segments that contained category descriptions of what the child did; categories included child ignores mother, asks for help, actively refuses clean-up, and vocalizes. And (3) overall rating of compliance which was a composite qualitative rating of the total six minute period.

Additional Measures

Developmental assessment. Each child was assessed with the Gesell Developmental Schedules (Gesell & Amatruda, 1952). Scores for all the subjects were summed to compute overall developmental age (DA) scores. In addition, separate developmental ages were computed for each sub-scale (gross motor, fine motor, adaptive, language, and personal-social). Developmental quotients (*DQ*) were computed using the formula: $DA/CA \times 100$.

Sustained attention task. The child was seated on the floor with a bucket of toys and told to "sit here and play with these toys." The bucket included a doll, baby bottle, necklace, hammer, puppets, small cars, comb, brush, a book, and a few other items. The mother was seated near the child and asked not to initiate any interactions with the child, unless the child left the toys and attempted to make contact with her. She was then to encourage the child to return to the toys. Six minutes of behavior were videotaped. Behavioral codes included time on-task and a measure of the cumulative duration of the child's engagement with toys.

Language production. All of the children produced some verbal utterances, although the most verbally facile children were found in the normally developing sample. In order to obtain a measure of output, we counted instances of discrete utterances, irrespective of length or complexity. This relatively crude measure presumably "penalized" children whose language was particularly rich, but acknowledged the production of less fluent children.

The frequency of production was tallied in the child clean-up task because both mother and child were involved, and the child could initiate-respond in interactive exchanges, or could talk to him/herself. Four codes were used, verbal interaction-task (clean-up) oriented, verbal interaction-non-task oriented, child monologue-task oriented, child monologue-non-task-oriented.

Examination of raw data revealed highly skewed, non-normal distributions for many of the measured variables. We rely primarily on descriptions, and non-parametric statistics, to report the data.

Delay Measure Findings

The validity and internal consistency of delay scores had been measured with a sizeable sample of *ND* children and found to be adequate. Details about stability across task, time, and situation are found in Vaughn, Kopp, and Krakow (in press). This information served as background for initial analyses with the handicapped groups.

Each group's performance. One telephone duration score and four raisin task (two for the short first six trials, and two for the long seventh trial) were examined. Table 5.4 provides the medians and ranges for each group and Fig. 5.1 shows the distribution of means, medians, and modes. First, with reference to Table 5.4, none of the overall differences were

TABLE 5.4
Median Delay Task Scores (and Ranges) by Diagnostic Groups

Delay task	Diagnostic Groups		
	ND	DS	DD
Touch telephone (sec.)	42.0 (1-150)	6.9 (1-93)	14.0 (1-150)
Raisin: First Six Trials:			
Not pick up raisin (trial)	5.0 (0-6)	1.0 (0-6)	1.3 (0-6)
Not eat raisin (trial)	5.7 (0-6)	2.5 (0-6)	4.0 (0-6)
Seventh Trial: Touch cup (sec.)	45.0 (1-120)	7.0 (1-120)	6.0 (1-120)
Eat raisin (sec.)	119.6 (2-120)	14.0 (4-120)	27.5 (3-120)

significant, although the one for the telephone task approached the conventional level of rejection (Kruskal-Wallis one-way anova x^2 (2) = 5.37, p = .068). As a group, normally developing children tended to be more likely to delay touching the telephone for an appreciable length of time than either of the two handicapped groups. Other trends emerged: more *ND* children were apt to refrain from picking up and eating the raisin during the first six trials, and to inhibit picking up and then postpone eating the raisin during the seventh trial than *DD* or *DS* children.

The *DS* children demonstrated the most difficulty in delaying or inhibiting a response to a higher salient stimulus. Their performance improved after practice (the six short raisin trials preceded the long seventh one), and in a situation structured so that examiner (and to some degree, mother) was available and interacting with the child.

Examination of Table 5.4 reveals a great deal of variability within each sample. Figure 5.1 provides description of the variability and the extent to which the samples overlapped in performance. The most distinctive pattern of group differences was found for the telephone task where the overlap of *ND* and handicapped groups was minimal. Overall, modal performance for the *ND* group was at task ceiling, but was often not the case for the two handicapped groups.

Age trends. In our first study with normally developing infants (Vaughn, Kopp, Krakow, in press) we analyzed age trends using three age groups, 18, 24, and 30 month olds. Significant age differences were found indicating an increase in ability to delay with age.

In the present study, our data pool was restricted, and the samples had been constituted with a *DA* age range from 22 to 44 months. Therefore, correlations test (non-parametric) were employed to determine the association

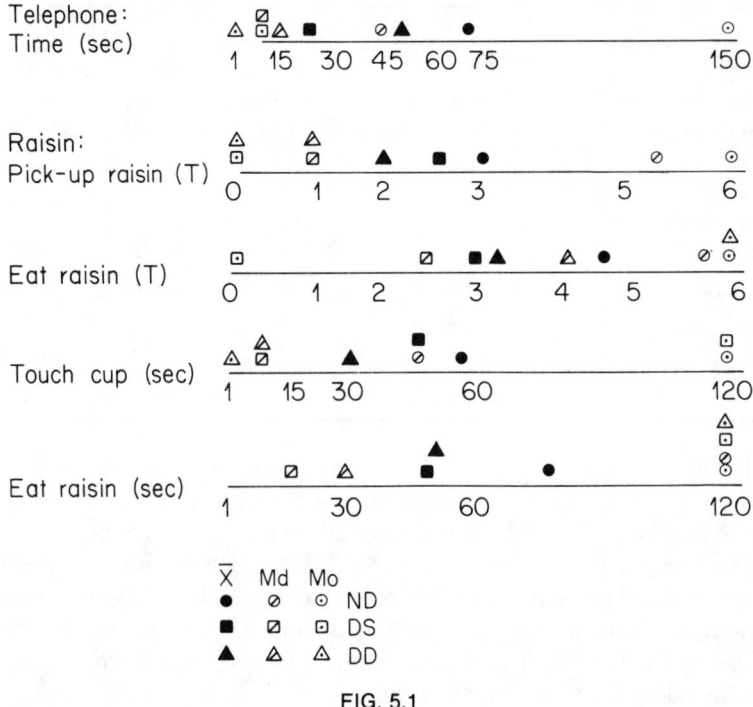

FIG. 5.1

between developmental age and delay performance. In addition, similar correlations were computed for chronological age and developmental quotients. Four scores (one from the telephone and three from the raisin tasks) were used for these analyses. As anticipated, for the *ND* sample, the *DA* and *CA* coefficients were sizeable, positive, and significant; our expectation that *DQ* would be unrelated to delay was borne out. Details are found in Table 5.5.

In contrast, the number of significant coefficients differed for the handicapped groups. For the *DS* children, a significant positive correlation appeared between the telephone task and chronological age, and a significant negative correlation emerged with telephone and developmental quotient. No developmental age coefficient was significant, although positive moderate trends were apparent. These findings indicate that, at least for the telephone task, chronologically older, lower functioning children were better able to delay than younger, higher functioning ones. Findings for the *DD* children showed no significant coefficients for developmental age, chronological age, and developmental quotients.

TABLE 5.5
Spearman Correlations Between Developmental Age (DA),
Chronological Age (CA), Developmental Quotient (DQ)
and Delay Task Scores

			Delay Tasks		
			Raisin Task (Tr. 1-6)		(Tr.7) Raisin Task
ND		Telephone	Not pick up raisin	Not eat raisin	Latency to eat raisin
	DA	.52*	.80***	.69**	.63**
	CA	.51*	.65**	.75***	.64**
	DQ	.05	.20	−.10	.03
DS					
	DA	.27	.36	.35	.36
	CA	.53*	.47	.40	−.15
	DQ	−62*	−.45	−.36	−.22
DD					
	DA	−.14	.26	.28	.17
	CA	−.18	.19	.21	.17
	DQ	−.01	.32	.16	.15

Note. Significance levels are based on two-tailed tests.
*$p < .05$
**$p < .01$
***$p < .001$

The pattern of these correlations reveals considerable organization in the growth of ability to delay among normally developing children in the second and third years of life. That is, the older the child, the more likely that delay will occur. In contrast, the correlations for the handicapped sample were not clearly interpretable from a developmental perspective. These data underscore the problems that can arise when attempts are made to elucidate the processes of development among some groups of handicapped children. This issue arises repeatedly, and is one that we will discuss in more detail later.

Compliance Task Findings

Each group's performance. Three general indices of compliance were analyzed, the amount of time until the child started the clean-up, the child's overall level of compliance (a seven point scale was used that ranged from active refusal [1] throughout the clean-up to active demonstration [7] of clean-up behavior throughout), and a dichotomous category that noted whether clean-up was completed by the child during the allocated period. In addition, discrete behavioral categories were defined to reflect instances of child "ignores" or "actively refuses" mother's request, or leaves task. A measure of negative affect was recorded which included frequencies of cry, fret, or tantrums.[4]

Table 5.6 presents a listing of medians and ranges of each group's performance for overall and specific compliance behaviors. Trends that emerged were as follows: (1) the three groups of children were remarkably similar in the rapidity of their response to mothers and compliance to her requests, (2) the groups were also similar in their demonstration of low levels of active or forceful refusals, (3) the groups were dissimilar in that ignoring mother,

TABLE 5.6
Compliance Task (Clean-up) by Diagnosistic Groups

Behaviors	Medians and Ranges		
	ND	DS	DD
Time to first Compliance (sec)	21 (5-148)	19 (7-170)	21 (5-125)
Overall Compliance rating	5 (1-7)	4 (2-7)	5 (2-7)
Ignores (freq.)	3 (0-14)	5 (1-14)	6 (0-13)
Active refusal (freq.)	1 (0-18)	1 (0-13)	1 (0-10)
Leaves task (freq.)	0 (0-5)	0 (0-3)	0 (0-4)
Completed clean-up (%)	41%	20%	18%

a passive form of refusal, was shown more frequently by handicapped groups than the *ND* group, (4) moreover, twice as many of the *ND* children completed the clean-up than did the handicapped children. The extent to which this last finding was a function of mother persistence has yet to be determined. Frequency of negative affect was also coded. Approximately one quarter of the *ND* (23%) and the *DD* (29%) samples displayed fussy behavior, whereas only 7% of the *DS* children displayed negative affect.

Overall, the clean-up task elicted few substantive group differences. Every child engaged in clean-up; in each group, a couple of children resisted strongly at one or another point, and a few complied immediately. Most children, however, had to be prodded moderately to cease their play. The characteristic that primarily distinguished the groups was the means selected to avoid maternal requests. Rarely did the *ND* children actually ignore their mothers as if they did not hear, rather they turned to more active forms of refusal to comply.

---

[4]A list of coding categories is available from the authors.

Age trends. Non-parametric correlational analyses were employed to determine the degree of association with overall compliance, time to first compliance, developmental age, chronological age, and developmental quotients. Table 5.7 provides details. The only significant relationship emerged between overall compliance and developmental age for the *DS* group. We

TABLE 5.7
Spearman Correlation Analyses of Clean-up Behaviors

		Time to first compliance	Overall compliance rating
ND	DA	−.05	.43
	CA	−.02	.22
	DQ	−.34	.01
DS	DA	.11	.61*
	CA	.09	.49
	DQ	−.37	.27
DD	DA	.15	−.01
	CA	.20	.42
	DQ	.07	.33

Note. Significance levels are based on two-tailed tests.
*$p < .05$

are puzzled about the lack of significant relationships for the *ND* group; however, this might have been due to the restricted range of ages in the sample. Finally, as found before in the delay analyses, no pattern of relationships appeared with the *DD* sample.

Relations with Cognitive Variables

We were also interested in the relations between self-control and cognitive variables other than those tapped by the developmental examination and reflected in the *DA* score. In particular, sustained attention and language represent two facets of cognition that (1) undergo important developmental changes during this age period, (2) exhibit suggestive theoretical and empirical relations to self-regulation among older children, and (3) offer a useful perspective for understanding the emergence of self-control. Accordingly, we examined the relations between delay/compliance and selected attention and language measures.

Sustained attention. Our previous research (Krakow, Kopp, & Vaughn, unpublished) indicated that, among *ND* children, the measure of sustained attention (i.e., time on task) was reliable week to week, showed significant and stable increases over the age period under study and was independent of *DQ*, but highly and significantly related to delay behavior. In other words, during the second and third years of life, *ND* children increased their tendency to become and to remain engaged in play. At the same time, individual differences remained important: children who sustained attention best at 12- and 18-months continued to do so during the third year, and also excelled in tasks that measured their ability to delay touching attractive stimuli.

In the present study, time on task was measured as a function of group membership, as was the relationship between sustained attention and self-control and developmental measures. Group differences did not emerge for time on task. In contrast, patterns of correlations varied by group.

Table 5.8 summarizes group-by-group correlational analyses of sustained attention and self-control and developmental variables; for the *ND* sample, the results largely replicated our prior work. Time on task showed a positive relation with developmental age and with the two delay variables. It was not, however, related to the overall compliance rating. Among the *DS* children, time on task increased with both chronological and developmental age but did not show a relationship with delay or compliance behaviors. Among the *DD* children, the pattern was even less consistent.

TABLE 5.8
Spearman Correlations of Sustained Attention (Time on Task) with Self-Control and Age Variables

	ND	DS	DD
Telephone	.38	.24	.01
Not pick up raisin	.41	−.25	.42
Overall compliance	.07	.26	−.07
DA	.42	.46	−.05
CA	.32	.52	−.42

Said differently, the inter-related constellation of delay ability, attention and age that we have observed among *ND* children appears not to hold among the handicapped, and particularly the *DD* groups. To examine this hypothesis more directly, we performed principal components analyses separately for each group. The percentage of variance accounted for by the unrotated first principal component in such analyses is a measure of the degree of underlying coherence among variables.

The principal components analyses were conducted with four variables: telephone, raisin, sustained attention, and developmental age. For *ND* children, the first principal component accounted for 65% of the common variance, with all variables loading at .67 or above. By contrast, for the *DD* and *DS* samples, the first principal components accounted, respectively, for only 45% and 46% of the variants, and item loadings were as low as .41 and .12. (Analyses substituting chronological for developmental age yielded similar results.) Thus, this approach offered preliminary confirmation in that the structure of delay, attention and age-related variables is more cohesive for *ND* than for handicapped young children.

Language. In order to examine the relationship between language and self-control variables, we utilized three language measures, (1) a language age score for the language sub-test of the Gesell, (2) frequency of task-oriented verbalizations (interactive or monolog) during the clean-up task, and (3) frequency of non-task oriented (interactive or monolog) during the clean-up. See Table 5.9.

The groups were virtually identical on task-oriented and non-task oriented verbalizations, whereas the ND children had a slightly higher mean language age (30 vs 26 and 28 months). In contrast, the groups differed markedly in the pattern of intercorrelations that was obtained between language variables and self-control performance. For the *ND* children, language competence was highly related to self-control behavior, and these relations were maintained with chronological age controlled statistically. By contrast, clean-up was independent of verbal productions. In other words, the *ND's* self-control was a function of their underlying language ability, but not of the amount of their production.

With the handicapped children, language age was unrelated to self-control, but task-oriented verbalizations, which increased with developmental age, were associated with compliance and delay for the *DS* group. Of interest, non-task oriented verbalizations were associated with decreased compliance for both the *DS* and *DD* children. These results suggest that the functional relationships between language and self-control may be different for *ND* and handicapped young children, at least in the setting that was measured. Implications are discussed below.

In this chapter, we have presented the results of a series of analyses designed to describe young handicapped children's abilities to monitor and moderate their own behavior. Three specific questions have been raised and addressed: (1) within the age span that we suggested encompassed the emergence and consolidation of self-control (Kopp, 1982; Vaughn, Kopp, Krakow, in press) (1), is self-control similar for handicapped and normally developing children; (2) within the handicapped population, are observed individual differences a function of diagnosis; and (3) do the variables of self-control, sustained attention, and language ability form the nexus of interrelationships suggested by the clinical literatures on hyperactive and deaf children?

With respect to the first issue, our data suggest that handicapped children

TABLE 5.9
Spearman Correlations of Language Variables with Self-Control
and Developmental Variables by Group

		Language Age	Task-Oriented	Non-task Oriented
ND				
	Telephone	.43	.16	.29
	Not pick up raisin	.78***	.43	.34
	Touch cup	.64**	.43	.32
	Overall compliance	.35	.29	−.42
	DA	.90***	.34	.12
DS				
	Telephone	.31	.34	−.12
	Not pick up raisin	.35	.55*	.17
	Touch cup	.07	.41	.28
	Overall compliance	.36	.77***	−.74***
	DA	.89***	.73**	−.41
DD				
	Telephone	.13	−.20	−.26
	Not pick up raisin	−.11	.06	−.56*
	Touch cup	−.05	.05	−.45
	Overall compliance	.03	.20	−.65**
	DA	.39	.73**	.31

Note. Significance levels are based on two-tailed tests.
*.05
**.01
***.001

(regardless of diagnosis) closely approximate the performance of normally developing children in our battery of self-control tasks. To some degree, all of the children initially inhibited a response when asked to delay (telephone and raisin tasks) and produced a sequence of active compliant behaviors when their mothers asked them to clean up the lab room. To the extent that these tasks measure self-control, the performances of the handicapped and the normally developing children were parallel. These findings are consistent with reports that the structure of behavior in other domains is similar for both mentally retarded and for normally developing children (e.g., Cicchetti & Serafica, 1981; Serafica & Cicchetti, 1975; Weisz & Zigler, 1979). In essence, the data suggest that differences between diagnostic groups may disappear for the broad domains of developmental phenomena when mental (or developmental) age is controlled.

Despite the fact that the diagnostic groups do not differ in their performances on our battery of tasks, we hesitate to assert that the course of developmental is identical for all groups. Several of our findings have proven difficult to interpret. In particular, it was our expectation that self-control would show age-related increases in capacity. This expectation had been met in our cross-sectional study of self-control in a normally developing sample ranging in *CA* from 18- to 30-months (Vaughn, Kopp, Krakow, in press). The same pattern of correlations was found for the present sample of normally developing children (i.e., older children waited longer in the delay tasks and tended to be more compliant). In contrast, the relations between age measures and self-control in the handicapped samples were quite modest and for the most part not significant. In less statistical terms, developmentally younger children in the handicapped groups were performing similarly to their developmentally older counterparts on our individual tasks.

This finding is counter-intuitive, and we are not fully able to account for it. However, a number of factors may be implicated. We recognize that our samples are limited to their rather small size and to the within sample heterogeneity (see Table 5.3). Although we made continued and intensive efforts to restrict sample composition on the basis of *DQ, DA,* and diagnosis, there are still many differences in the three groups. The handicapped groups differed from the *ND* group in health histories, maternal education, sensory abilities, and age. It is unclear from the data which of these factors, if any, interacted to suppress the expected relationship between self-control and developmental age. Unfortunately, these issues can only be addressed in future research with larger samples.

While recognizing the methodological limitations of this study, we are not inclined to attribute the paucity of developmental correlations entirely to them. In point of fact, we believe that weak relationships between *DA* and self-control are a function of complex conditions, including the handicap *per se* and the nature of the learning and social experiences encountered by the child.

For example, some handicapping conditions (e.g., Down syndrome) that involve central nervous system impairment, are associated with a leveling off of cognitive growth at an early age (see Gibson, 1978; Kopp & McCall, 1982). With Down syndrome this reduction in the rate of cognitive growth often begins during the sensorimotor period (as a consequence, *DQ* scores are often seen to drop). Further, a number of these children show minimal growth in cognitive abilities after the preoperational period (Gibson, 1978). For these children, the slope of the curve for cognitive developmental abilities is less steep and reaches assymptote at a different level than in normally developing children. At the same time, however, some Down syndrome children function successfully in protected environments because they use effective social skills and are able to initiate and perform routine repetitive tasks (see Gibson, 1978).

It is possible that some of the chronologically older Down syndrome and *DD* children in our samples were in the process of reaching asymptote, and were simply not showing the same rates of developmental progress as the chronologically young children. Though these children had acquired some rudimentary self-monitoring skills, the rate of increase in such skills would have been consistent with other intellectual skills. This would, of course, have the result of suppressing the relationship between self-control and *DA*.

It is also clear that the socialization and educational histories of the handicapped groups are considerably different from those of the normally developing children. Many developmentally delayed infants, especially those who have a diagnosis invariably associated with later mental retardation, enter into intervention programs as early as six months of age. The programs are designed to enhance cognitive and social skills of these children and often use the format of small groups with activities scheduled throughout the period of attendance. Thus, children in such programs are offered a variety of rich experiences along with systematic formal training for a number of years.

Every handicapped child in our study had been in an intervention program, and had been exposed to formal training experiences for three or more years. We believe that the effects of this early training may be accumulative so that the handicapped child functioning at a cognitive developmental age of 2-years may actually have and use social skills consistent with a developmentally older child (see Table 5.3, personal-social scores from the Gesell schedules). In this case, we offer the speculation that the socialization skills implicit in our delay and compliance tasks (e.g., not touching an attractive stimulus in the absence of an external control; changing from play to clean-up at an arbitrary signal) may actually deteriorate when cognitive capacities reach the (initial) level of social skills. This is to say, the handicapped child may reach the period of autonomy and social independence *cognitively* and chronologically later than would be expected from their earlier level of socialization skills. Using the language, memory, and symbolization skills that mark the end of the sensorimotor period, the cognitively older handicapped child may try out and test his/her abilities with little or no regard to the social constraints of the situation.

Finally, we do not wish to discount the influence of motivational or affective factors (e.g., Harter, 1981; Harter & Zigler, 1974). It has been shown that older handicapped and mentally retarded children become increasingly aware of their own limitations in cognitive and social realms. As a result of this awareness, they derive little pleasure in *doing*. Intuitively, it seems reasonable to expect developmentally older children will be more aware of limitations, and that perhaps this might lead to less concern over performing in our delay and compliance tasks.

In sum, we have offered several admittedly speculative hypotheses to account for the failure to find significant developmental age trends in the self-control data for handicapped children. We have emphasized these findings, because if they replicate, they have considerable theoretical and practical implications. It is possible, for example, that developmentally delayed children reach a particular point in development (e.g., *DA* 2 years) by a number of different routes, and that their particular developmental histories either enhance or inhibit the cognitive and social skills seen at that point in development. Quite possibly, this type of variability plays an important role in later growth and development.

Many of the preceding comments about the similarities and differences found among normally developing and delayed young children pertain to comparisons between the *DS* and *DD* groups. In many ways, the children showed similarities in performances on our tasks when developmental age was controlled. Nonetheless, striking differences were found in the pattern of correlations within groups when self-control scores were correlated with developmental age. This appears to be especially true of compliance during the clean-up task where *DA* and compliance are significantly related for the *DS* children and nonsignificantly and *negatively* related for the *DD* children. Though the sample sizes preclude between group tests for the significance of the differences between these correlations, the data are suggestive of group differences. Whether the "uniqueness" of each group is a function of particular characteristics associated with a specific handicap (e.g., the problems that young *DS* children appear to have with certain visual stimuli), remains to be determined.

Our final question concerned the interrelationship of self-control and several cognitive variables. Again, the findings were intriguing, but raise as many questions as they answer. Among normally developing children we obtained a coherent and predictable pattern of interrelationships among measures. The delay tasks were themselves correlated and covaried with sustained attention and *DA* (and by implication with language age as measured by the Gesell). For the handicapped groups, the delay tasks did not show the same degree of relationship to each other, nor to sustained attention and *DA*. Perhaps most interestingly, self-control did not show a similar relationship to language age as for the normally developing children. Rather, the number of utterances produced during the clean-up task was related to the compliance rating. Children rated as more compliant (*DS*) produced more task-oriented verbalizations. Children rated as less compliant (both *DS* and *DD*) produced more non-task oriented verbalizations. Thus, unlike the normally developing group, the verbal productions in the handicapped children were directly related to their ongoing behavior. We believe that this may reflect an explicit training effect in the handicapped groups. That is, parents and intervenors often orient and maintain the attention in young handicapped children to tasks by encouraging the child's own verbal productions about what s(he) is doing. In this way, speech might come to guide behavior to a certain extent. Of course, as in the case of the less compliant children, when the child's goal differs from that of the adult, speech might be used to guide behavior in opposition to the wishes of the parent. That a similar relationship was not found for the normally developing group could well be due to the explicitness and length of training for the delayed groups.

In sum, this first pass over the data on self-control for handicapped children has left us with many unanswered questions. Though we continue to hold to the belief that self-control is an age-related function, our data suggest that the paths to developmental competencies may be very different for handicapped and normally developing children, and these differences in developmental routes may be important in determining the ease with which children can invoke and use their personal resources. Given sensitive caregivers and a non-depriving environment, the normally developing child matures and acquires information in such a way that developmental resources can be marshalled and applied flexibly in meeting the demands of daily living. The handicapped child lacks this range of resources and very likely depends very heavily on the resources available, both personal and in the environment, to meet those same demands. Consequently, the production of situationally appropriate behaviors may not be as easy or likely as for normally developing children. That is, the handicapped child's behavioral control may be tied to particular persons or situations and is not flexibly and adaptively modulated by dynamic situational demands.

CONCLUSION

In the first part of this chapter, we presented two theoretical positions. One described a series of developmental phases (neurophysiological modulation, sensorimotor modulation, control, self-control, and self-regulation), that comprise an ontogenetic course for self-regulation. The other focused upon individual differences and highlighted findings showing the interrelationship between self-regulation and other facets of behavior in clinically designated groups of children. In the second, data portion of this chapter, findings obtained from normally developing and handicapped children were described in relation to the phase labeled self-control. Admittedly descriptive, the findings nevertheless pointed to a reasonable level of coherence between the self-control behaviors of delay and compliance and other cognitive processing skills for normally developing children, whereas low or absent relationships were obtained for handicapped children.

In our view, the emergence and consolidation of self-control can be seen as a developmental structure or organizer during the second, third, and fourth years of life. That is, the ability to monitor, modulate, and adapt behavior to fluctuating environmental circumstances is a major developmental accomplishment of this age *and* an important underpinning of the subsequent development of self-regulation. It is possible that self-control also serves as a foundation for later growth in other cognitive and social domains.

To the extent that the nexus of interrelated self-control and cognitive competencies are not seen in the development of handicapped children, aspects of development are based on an unsound foundation. That is, the within-child supports (e.g., cognitive processing skills) that are weak or erratic for some handicapped children will make it difficult to plan and apply behavior to the physical and social environment. Further, if our interpretation of the data presented here are correct, the external environment of the young handicapped child may give the child's behavior the appearance of self-control without the substance of interwoven abilities to sustain and direct attention and to understand, organize, and communicate information. Without the supports of specific individuals or specific situations, self-control is inconsistent and tied to the vagaries of particular situations. In contrast, when children's developmental competencies and resources are on a par with one another, then they can select the skill most appropriate to use to meet challenges of various situations.

We believe we are beginning to understand why the clinical literature is replete with descriptions in which deficits or problems in self-regulation, sustained attention, activity level, and language have been cited. Clearly our data do not point to causal directions, but only to the fact that we have obtained evidence about lack of coherence to behavior as early as the second year of developmental age. We feel that our line of research is sufficiently promising to pursue vigorously.

ACKNOWLEDGMENTS

Presented at the Minnesota Symposium on Child Psychology, October 1981. Preparation of this paper was supported in part by contract #330-77-0306 from the Bureau for the Education of the Handicapped (now Office of Special Education). Appreciation is extended to Kim Johnson for her assistance in many phases of the research, to Anne Weickgenant, Jeanne Doyle, Diane Parham, and Marvin Lee for coding and data analysis help, and to Linda Cullian for statistical advice.

REFERENCES

Als, H. Assessing an assessment: Conceptual considerations, methodological issues, and a perspective on the future of the Neonatal Behavioral Assessment Scale. In A. J. Sameroff (Ed.), *Organization and stability: A commentary on the Brazelton Neonatal Behavior Assessment Scale. Monographs of the Society for Research in Child Development,* 1978, *43,* (506, Serial No. 177).

Altshuler, K. Z. The social and psychological development of the deaf child: Problems, their treatment and prevention. *American Annals of the Deaf,* 1974, *119,* 365-376.

Benezra, E. Learning and memory in hyperactive, reading disabled and normal children. Unpublished manuscript, Department of Psychology, McGill University, 1978. Cited in Douglas, Z. I., Treatment and training approaches to hyperactivity. In C. K. Whalen & B. Henker (Eds.), *Hyperactive children: The social ecology of identification and treatment.* New York: Academic Press, 1980.

Cicchetti, D., & Serafica, F. C. Interplay among behavioral systems: Illustrations from the study of attachment, affiliation, and wariness in young children with Down's syndrome. *Developmental Psychology,* 1981, *17,* 36-49.

Clausen, J., Udsky, A., & Sersen, E. A. Measurements of autonomic function in mental deficiency. In R. Karrer (Eds.), *Developmental psychology of mental retardation.* Springfield, Ill.: Charles Thomas, 1976.

Collins, J. T., & Hagen, J. W. A constructivist account of the development of perception, attention, and memory. In G. A. Hale & M. Lewis (Eds.), *Attention and cognitive development.* New York: Plenum, 1979.

Douglas, V. I. Treatment and training approaches to hyperactivity: Establishing internal or external control. In C. K. Whalen & B. Henker (Eds.), *Hyperactive children: The social ecology of identification and treatment.* New York: Academic Press, 1980.

Douglas, V. I. & Peters, K. Toward a clearer definition of the attentional deficit of hyperactive children. In G. A. Hale & M. Lewis (Eds.), *Attention and cognitive development.* New York: Plenum, 1979.

Freedman, D. C., Cannady, C., & Robinson, J. A. Speech and psychic structure: A reconsideration of their relation. *Journal of the American Psychoanalytic Association,* 1971, *19,* 765-779.

Gibson, D. *Down's syndrome. The psychology of mongolism.* Cambridge: Cambridge University Press, 1978.

Gibson, E. & Rader, N. Attention: The perceiver as performer. In G. A. Hale & M. Lewis (Eds.), *Attention and cognitive development.* New York: Plenum, 1979.

Greenacre, P. General problems of acting out. *Psychoanalytic Quarterly,* 1950, *19,* 455-467.

Greenfield, P. M., Nelson, K., & Saltzman, E. The development of rulebound strategies for manipulating seriated cups: A parallel between action and grammar. *Cognitive Psychology,* 1972, *3,* 291-310.

Harris, R. I. Impulse control in deaf children: Research and clinical issues. In L. S. Liben (Ed.), *Deaf children: developmental perspectives.* New York: Academic Press, 1978.

Harter, S. A developmental perspective on some parameters of self-ruleation in children. In P. Karoly & F. H. Kanfer (Eds.), *Self-management and behavior change: From theory to practice,* in press.

Harter, S. A model of mastery motivation in children: Individual differences and developmental changes. In W. A. Collins (Ed.), *Minnesota Symposium on child psychology.* Vol. 14, Hillsdale, N.J.: Erlbaum, 1981.

Harter, S. & Zigler, E. The assessment of effective motivation in normal and retarded children. *Developmental Psychology,* 1974, *10,* 169-180.

Honzik, M. P., McFarlane, J. W., & Allen, L. The stability of mental test performance between two and eighteen years. *Journal of Experimental Education,* 1948, *17,* 309-324.

Johnson, K., & Kopp, C. B. *Use of diversionary strategies: 2-year-olds in a delay situation.* Presented at the Society for Research in Child Development, Boston, April 1981.

Kagan, J. *Change and continuity in infancy.* New York: Wiley, 1971.

Kagan, J., & Kogan, N. Individual variation in cognitive processes. In P. H. Mussen (Ed.), *Carmichael's manual of child psychology.* New York: Wiley, 1970.

Karrer, R., Nelson, M., & Galbraith, G. Psychophysiological research with the mentally retarded. In N. R. Ellis (Ed.), *Handbook of mental deficiency, psychological theory and research,* 2nd ed. New Jersey: Lawrence Erlbaum Associates, 1979.

Kopp, C. B. Infancy studies. In B. K. Keogh & C. B. Kopp, *Research on early abilities of children with handicaps.* Proposed submitted to the Bureau of Education for the Handicapped, 1978.

Kopp, C. B. The antecedents of self-regulation: A developmental perspective. *Developmental Psychology,* 1982, *18,* 199-214.

Kopp, C. B. Risk factors in development. In M. Haith & J. Campos (Eds.), *Biology and Infancy. Vol. 2.* In P. Mussen (Eds.), *Manual of Child Psychology.* New York: Wiley, in press.

Kopp, C. B., & McCall, R. B. Stability and instability in mental performance among normal, at-risk, and handicapped infants and children. In P. B. Baltes & O. G. Brim (Eds.), *Lifespan development and behavior,* Vol. 4. New York: Academic Press, 1982.

Kopp, C. B., & Vaughn, B. E. Sustained attention during exploratory manipulation as a predictor of cognitive competence in pre-term males. *Child Development,* 1982, *53,* 174-182.

Krakow, J. B., Kopp, C. B., & Vaughn, B. E. Sustained attention during the second year: Age trends, individual differences and implications for development (in preparation).

Krakow, J. B., Johnson, K., Kopp, C. B. Clustering behaviors in young children, unpublished manuscript.

Lesser, S. R., & Easser, B. R. Personality differences in the perceptually handicapped. *American Academy of Child Psychiatry,* 1972, *11,* 458-466.

Levine, E. F. *Youth in a soundless world; A search for personality.* New York: New York University Press, 1956.

Lidz, T. Developmental concept of acting out. Discussion. In E. N. Rexford (Ed.), *A developmental approach to problems of acting out.* Rev. Ed. New York: International Universities Press, 1978.

Luria, A. R. Verbal regulation of behavior. In M. A. B. Brazier (Ed.), *Conference on central nervous system and behavior.* New York: Josiah Macy Foundation, 1960.

Malone, C. A. Some observations on children of disorganized families and problems of acting out. In E. N. Rexford (Ed.), *A developmental approach to problems of acting out.* Rev. Ed. New York: International Universities Press, 1978.

McCall, R. The development of intellectual functioning in infancy and the prediction of later I.Q. In J. Osofsky (Eds.), *Handbook of infant development.* New York: Wiley, 1979.

Mischel, W., & Patterson, C. J. Effective plans for self-control in children. *Minnesota Symposium on child psychology.* New Jersey: Lawrence Erlbaum Associates, 1978.

Parmelee, A. H., Kopp, C. B., & Sigman, M. Selection of developmental assessment techniques for infants at risk. *Merrill-Palmer Quarterly of Development and Behavior,* 1976, *22,* 177-199.

Piaget, J. *The origins of intelligence in children.* New York: International Universities Press, 1952.

Rebelsky, F., Beavey, C., Blotner, R. Maternal control techniques and resistance to temptation in young children. Presentation at the meeting of the Society for Research in Child Development, Minneapolis, 1971.

Rexford, E. N. *A developmental approach to problems of acting out,* Rev. Ed. New York: International Universities Press, 1978.

Ricciuti, H. N. Object grouping and selective ordering behavior in infants 12 to 24 months old. *Merrill-Palmer Quarterly,* 1965, *11,* 129-148.

Sackett, G. P. Response to differentiated visual complexity in four groups of retarded children. *Journal of Comparative and Physiological Psychology,* 1967, *64,* 200-205.

Sander, L. W. The longitudinal course of early mother-child interaction. In B. M. Foss (Ed.), *Determinants of infant behavior* (Vol. 4). London: Methuen, 1969.

Tant, J. L. Problem solving in hyperactive and reading disabled boys. Unpublished doctoral dissertation, McGill University, 1978. Cited in Douglas, Z. I., Treatment and training approaches to hyperactivity. In C. K. Whalen & B. Henker (Eds.), *Hyperactive children: The social ecology of identification and treatment.* New York: Academic Press, 1980.

Uzgiris, I. C. Ordinality in the development of schemas for relating to objects. In J. Hellmuth (Ed.), *The exceptional infant: The normal infant,* Vol. 1. Seattle, Wash.: Special Child Publications, 1967.

Vaughn, B. E., & Kopp, C. B., Krakow, J. B. The consolidation of self-control and the emergence of self-regulation from 18 to 30 months of age: Normative trends, individual differences and external correlates. Child development, in press.

Vygotsky, L. S. *Thought and language.* Cambridge, MIT Press, 1962.

Wellman, H. M. The early development of intentional memory behavior. *Human Development,* 1977, *20,* 86-101.

Werner, H. & Kaplan, B. Symbol formation. New York: Wiley, 1963.

Whalen, C. K. & Henker, B. (Eds.) *Hyperactive children: The social ecology of identification and treatment.* New York: Academic Press, 1980.

Zigler, E. Developmental versus difference theories of mental retardation and the problem of motivation. *American Journal of Mental Deficiency,* 1968, *73,* 536-556.

6 Comments on Kopp, Krakow, and Vaughn's Chapter

Byron Egeland
Department of PsychoEducational Studies
University of Minnesota

Kopp, Krakow, and Vaughn are to be congratulated for their commitment to do research on a topic as complex and difficult to understand as self-regulation. Issues of self-control and regulation have preoccupied educators, mental health professionals, and others working with children for a number of years. However, there has been relatively little research in the area, and those who have written on the topic have done so from very different perspectives and orientations. The work of Kopp and her associates reported here, and other studies from Project REACH represent a systematic effort to understand the development of self-monitoring behavior in normal and handicapped children.

Before I discuss the basic assumption underlying the chapter, I would like to comment on the use of handicapped samples in the study of self-monitoring behavior. Comparisons were made among a sample of 17 normal children between the ages of 18 and 31 months, 15 Down's Syndrome children between the ages of 31 and 60 months, and 17 developmentally delayed children between the ages of 32 and 53 months. Group differences were examined and developmental age, *CA, DQ,* and the cognitive measure for each group were correlated with delay scores and compliance. The normal children were found to have significantly higher delay scores than the handicapped groups, while there were basically no differences between groups on the compliance task. The age factor and cognitive measures correlated with the delay tasks for the normal group but the correlations for the handicapped groups were inconsistent and generally nonsignificant.

It is difficult to draw any conclusions from the correlational patterns presented by Kopp, Krakow, and Vaughn because of the small sample sizes and the heterogeneous nature of the two handicapped groups. In addition, the handicapped groups differed from the normal group on parent education and occupation. No doubt there were other, perhaps more significant, differences related to caretaking history, life circumstances, separations of child from caretaker, and early educational and peer group experiences. Such variables are likely to have affected the development of self-monitoring behavior and the relationship between cognitive measures and monitoring behavior. The difference in delay scores between normal and handicapped groups could be attributable to differences in early caretaking and educational histories of the groups rather than cognitive developmental status. Thus, the use of small groups of handicapped children in the study of the development of self-monitoring behaviors in young children, particularly the cognitive correlates of such behavior, would appear to complicate an already difficult area of study. I would argue that it would be easier and more meaningful to establish the cognitive correlates of self-monitoring behavior for a sample of normal children.

Beyond my concern with sample selection is a question about Kopp, Krakow, and Vaughn's assumption that monitoring behavior is a product of the child's cognition, and that cognitive development framework provides a good foundation for understanding self-regulation. To establish the link between monitoring behavior and cognitive skills Kopp and her colleagues report findings from the clinical literature, which suggests that acting out and hyperactive children have difficulties with sustained attention and self-monitoring. An inability to sustain attention means that the child is unable to identify relevant cues in complex social situations and consequently he/she will have problems in self-regulation. Even though sustained attention may be a prerequisite for self-regulation, it does not mean there is a causal relationship.

Deaf children are used to exemplify the association of linguistic development and problems in monitoring behavior. Deaf children's problems with impulse control are linked to limited linguistic development. Schein (1975) and Schildroth (1980) report the percentage of deaf children in residential settings with emotional problems (most of which are problems with impulse control) range from 6% to 11%. Even though these figures are quite high, the majority of the deaf children did not have impulse control problems. Since the incidence figures were based on students in residential schools, it can be assumed that they were all deaf rather than hard of hearing, which suggests that they had communication problems. If they all had communication problems, why was the incidence figure for impulse control problems so low? It should also be noted that three of the four current etiologies of deafness—maternal rubella, prematurity, and emotional-fetal Rh incompatibility—are associated with additional handicapping conditions, including neurological handicaps that may have behavioral consequences (Goulder & Trybus, 1977). The impact of etiology on behavior may be especially great in deafness caused by maternal rubella during pregnancy. Vernon (1967) found rubella deaf children to be significantly poorer in emotional adjustment than children who were deaf due to heredity or meningitis. When the etiological agent causing deafness can also cause other problems, it is difficult to distinguish the secondary effects of the deafness from the other primary effects of the etiological agent (Rosen, 1983).

Kopp and her associates conclude that "to the extent that cognitive skills are limited then self-regulation will be limited" (p. 10). It is assumed that under normal circumstances the adequate development of cognitive skills will result in the normal development of self-regulation. The fact that both increased self-regulation and significant changes in cognitive development occur during the second and third years of life does not establish a causal relationship nor can one draw any causal inferences from the clinical literature. I would agree that cognitive components are important, but would place more emphasis on social and emotional factors, particularly the development of the caretaker/infant attachment relationship.

In an attempt to illustrate the importance of social/emotional factors on the development of compliance and self-regulation, I would like to report some data from our longitudinal study of the development of competence in a group of high risk children. A sample of 267 families from the Minneapolis Public Health Clinic were enrolled in the study during the mother's last trimester of pregnancy. The children were assessed at regularly scheduled intervals starting at birth and continuing through the preschool period. Detailed and comprehensive information on the families and the children's life circumstances was also collected at regularly scheduled intervals.

Using some of the data from our prohibition situation, Joffe (1980) looked at various factors related to compliance in children 12 and 18 months of age. The prohibition situation (Egeland, Brunnquell, & Joffe, 1977) is a procedure designed specifically to assess individual differences in mother-infant interaction in a limit-setting situation. Mothers and their infants were videotaped in a waiting room which contained a number of objects designed to elicit the infant's curiosity and exploration. Ratings were employed to assess the nature and extent of mother's attempts to prohibit the child from exploring and playing with certain items, and the child's response to the prohibitions and limit setting. Infants were rated on compliance, activity level, quality of object exploration, and predominant affective state. Quality of mother-infant attachment was also assessed at 12 and 18 months using Ainsworth's Strange Situation (Ainsworth, Blehar, Waters, & Wall, 1978). Children were given the Bayley Scale of Infant Development (BSID) at nine months and the Uzgiris and Hunt Ordinal Scales of Psychological Development (1975) at 12 months. The latter is designed to measure the cognitive development of young children and is based on Piaget's notion that development proceeds in an invariant sequence. It included three scales: The development of Visual Pursuit and the Permanence of Objects; the development of Means for Obtaining the Desired Environmental Events; and the Constructs of Object Relations in Space. No significant relationship was found between BSID scores and the ratings of compliance in the Prohibition Situation, nor was there a relationship between performance on the Uzgiris and Hunt Scales and compliance. Infants classified as securely attached complied more readily with maternal prohibitions than did anxiously attached infants. Joffe points out that there is little evidence in the socialization literature that says obedience is fostered through specific training practices. This does not, of course, obviate the role of learning in socialization but simply suggests that the affectional tie itself may dispose the infant to comply with maternal signals. Following Stayton, Hogan, and Ainsworth (1971), we do not see attachment as a socialization technique per se, but rather as a reflection of quality of the infant-mother interaction that has developed over time. As an affectional relationship, attachment is based on interaction, and it is therefore not surprising that the quality of those interactions might have predictable effects on subsequent mother-infant interaction in a variety of developmentally salient situations. Where the history of interaction has led to the development of a secure attachment relationship, maternal effectiveness and infant compliance seem to result as both partners negotiate the infant's transition into the broader social world of rules, regulations, increasing competencies, and growing autonomy. Where the history of interaction has led to the development of an anxious attachment relationship, the outcome seems to be less positive in terms of infant compliance and maternal effectiveness. The data indicate that the effectiveness demonstrated by the securely attached pairs is not easily attributed to individual cognitive differences in either member of the pair. I wouldn't deny the importance of learning in the acquisition of control and self-regulation, however, I would highlight the importance of the child's willingness to learn the behaviors deemed appropriate for control and self-regulation.

Using data obtained in a tool-using problem-solving situation at age two, Erickson (1981) reported findings similar to those obtained by Joffe on the children at an earlier age. A number of mother and child behaviors were rated from videotapes of the pairs interacting in a series of increasingly more difficult problem-solving tasks. The tasks were designed to stress the children's capacity to use their own resources and the resources of the mother. Erickson looked at the child's compliance with maternal directives and found that quality of attachment assessed at 12 and 18 months was highly related to compliance at age two. She also found that the BSID scores obtained at age two related to compliance. For the two-year-old, compliance is a function of the quality of the child's relationship with his/her caretaker as well as overall developmental level.

Finally, I looked at compliance and self-control for the children in our sample who have attended preschool. These findings are preliminary, since we have not completed the observations of the children in preschool, nor have we completely analyzed the data. At this time we have collected observational data and teacher ratings on 80 children. Forty of these children were in a preschool organized by Sroufe specifically for a subsample of our children. (It is on this subsample that the data reported by Sroufe in this volume is based.) The additional 40 children attended various preschools in the Twin Cities. Each child was observed for at least two half days by two of our observers and at least one teacher rated each child. Our observers rated each child on a series of seven point scales, including a scale on compliance with teacher directions. The teacher rated each child on the same scales and also completed the Behar Preschool Behavior Questionnaire and a checklist of behavior problems. The California Q-sort was also completed separately by the observer and teacher. Based on this data, a group of 18 compliant and 14 noncompliant preschool children were identified. Correlations between our observations of compliance and teachers' ratings was .75, and agreement at the extreme ends of the scale was beyond 90%.

I looked at differences between the compliant and noncompliant groups on a variety of factors having to do with the child's past developmental and caretaking history. Specifically, how do quality of attachment, various cognitive measures, and other factors relate to compliance assessed in preschool? Surprisingly, there were very few group differences. The compliant groups tended to consist of more securely attached children, and they tended to have higher scores on certain cognitive and language measures, such as the Zimmerman Preschool Language Scale. Even using a number of caretaking, cognitive, and life circumstances variables in combination, we were not able to predict the child's membership in the compliant or noncompliant groups using multiple discriminant function analyses.

The reason I was unable to find any social/emotional, cognitive, or caretaking correlates to compliance in preschool children was that these factors were highly variable for the noncompliant group. The range of IQ and language scores for the group extended from the mentally retarded range (<70) to greater than 130. Quality of caretaking as assessed in the problem-solving situation at age two and the teaching task at 42 months was highly varied, and the home situations in general ranged from the best to the worst. It was also true that earlier assessments of compliance were highly varied for the noncompliant preschool group. Noncompliant preschool children were heterogeneous in terms of earlier ratings of compliance in the 12 and 18 month prohibition situation and the 24 month problem-solving situation. There seems to be little continuity in the area of noncompliance across the toddler and preschool period. The compliant group, however, was found to have a history of compliant behavior, and in general, they were judged to be competent at each assessment period. It appears that the factors related to compliant behavior in preschool are a secure attachment and good quality caretaking, a past developmental history of competence and compliance, and at least a minimum of cognitive and linguistic skills. These same factors (or lack thereof) are not necessarily critical, however, in the development of noncompliance in preschool children. Many of the children in the noncompliant group were securely attached, had a past history of competence, and had the necessary cognitive and linguistic skills.

The roots of noncompliance are varied, and, in fact, closer examination of the children in the noncompliant preschool group indicated that there were different patterns of behavior or types of noncompliant children. As expected, large differences were found when the competent and noncompetent groups were compared on the various items and scales of the Preschool Behavior Questionnaire. Generally, the compliant children were rated positively while the noncompliant group was highly varied. Large differences were found on the items and subscales having to do with anxiety, anger, and peer relations. Compliant children were rated as relaxed, not hostile or angry, and as having good peer relations and social skills. The noncompliant group distributed themselves in a bimodal fashion on each of these dimensions. Noncompliant children were rated as either relaxed or tense. Some noncompliant children were rated as angry, others were rated as not displaying anger. The same was found for peer relations and social skills in that the noncompliant children were rated at one extreme or another. It was clear from the data that subtypes of noncompliance existed. With the noncompliant group divided into subgroups along the dimensions of anxiety, anger, and peer relations, some coherence with earlier development and caretaking histories was found. Even though the subgroups were small, the angry noncompliant children were anxiously attached at 12 and 18 months, and the quality of caretaking as observed in the 24 month problem-solving situation was poor. Noncompliant children who were rated as having good social skills and peer relations had a history of secure attachment and good quality caretaking. The children in this subgroup also had higher IQ and language scores compared to the remainder of the noncompliant group.

In conclusion, perhaps it will be necessary to identify subtypes of noncompliant children and study these subgroups using a multivariate approach in order to understand the development of self-monitoring behavior. Kopp, Krakow, and Vaughn's data (and review of the clinical literature) provides only limited support for the cognitive roots of self-monitoring behavior. The data I presented indicates that the relationship between cognitive factors and compliance is not clearly demonstrated; however, neither is the relationship between social/emotional factors and compliance. Age is a crucial variable: Compliance at 12 and 18 months was related to quality of attachment but not to *DQ* and cognitive measures. At

24 months it was related to both quality of attachment and cognitive factors, and at the preschool level the picture is very confusing. Compliant preschool children have a history of social/emotional and cognitive competence. Noncompliant preschool children have highly varied histories. However, when this group was divided into subgroups on the basis of anxiety level, anger, and peer relations, the picture is somewhat clearer.

REFERENCES

Ainsworth, M., Blehar, M., Waters, E., & Wall, S. Strange-Situation behavior of one-year-olds: Its relation to mother-infant interaction in the first year and to qualitative differences in the infant-mother attachment relationship. Hillsdale, N.J.: Lawrence Erlbaum Associates, 1978.

Egeland, B., Brunnquell, D., & Joffe, L. Manual for Prohibition Situation. Unpublished manuscript, University of Minnesota, Minneapolis, Minnesota, 1977.

Erickson, M. F. Antecedents of compliance in two-year-olds from a high-risk sample. Society for Reseach in Child Development, Boston, Massachusetts, April 2-5, 1981.

Goulder, T. J., & Trybus, R. J. *The classroom behavior of emotional disturbed hearing impaired children.* Washington, D.C.: Office of Demographic Studies, Gallaudet College, 1977.

Joffe, L. The quality of mother-infant attachment and its relationship to compliance with maternal commands and prohibitions. Unpublished doctoral dissertation, University of Minnesota, 1980.

Rosen, M. Language, interaction, and the development of deaf children. Unpublished doctoral dissertation, University of Minnesota, 1983.

Schein, J. D. Deaf students with other disabilities. *American Annals of the Deaf,* 1975, *120,* 92-99.

Schildroth, A. N. Public residential schools for deaf students in the United States, 1970-78. *American Annals of the Deaf,* 1980, *125,* 80-91.

Stayton, D. J., Hogan, R., & Ainsworth, M. Infant obedience and maternal behavior: The origins of socialization reconsidered. *Child Development,* 1971, *41,* 1057-1069.

Vernon, M. Psychological, educational, and physical characteristics associated with post-rubella deaf children. *Volta Review,* 1967, *69,* 176-185.

7 Toward a Model for the Attention Deficit Disorder

Marcel Kinsbourne
Department of Behavioral Neurology
Eunice Kennedy Schriver Institute for Mental Retardation

The pattern of behavior described as "hyperactive" (hyperkinetic, etc.) has justifiably triggered a massive research effort. Not only does it represent the most prevalent childhood psychopathology (Ross & Ross, 1976), and one with serious consequences for child and family, but it presents contentious issues for those concerned with its management. Beyond doubts about such specifics as prevalence, and the proper criteria for inclusion in a sample of hyperactive children, lie broader uncertainties about treatment, and even about the nosological status of the entity. Taxonomy presents a problem because, although the behavior in question presumably results from disorder of some basic brain mechanism (controlling a particular component of behavior), there is no agreement as to what that basic component or mechanism might be. Instead, we remain at the level of surface symptomatology. Luxuriant as this symptomatology certainly is, its very richness undermines its specificity, and therefore, in the eyes of some, its credibility.

If hyperactive behavior were qualitatively deviant, this would not necessarily be problematic; but what hyperactive children do frequently, other children do sometimes. Therefore, every one of the many manifestations of hyperactivity, as found, for instance, in questionnaires, lends itself to diverse causal attribution. These broad categories, as represented, for instance, in the latest classification favored by the American Psychiatric Association, the DSM-III (Table 7.1) could be the behavioral endpoints of many causes, both environmental and biological. The problem is not solved by looking for a diagnostic pattern of descriptors, instead of a single one, because (as recognized in the scoring recommended by DSM-III) hyperactive children differ in their most frequent behaviors. Few, if any, show the

TABLE 7.1
DSM-III Checklist for Attention Deficit Disorder

Hyperactivity

(1) Excessive running or climbing.

(2) Difficulty sitting still or excessive fidgeting.

(3) Difficulty staying seated.

(4) Motor restlessness during sleep. (Parents) Motor restlessness. (Teachers)

(5) Always on the go or acts as if "driven by a motor".

Inattention

(1) Often fails to finish things he or she starts.

(2) Often doesn't seem to listen.

(3) Easily distracted.

(4) Difficulty sticking to a play activity.

(5) Difficulty concentrating on school work or other tasks requiring sustained attention.

Impulsivity

(1) Often acts before thinking.

(2) Excessive shifting from one activity to another.

(3) Has difficulty organizing work (not due to cognitive impairment).

(4) Needs a lot of supervision.

(5) Frequent calling out in class.

(6) Difficulty waiting for turn in games or group situations.

full range of behaviors designated in a typical checklist used for ADD diagnosis.

All this is not to deny that there is a "style" of behavior (far transcending in its generality and impact the aspect of activity level, for which the disorder was originally named), which is readily apparent to the experienced clinician. This style is not adequately described entirely in terms of abnormal or even maladaptive behaviors. In a recent study (Kinsbourne, in preparation) we gathered responses from the parents of 69 hyperactive and 70 age and sex-matched behaviorally normal control children to a series of questions following the format: "If your child is *x*, does he/she *y* or *z*?" Significant differences characterized the outcomes not only of questions indicating attention deficit (in work habits, hasty and sloppy rather than slow and meticulous; flit from one thing to another rather than concentrate long and hard), but also of questions indicating difference in personal style unrelated to maladaptive behavior—the hyperactive children more often prefer continuous adult attention to being left alone, and in social situations to be at the center of attention, rather than on the sidelines. In Achenbach and Edelbrock's (1978) "broadband dichotomy," one would clearly put the ADD children within the externalizing band rather than the internalizing band (as Achenbach & Edelbrock indeed do). We are dealing with a personality type that is maladaptive only at its extreme.

This style, however, is not invariant during development or impervious to environmental influence. On the contrary, the surface manifestations change dramatically as the individual transverses the various stages of the life span (a generally-recognized fact which is, however, not addressed by any of the commonly used checklists or questionnaires). They could also vary in relation to the child's social circumstances, and the rest of the child's personality. People differ from each other in how they behave in many respects and how a person who, for instance, is of an impulsive and inattentive disposition will manifest these traits will clearly be modified by whether he is active and outgoing, or passive and shy. In other words, how the hyperactive temperament expresses itself in overt behavior must be affected by the individual's status on temperamental traits other than the one that is directly under the control of "hyperactive" tendencies. Given such malleable surfaces' structure, the incentive for elucidating the deep structure of the disorder is great indeed.

If one adopts a "disease" model of hyperactivity, he could conceivably circumvent the need for further analysis at the behavioral level by discovering diagnostic signs at the neurological level.

NEUROLOGICAL MODELS OF HYPERACTIVITY

Some investigators regard ADD as due to brain damage, some as representing a developmental lag, and some as arising from individual variation with respect to a personality dimension that governs cognitive style (Kinsbourne, 1977) (i.e., as an extreme of a continuum of normal variation).

The possible role of brain damage in generating hyperactive behavior has been suggested because patterns of hyperactive behavior have been observed in children who have demonstrable brain damage. Early in this century it was noted that the post-encephalitic behavior of children was characterized by restlessness, inattentiveness, impulsivity, anti-social behavior, and irritability (Ebaugh, 1923). A similar pattern of behavior was noted by Strauss and Kephart (1955) and Strauss and Lehtinen (1968) in studies of the psychological characteristics of a group of children who were mentally retarded due to brain injury. Many children in whom brain damage was not apparent also had similar behavior patterns. Strauss & Lehtinen (1948) proposed that these children, too, were probably brain-damaged, but that the customary neurological examination simply failed to detect the presence. Some have suggested that this is perhaps because the brain damage occurs at or before birth, and due to plasticity of the immature organism, the neurological symptoms dissipate rapidly; when the child starts school, only the behavioral effect is apparent. Two conferences have been held on the question of "minimal brain damage" (Bax & MacKeith, 1963; Clements, 1966). In both cases, the consensus was that brain damage in children should not be inferred from behavioral signs alone (when these represent slower than normal development rather than loss of established function). The parallels between behavior due to brain damage and hyperactivity have not led us to identify a cause for the disorder. The term "minimal brain damage" is seldom used these days, but the term "minimal brain dysfunction" is often used (Clements, 1966; Wender, 1971) to satisfy those who have a medical orientation.

Hyperactivity has also been regarded as a neurodevelopmental lag. The findings that lead to a diagnosis of minimal brain dysfunction in a particular child are considered abnormal only with references to that child's age. If the child were younger, the finding would be considered normal (Kinsbourne, 1970). Viewed in this way, the behavior of the hyperactive child—whether it reflects motor immaturity, failure to focus attention, cognitive deficiencies, or lack of emotional control—is assumed to resemble the normal behavior of younger children, rather than an arbitrary symptom complex. It is well established that activity level is highest early in life (Routh, Schroeder, & O'Tauma, 1974). Thus one might regard a hyperactive person as retaining the activity level of a younger normal child. The apparent resolution of many instances of hyperactivity at adolescence would then be regarded as a final closing of the gap between the lagging individual and others. The reports of relatively slow rhythms on the electroencephalogram of some hyperactive people (Hastings & Barkley, 1978) would fit into such a notion. Slow rhythms represent maturational immaturity of the brain, and in general, basic EEG rhythms accelerate in the course of development. Some research using the averaged evoked potential derived from the EEG also reflects a pattern of immaturity (Buchsbaum & Wender, 1973; Satterfield, Cantwell & Satterfield, 1974; Satterfield & Braley, 1977).

One difficulty with the developmental lag model is the repeatedly-reported clinical observation that hyperactive individuals were, at least retrospectively, abnormal right at or soon after birth. Also, it is difficult to think of any normal child (at any age) behaving in the way that some of the extremely hyperactive children act.

The fact that the severity of hyperactivity varies fits well in the context of an individual differences model. Moreover, it has become clear that at least some cases persist into the adult years as a temperamental deviation taking an age-appropriate form. Thomas and Chess (1977), in their 20-year longitudinal study, noted that children seem to express the same temperamental pattern at different ages despite dramatic developmental changes in abilities and behavior. Perhaps hyperactivity is due to an inherited temperament and represents an extreme placement on a dimension of personality or cognitive style.

We advocate a model which appears to combine the merits of these various approaches. Hyperactive behavior is regarded as differing only in degree from comparable behavior manifest in the general population. We suppose a continuum of individual difference between the extreme of underfocused attention or concentration, manifested as inattentive and noncompliant behavior and the extreme of overfocused attention or concentration manifested as withdrawn and inflexible behavior. We assume that the attentional style of any one individual is determined by his placement on this continuum, which we regard as representing the resultant of opposing influences from separate brain structures. We consider the balance between these structures to be subject to bias, through brain damage or through genetic diversity.

LABORATORY STUDY OF ADD CHARACTERISTICS

Hyperactive behavior varies greatly between patients, and also within the patient at different times. This is because of the contextual dependence of the behaviors and because of the complex and largely unpredictable circumstances that lead to exacerbations. Such phenomenology lends itself well to clinical description at the level of anecdote but is very difficult to systematize by means of objective observation in real life settings. While such work is a useful source of hypothesis, inevitable confounds complicate interpretation. The formulations that result, if they venture beyond the trivially obvious, remain conjectural. Only in the controlled conditions of the behavioral laboratory can one anticipate results which are unequivocal and also revealing.

The laboratory setting is prone to generating errors of omission when it is used to appraise hyperactive behavior. The setting has both negative and positive effects on the expression of the ADD: negative in that it excludes many of those real life situations in which hyperactive behavior tends to be at its most extreme; positive in that the novelty, structure, and individualized attention intrinsic to many experimental arrangements might attenuate the very phenomena one wishes to study. An otherwise hyperactive child might fail to behave in hyperactive ways in the laboratory. But, if even in the laboratory one can elicit and measure ADD manifestations then one is enabled to gain a more specific and unambiguous insight than would otherwise be possible.

The present discussion is confined to laboratory studies whose outcomes may contribute toward a valid model of the ADD deficit.

Attention as the Relevant Construct in Hyperactivity

A recent change in nomenclature from the term hyperactivity to Attention Deficit Disorder (ADD) has dramatized the shift of emphasis from the motor to the attentional symptoms. Certainly the restlessness that impressed clinicians at the time when this disorder was first described and named (Bradley, 1937) is quite inconstant, both between individuals and within the lifespan of a single individual (Staton & Brumback, 1981). The current DSM-III classification distinguishes between ADD and ADDH, dichotomizing ADD children into whether they are or are not in addition hyperactive. This also seems inappropriate as the difference in restlessness among ADD children is one of degree and empirical studies (Achenbach & Edelbrock, 1978) do not provide justification for this distinction.

The repeatedly reported failure to find high correlations between restlessness, impulsivity, and inattentiveness and the fact that, in general, a single symptom has little diagnostic utility (Shaffer & Greenhill, 1978) need not be interpreted as showing ADD children to be heterogenous in any fundamental way. Quite apart from questions about the stability and validity of the subjective ratings on which these judgements are based, one may be dealing with second-order characteristics. A proper organizational principle for the behavioral mechanism of ADD might reveal a more basic and stable measurable characteristic. Would this, as the DSM-III suggests, be an attentional variable?

HYPERACTIVITY, IMPULSIVITY, INATTENTIVENESS

At a single viewing, some children who satisfy DSM-III criteria for an attention deficit disorder may appear constantly restless and overactive, whereas others may not (Staton & Brumback, 1981). But for children of a given age, the difference appears to be more one of degree than kind, and the judgement is additionally confounded by the fact that development has been ignored in the construction of the DSM-III criteria. Using the DSM-III criteria for ADD as a questionnaire with a four point rating scale, Swanson, Logan, and Pelham (in preparation) have found a systematic decline in teacher ratings of hyperactive, impulsive, and inattentive behavior in normal children, with increasing age, with a particularly steep decline in ratings on the hyperactivity scale. Conners questionnaire norms show similar developmental trends (Goyette, Conners, & Ulrich, 1978). This shifting developmental baseline against which hyperactivity manifests itself could explain why restlessness is clinically inconspicuous in post-pubertal children, and ADD, as classically understood, is altogether less conspicuous in adolescence, to the point that it used to be believed that hyperactivity remits at adolescence. Increasing information about the serious outlook for individuals who were diagnosed as hyperactive in childhood (Hopkins, Perlman, Hechtman, & Weiss, 1979; Weiss, Minde, Werry, Douglas, & Nemeth, 1971; Wender, Reimherr, & Wood, 1981), as well as about the familial incidence of psychopathy, alcoholism, and hysteria in relation to hyperactive probands (Cantwell, 1975), suggest that the inattentive, impulsive temperament often, if not always, persists, only the surface symptomatology changes, in a manner which becomes intelligible when the subject's stage in the life span is taken into consideration.

The very organization of the DSM-III checklist is tendentious, in that it presents as a given the tripartite predominance of hyperactivity, impulsivity, and inattentiveness, arbitrarily subordinating other alleged characteristics (e.g., emotional lability, noncompliance; cf. Wender, 1971). Nevertheless, taking this at face value, we shall now discuss an effort to subtype ADD children who are primarily impulsive versus primarily inattentive.

Mock and Kinsbourne (unpublished) gave the Matching Familiar Figures Tests (MFF; Kagan, 1965) to ADD children whose symptomatology had been independently classified into mainly impulsive versus mainly inattentive. Those children, all of whom had in common documented favorable response to stimulants, were contrasted with a control group which consisted of ADD children who had been classified as stimulant non-responsive based on laboratory learning tests. The results showed that both the impulsive and the inattentive subgroups made significant numbers of errors on the MFF and both subgroups made fewer errors when given stimulants. In contrast, the control group's performance did not improve on stimulants. The striking aspect of the outcome pertained to the response latency. The impulsive ADDs responded with relatively short latency, as originally described by Kagan. But the inattentive ADDs did not conform to the conventional MFF dichotomy into fast/inaccurate and slow/accurate. They were slow and inaccurate. On stimulant medication, the impulsives become slower, and the inattentives faster, in their decision times.

Thus the groups had a similar response to stimulant in terms of increased accuracy. With respect to latency, stimulants induced a normalizing effect, reducing the overall variance of the MFF performance within the experimental ADD group, bringing extreme values in both subgroups toward a midpoint. The study is suggestive in terms of a possible subtyping of ADD.

We have further studied ADD children's decision process when selecting the exact match from within a confusable array in the context of a computer-driven CRT display and while monitoring eye movements (Flintoff et al., in press). The outcome of this study was intriguing in that we were able to demonstrate changes in attentional style between placebo and stimulant state in the absence of changes in accuracy of performance. On stimulants, the ADD children make more eye position switches between exemplars in the array, and between the target and exemplars, than on placebo (without further improving the accuracy of the match). This is an example of a task in the performance of which hyperactive children were not helped by stimulants (although they were known to be favorable stimulant responders in the field). The task was fairly difficult, and the computer-driven arrangement was attention-catching and interesting to these children. This illustrates the task-specificity of the response to stimulant administration—a topic to which we shall return. For present purposes, we note that we have seen in the laboratory a stylistic shift between the untreated and treated child orthogonal to adaptive outcomes as it were, a chemically induced personality shift.

The Type of Attention Implicated in ADD

An initial classification of attention is into its intensive and its selective aspect. The intensive aspect determines the organism's general readiness to respond. Its physiological index is the generalized orienting response (Sokolov, 1957). The selective aspect relates to choice between alternative possible foci of attention within a multistimulus or multiattribute array. The prototype is the selective orienting response, in which, in concert with the hallmarks of general alerting, one observes receptor positioning so as to maximize perception of the selected object or locus: grossly observable turning of body, so as to aim head and eyes. More subtle forms of orienting response exist in which gross body position remains unchanged, but a premotor shift of attention across the visual field (Posner, Nissen & Odgen, 1978) or to one or side of auditory space may suffice to implement the selective information processing.

In brief, no consistent abnormality in either aspect of orienting has been found in ADD. This does not imply that the selective element in attention is intact in ADD. Far from it, but for a test to show up the deficit, it has to extend over time. Apart from the nature of the task, the time involved, in terms of number of trials, number of presentations of a list to be learnt, length of time during which a subject monitors, tracks, or otherwise engages in continuous performance, is a prime determinant of an overt attention deficit in ADD.

The Double-Blind Acute Drug/Placebo Paradigm

We have studied the adequacy of the concept of curtailed attention for ADD within the context of an acute double-blind, stimulant drug/placebo paradigm (Kinsbourne, Swanson, & Herman, 1979). This offers an opportunity to study attention deficit disorder on a repeated measures basis; that is, in the same child both when hyperactive (on placebo) and when normal (on stimulant drug). The use of this paradigm is based on the following assumptions for which we have independent experimental evidence: (1.) that stimulant drugs normalize ADD (rather than merely suppressing or substituting symptoms); (2.) that a single administration of stimulant produces, for the duration of its behavioral effect, changes essentially identical to those found in the course of long-term therapy with that drug at that dose level; and (3.) that the effect of an acute administration has fully dissipated the next day, so that successive days of a drug trial are uncontaminated by cumulative effect.

Using this paradigm, we first subtype all children meeting ADD behavioral diagnostic criteria into those who respond favorably to some level of stimulant drug on a paired associate learning test and those who respond adversely (i.e., those who do better on the drug condition vs. those who do better on the placebo condition). Given the potent effect of stimulants in normalizing the behavior of many of these children and the total absence of such an effect in others, given that the stimulants are catecholaminergic, and assuming they act at central loci directly related to the deviant physiology of these children, diametrically opposed effects of the same set of agents must index disparate disorders and neurophysiology (i.e., opposite base states of some mechanism in imbalance). If one is going to study the effect of stimulant administration on ADD children in the laboratory, one should first ascertain that they have exerted beneficial effect on the sample of ADD children to be studied, in the laboratory where they will be studied. It could be that the formal, structured and novel circumstances of the laboratory, as well as the typical one-to-one attention typically given the child, so affect their state that transiently they become adverse responders to stimulants (being in this respect analogous to normal children). These would not be suitable subjects for laboratory demonstrations of the nature of the ADD deficit.

Within the double blind drug/placebo paradigm, one has the opportunity of controlling one's observations in three ways: One may compare the findings on ADD with those on normal control children. This obvious manner of controlling is relatively little practiced because of ethical objections to giving stimulant drugs to children who do not need them. For that reason, normal sample sizes tend to be very small (Swanson & Kinsbourne, 1976) and also atypical (e.g., children of the investigators and research staff; cf. Rapoport et al., 1980).

One may compare the child untreated with himself treated. This invokes the more powerful repeated measures design, and is ideal given two conditions: one practical, that the dose of drug be truly optimal (so that one is not, in the drug condition, observing a partially treated, or conversely, an overdosed, child), and the other more fundamental, that we are correct in supposing that the optimally treated ADD child approximates the normal condition, and therefore behaves much as a normal control would. The direct test would be to compare treated ADD children with normal controls, and determine whether residual differences exist. The study has not been done. But whether normality is achieved or not, there is no question about the direction of change on treatment in most ADD children. It is justifiable to use the extent of a treatment effect in normalizing any specific aspects of behavior as an approximate indicator of how far from the norm the untreated ADD child typically is on this parameter.

A third way of controlling findings on ADD children who respond favorably on stimulants is to compare their behavior with that of children who are referred for similar surface symptomatology, but who respond adversely to stimulant therapy. The interpretation of this response depends crucially on how one conceptualizes the nature of these children's problems, and whether one regards favorable or adverse response to stimulants as "normal".

Having mentioned the possibility of laboratory demonstrations of attentional deficits corrected by stimulant drug, we shall briefly review selected data about the direction of stimulant effects in ADD and normal individuals in the laboratory.

Stimulant Effects on ADD

Since Bradley's (1937) pioneering study, a massive literature attests to the benefits, for concentration and conduct, of stimulant therapy on the majority of ADD children (Eisenberg, 1972). These include many objective studies in the field and some in the laboratory. Douglas and Peters (1980) list the laboratory tests on which ADD children have been found to be impaired, the impairment being corrected by stimulant therapy (Sroufe, 1975).

They include paired associate learning (Conners, Eisenberg, and Sharpe, 1968). We have demonstrated stimulant effects with paired associate learning (Swanson & Kinsbourne, 1976; Swanson, Kinsbourne, Roberts, & Zucker, 1978; Dalby, Kinsbourne, Swanson, & Sobol, 1977; Conte, 1982) avoidance learning (Freeman, 1978), motor learning (Humphries, Swanson, Kinsbourne, & Yu, 1979), risk taking (Freeman, 1978), intentional versus incidental learning (Thurston et al., 1979), continuous performance (Swanson, Barlow, & Kinsbourne, 1979), matching familiar figures (Mock & Kinsbourne, unpublished), and analogous tests (Flintoff, et al., in press). The favorable response of hyperactive children to stimulant therapy has been labelled paradoxical. In the symptomatic sense that stimulants "stimulate" normal children but "calm down" hyperactives (Wender, 1971), this notion must be rejected. There is no evidence that hyperactive children are more calm on stimulants (or that they are not calm when off). Nor is it clear that on the low doses that fall within the therapeutic range normal children would show behavioral stimulation. If by paradoxical is meant a behavioral change in a direction opposite to that which is customary, then in terms of performance on higher-level mental tests (paired associate learning, maze learning, and incidental avoidance learning), the response to stimulants of ADD children is paradoxical. Such a use of the term paradoxical would encompass normalizing effects that reduce within group variability, bringing outlying values on the relevant dimension toward the mean. Stimulants have such effects.

But the mechanism of that contrary directionality of effect nevertheless could invove a unidirectional change along a critical dimension, but with "U-shaped" consequence for behavior. Given a base state at the low end of the range of variation of the dimension in question, an increase leads to improved performance. Given a higher base state, the same amount of further increase might not improve, or even impair performance. Thus we attribute to ADD children underactivation of certain behavioral control mechanisms and to stimulants the effect of raising the activation levels of these mechanisms (i.e., enabling them to participate to a greater extent in the formulation of decisions about how to act). Over- and under-participation of these mechanisms in behavioral decision making yields suboptimal cognitive processing and suboptimal conduct. With a given child suffering from ADD the decision has to be made: would stimulants at some optimal does help him toward more normal and effective behavioral control? Or is the problem such that giving the child stimulants might actually impair his functioning by rendering him overly dependent on the control mechanisms in question (putting him into a state we have elsewhere designated as "overfocused") (Kinsbourne & Caplan, 1979)? In the studies listed not all hyperactive children benefited. Some performed worse in the drug than in the placebo condition. We have suggested that the majority of favorable and minority of adverse responses define two subtypes of ADD (Kinsbourne, 1977). However, we have also pointed out that whether a child (hyperactive or normal) performs better on stimulants or not depends on the nature of the test (Swanson, Barlow, & Kinsbourne, 1979). Finally, the possibility has not been ruled out that an ADD child might respond paradoxically on one test, but not on another.

Interaction of Task and Drug

Clear evidence for the view that the performance deficit of ADD children evolves in the course of a task is presented by Humphries, Swanson, Kinsbourne and Yu (1979). In this study, ADD children performed a maze-tracking task and compared their performance when on methylphenidate and when on placebo. The maze was composed of six identical segments, and children's performance was compared across these six stages of the task. The ADD children made fewer errors overall in the drug condition, but this difference was entirely contributed by segments three to six. On the first two segments, performance was fairly accurate under both conditions. The children in the medicated condition continue at roughly the same level of accuracy, but in the unmedicated condition performance grossly deteriorates from the third segment on. This result is important in that it shows that the unmedicated child was quite capable of good performance, but failed to *persist* at that level. Such performance decrement over trials within a task is often found in normal subjects, but only if the task was lengthy indeed. Over as little as two minutes, which was the average length of time it took to complete the maze, no such performance decrement would normally be expected.

Thurston, Sobol, Swanson, and Kinsbourne (1979) gave hyperactive children an intentional learning task with opportunity for incidental learning which was then measured. The hyperactive children on placebo learned less of the central and more of the incidental material than they did on stimulant. This demonstration of diminished selectivity of attention in ADD is complemented with respect to the issue of sustaining selectivity over time by the use of continuous performance tasks.

Working in our laboratory with a computer-generated visual tracking task, Kapelus demonstrated a steeper decline over time of accuracy of performance (increase in mean square error) of the favorable responders on placebo than on the stimulant. Over the duration of the task, adverse responders showed no performance decrement at all under either condition.

Virtually all ADD children perform vigilance and continuous performance tests better when on stimulants than on placebo (Sykes, Douglas, Weiss, & Mind, 1971; Swanson, Barlow, & Kinsbourne, 1979). But then, stimulants are well known to improve vigilance in normal people (Solandt &

Partridge, 1946; Mackworth, 1950, 1965; Loeb et al., 1965). Weingartner et al. (1980) have shown improvement in both hyperactive and normal children on vigilance tests as well as on simple reaction time, coding, and one-trial free recall tests. These test findings are consistent with Weiss and Laties' (1962) summary statement that performance on tests such as reaction time tends to be improved by stimulants. They pointed out, however, that on higher level cognitive tests, stimulants impair the performance of normal adults. In his pioneering study, Bradley (1937) pointed out that stimulants failed to improve the performance of many children. Flory and Gilbert (1943) found no improvement or even decline after stimulants on certain higher level tasks.

Working with the acute double-blind drug/placebo paradigm, Swanson, Barlow, and Kinsbourne (1979) gave a vigilance test to ADD children. Two levels of task were used: simple and complex, and two drug states, methylphenidate and placebo. Performance was, as expected, slower on the difficult version. Methylphenidate improved performance on the easy version, but not on the difficult one.

This is a demonstration of the task-specificity of the stimulant response. The complex version of the task was of a "higher-level" to the extent that it sufficiently stimulated the sluggish ADD attentional system to make the stimulant effect redundant. One can hardly engineer so challenging an environment on an ongoing basis outside the laboratory. But the observation that a selected task can have such an effect may point the way to a more general understanding of the nature of the attentional weakness in ADD.

Optimal Dosage Levels

The optimal level of stimulant dose in the laboratory might be relatively low. Doses which optimally control behavior elsewhere could amount to overdose in the laboratory, as manifest in impaired performance. This type of artifact could well explain the finding of Sprague and Sleator (1977). They compared the dose level for optimal response to a cognitive task in the laboratory (two hours after administration) with that for improved conduct in the *classroom* (across the day). They concluded that fundamental dose-response chracteristics differ for cognitive and behavioral deficits in ADD. The discrepancy can be more conservatively interpreted as due to comparing a laboratory measurement with one taken under classroom conditions. To arrive at valid conclusions about dose-response for different dimensions of behavior, one must test them in the *same situation,* as well as at the same time after drug administration, which was not done by Sprague and Sleator. Sprague and Sleator gave one morning dose of methylphenidate only; yet solicited ratings across morning and afternoon classroom sessions. Much of the rating must have been based on the child's behavior in the untreated state. A more valid comparison would be based on classroom ratings for children for whom stimulant therapy is maintained across the school day. It will then be possible to determine whether laboratory outcomes indeed predict outcomes within the classroom (directly or after an empirically-derived correction factor is applied).

In the light of these considerations, we can now discuss the relative merits of the following three alternative interpretations of adverse response to stimulant in the laboratory:

1. The adverse response is abnormal (an indication of some abnormality in the child). This is a logical extrapolation of Rapoport's claim that normal people perform any task better on stimulant.
2. The adverse response is normal (and indicates that the child's problem, for which he was referred, is of some kind other than that of most ADD children).
3. The adverse response represents an atypical state in what could be a typical ADD child in a more natural environment than the laboratory. The laboratory circumstance has induced a temporarily normal control over sustained attention.

We are able to reject (1.) It is factually incorrect that normal people respond favorably to stimulants on all tasks, and we have already cited literature to that effect. If one were to demonstrate an adverse stimulant response for a task on which normal people are helped by stimulants (e.g., a vigilance task), then an argument for abnormality of that response could be made. However, in the case of higher level tasks (e.g., learning tests), no such argument can be sustained.

Interpretation (2.) would require validation from a follow up of drug response in the field. This is in progress. Pending the outcome, we cannot chose between (2.) and (3.).

This leaves an important practical question temporarily unanswered. But from the standpoint of a control for laboratory investigation of ADD, it makes no difference whether the normal adverse response indicates a trait characteristic (option 2.) or a state characteristic (option 3.). In either case, the adversely response subjects referred for ADD constitute a valid control group for the more typical and plentiful favorably responsive ADD subjects.

ADD children can at times attend normally, respond selectively, conduct themselves appropriately. It is therefore hardly reasonable to talk of a deficit, in the strict sense. Instead, we are dealing with a failure to deploy existing brain mechanisms under circumstances in which they normally would be deployed. Under a more restricted set of circumstances' they are deployed even by the ADD child. Thus we are dealing not with a lack of competence but with a performance deficiency. Some behavioral control mechanism is only intermittently rather than continually active; we cannot regard this as some autonomous fluctuation in brain state as the circumstances under which behavioral control is established are not random but lawful. In order to arrive at a viable model of the ADD deficit we must establish the general nature of the conditions that do permit adaptive functioning in ADD. To this issue we now turn.

We begin by considering the effect of stimulation on the performance of normal people. It depends both on the stimulation and on the base state of the recipient.

Stimulant Level and Performance

People perform less well at very low and at very high levels of stimulation than at intermediate levels (e.g., Broadbent, 1958). The resulting U-shaped curve relating performance to level of stimulation has been widely discussed (Hebb, 1958; Stennett, 1957; Malmo, 1959; Duffy, 1962). Its gradient depends on trait characteristics intrinsic to the organism. The hyperactive (ADD) individual can be viewed as requiring more stimulation in order to faciliate optimal performance than do normal individuals (Zentall, 1975); this disparity is corrected by appropriate stimulant therapy. Excessive stimulant dosage would presumably induce the opposite: an overstimulated state. The administration of tranquilizers to those in need of such treatment might induce "understimulation." It would follow that different levels of extrinsic stimulation should be called for in different conditions and under the influence of different drugs in order to maximize performance.

Many investigators in this field have conceptualized the effect of the level of stimulation in terms of the organismic construct of arousal (Hastings & Barkley, 1978); however, at this time, this concept is so beset with pitfalls and surplus meaning that we will avoid it as nonessential to the proposed line of reasoning. We instead use the term "level of stimulation". Operationally, this designates the point of functional covergence of the effects of certain task-related variables.

The parameters involved in our search for dependent variables that determine "levels of stimulation" derive largely from the vigilance/continuous performance literature (Davies & Parasuraman, 1982).

We now summarize the effects on sustained attention of normal observers of five task-related parameters.

DETERMINANTS OF THE VIGILANCE DECREMENT

1. *Stimulus salience.* The vigilance decrement becomes less or disappears with increases in signal intensity (Loeb & Schmidt, 1963; Webb & Wherry, 1960), signal duration (Baker, 1962, 1963; Fraser, 1957), and the spatial dispersion of signals (Broadbent, 1951; Jerison & Wing 1961).

2. *Stimulus frequency.* The greater the signal frequency, the less is the vigilance decrement (Kappauf & Powe, 1959). But at very high signal frequencies, performance also declines, yielding an inverted U-shaped relationship between performance and signal frequency (Ellis & Ahr, 1960).
3. *Manner of pacing.* Unlike paced tasks, unpaced (i.e., self-paced) tasks show little or no vigilance decrement (Broadbent, 1953).
4. *Incentives.* Both verbal (Neal, 1967) and financial (Grunzke, 1966) incentives can counteract the vigilance decrement.
5. *Extraneous stimulation.* Continual varied auditory stimulation (music, traffic noise, etc.) diminish vigilance decrement (Davies, Hockey, & Taylor, 1969; McGrath, 1963, Wokoun, 1963).

In overview, manipulations that would intuitively appear to enhance the immediacy, relevance, and vividness of the test situation diminish the tendency for attention to dwindle during a monotonous task. If for ADD children almost any task, however varied and brief, is potentially "monotonous", then the same manipulations that support vigilance should enhance hyperactives' performance in a much wider range of situations. This hypothesis parallels a generalization that describes stimulant effects on hyperactives: stimulants that support the performance of normals on low-level boring tasks, help hyperactives with a much wider range of tasks, including many that normals would not regard as low-level or boring. Given such a functional convergence of task-related stimulation effects and stimulant drug effects one could trade off one against the other.

If some central state is altered in normal people by protracted performance which is comparable to that generally present in the patient with ADD, what is the nature of this state? Is it arousal, conceived as a generalized level of central excitation that determines the degree of the organism's readiness to respond and is indexed by such psychophysiological variables as heart rate and skin conductance level? Or does the attentional variable reflect the degree of engagement of a more specific mechanism, not indexed by the psychophysiological concomitants of arousal?

AROUSAL DURING VIGILANCE DECREMENT

Many investigators have invoked arousal change to explain vigilance decrement, and many others have invoked an altered level of arousal to explain hyperactive behavior. Indeed, tests of these views have yielded parallel results in the two cases. Although indices of arousal have repeatedly been shown to indicate a decreasing arousal level during a lengthy vigilance period, the degree of such change does not correlate with the degree of decrement in performance. When a task-related parameter is manipulated and as a consequence performance level changes, that manipulation has no consequences for the psychophysiological measures. Thus, Corcoran (1963) found no relationship between vigilance performance and heart rate. Eason, Beardshall, and Jaffee (1965) also found no drop in heart rate while vigilance performance was decreasing; when they induced change in level of performance by varying signal rate, neither heart rate nor skin conductance levels changed. Stern (1966) also varied signal rate, and found better performance at higher rates, but no corresponding change in skin conductance.

AROUSAL IN ADD

Efforts to document underarousal in ADD children have been similarly inconclusive. Satterfield and his colleagues obtained contradictory results. Satterfield and Dawson (1971) found hyperactive children to have lower resting skin conductance levels than normal children. Satterfield, Cantwell, Lesser, and Podosin (1972) found no difference, and Satterfield, Atoian, Breshers, Burleigh, and Dawson (1974) found the skin conductance levels to be higher in the hyperactives. Failures to find skin conductance differences were reported by Cohen & Douglas (1972), Spring, Greenberg, Scott and Hopwood (1974), Conners (1975), and Zahn, Abate, Little, and Wender (1975). Two of the above cited studies subtyped their subjects into those responsive to stimulants and those not responsive (Satterfield, Cantwell, Lesser, & Podosin, 1972; Spring, Greenberg, Scott, & Hopwood, 1974). Neither found any reliable difference in skin conductance between their groups. Heart rate comparisons have similarly yielded negative results (Cohen, Douglas, & Morgenstern, 1971; Sroufe, Sonies, West, & Wright, 1973).

Stimulants improve performance of most ADD children. Do they act via arousal change? Moderate doses of stimulant, sufficient to enhance performance, exerted no effect on skin conductance level (Satterfield & Dawson, 1971; Satterfield et al., 1972; Spring et al., 1974). Only with high doses did skin conductance increase (Cohen, Douglas, & Morgenstern, 1971). Heart rate, on the other hand, is regularly increased by stimulants (Cohen, et al., 1971; Knights & Hinton, 1969; Porges, Walter, Korb, & Sprague, 1975) in a dose-related fashion.

Electrodermal lability (as indexed by spontaneous skin conductance responses) also differs little if at all between hyperactive and normal children. (Barkley & Jackson, 1977; Conners, 1975; Satterfield & Dawson, 1971; Spring et al., 1974; Zahn et al., 1975).

In contrast to the negative findings with tonic psychophysiological variables, phasic orienting response of hyperactives is known to be relatively limited, as indexed by skin conductance responses (Conners, 1975; Satterfield & Dawson, 1971; Spring et al., 1974; Zahn et al., 1975). However, stimulant administration does not increase the amplitude of the orientation response (Satterfield & Dawson, 1971; Spring et al., 1979; Zahn et al., 1975).

Conte (1983), working in our laboratory measured heart rate (HR), skin conductance level (SCL) orienting response (OR), habituation, and spontaneous skin conductance responses ($SSCR$) in ADD children participating in a double-blind acute methylphenidate/placebo trial extending over two successive days. On each day children were given methylphenidate morning or afternoon, alternating with placebo morning or afternoon, and the order of days was counterbalanced between subjects. Some two hours after each administration, that is, when the drug effect was at its height, the children were given a paired associate learning test at each of two presentation rates: "fast" (8 seconds per pair) and "slow" (12 seconds per pair). Physiological measurements were taken before and during each test.

The children divided up into those who learnt at a faster rate on drug (favorable responders, FR) and those who learnt better on placebo (adverse responders, AR). This design enables one to make the following comparisons: (1.) FRs on placebo with FRs on drug. Variables that change in correlation with improved performance could clarify the mechanism of the stimulant effect. If the stimulant controlled state is considered as approximately normal, that is, if stimulants are accepted as having a normalizing effect, then at least some of those variables that change may be related to the physiological abnormality in ADD. (2.) FRs with ARs in their (placebo) base state. Do any variables predict the differential drug response? (3.) Third, one compares the nature of changing variables (and direction of change) when AR are given stimulant to when FRs are given stimulant. Are physiological systems differently modified by comparable amounts of drug in these two responder types?

Considering first the FRs, who are the classically hyperactive children, if one includes favorable stimulant response among the diagnostic criteria (Laufer & Denhoff, 1957) versus ARs. Conte found no difference in OR amplitude or habituation or $SSCR$ between responder types, and $SSCR$ increased equally on drug in both groups. Resting heart rate did not differentiate groups, and this too increased in both groups with drugs. Phasic heart rate response during learning yielded more acceleration in the placebo condition for the FRs. In so far as cardiac acceleration indexes mental effort, this suggests that FRs are not undermotivated, but try to learn. Presumably their learning on stimulants is better organized and therefore less effortful.

Skin conductance was unaffected by drug administration in FRs, and there was no relationship between degree of learning improvement in drug and any parallel SCL changes. In other words, the mechanism that is indexed by *SCL* does not mediate the favorable effect of stimulants, and probably is not involved in the ADD deficit. ARs had resting SCLs comparable to those of FRs in the placebo state, but in the drug state the resting SCL increased (both before and during learning) in proportion to the extent to which the drug impaired learning as compared to placebo. We have here an indication of a different type of ADD child—different not in some stable trait characteristic, but in the nature of response to stimulant, that is, a response by elevation of SCL, correlated with impaired performance. These children seem to react to drug in a qualitatively different way, perhaps with anxiety, and for them any potential benefit of stimulant therapy is more than counteracted by this additional autonomic response. Note that not only with *FRs*, but also with *ARs*, the notion of generalized arousal change is not useful. In *FRs SCL* and *HR* behave orthogonally when placebo and drug states are compared. In *ARs*, they change in the same direction; but whereas the *ARs' SCL* change is correlated with the degree of performance change, their *HR* change is not.

We conclude that arousal theories of ADD fail to explain stimulant responsivity, and that the arousing potential of stimulant drugs fails to explain the ADD child's favorable response to these agents. When children respond adversely to stimulants, a further system comes into play that is not affected in the FRs.

How do these results bear on the vigilance model for ADD? As we have noted, during the time period of vigilance testing, indices of generalized arousal show decrement. But that decrement does not correlate with the decrement in the vigilance performance. When event rate (and thereby performance) is varied, *SCL* and *HR* do not change. When event rate is varied in ADD, these variables did not change either (Conte, 1983). One difference does exist: electrodermal lability predicts degree of vigilance decrement (Sostek, 1978), but it had no differential predictive value in the ADD study. In general, though, one concludes that the vigilance decrement, like the ADD state, is unrelated to generalized arousal, and must be mediated by some other more selective system.

These conclusions, however, may not apply to those children referred for hyperactivity who responded to stimulants with deteriorating learning performance. In the placebo state, they did not differ from the FRs in psychophysiological variables. But they did differ in their behavior relative to the presentation rate variable in the learning test, in that they did not show the presentation rate effect (i.e., their learning rate conformed to the total time principle, and was not controlled by the 8 versus 12 seconds per item event rate difference). Thus either they were not suffering from the particular attention deficit that generated this presentation rate effect in the *FS*s, or they were at least temporarily in a non-hyperactive state. The novelty of the situation, the personal attention offered in the laboratory setting, and the intrinsic interest of the computer driven display, could have lent a focus to their attention that it does not customarily have. The fact that *SCL* and *HR* did not distinguish them from the *SR*s in the placebo condition further illustrates the irrelevance of these indices of generalized arousal for ADD. But when the *AR*s were given stimulants, *SCL* did rise (as did *HR*, but only in the same proportion as in *FR*s). Indeed, the higher the rise, the greater was the drug induced performance decrement. A possible interpretation is that in those children, who did not have, or at least at the time did not exhibit, ADD in the stimulant responsive sense, stimulant dosage had the same effect on performance of a "higher level" task as it does in normals, that is, it impairs it. It could be that the drug made the children feel anxious and that this is what the *SCL* elevation indexed (cf. Conners, 1975). Weinberger and Ragan (1978) have demonstrated a U-shaped relationship between performance and psychological stress. Furthermore, subjects low in trait anxiety did relatively better under high stress. In one comparison, Conte found that adverse responders (ARs) actually learn faster at the slower presentation rate. These findings also are compatible with the view that the adverse responders were, at least temporarily, not exhibiting ADD. In this normal state, the superadded drug would lead to anxiety, better performance at the probably less stressful slower presentation rate, and overall learning impairment. An ongoing study attempts to determine whether adverse response in the laboratory indexes the subjects' current state only, or a trait characteristic that generalizes to everyday life (Wender & Kinsbourne, in preparation).

In the absence of information about how normal children would respond to stimulant administration in this paradigm, we cannot say whether the effect of stimulants in increasing *SCL* in *AR*s, or their lack of such an effect in *FR*s, represents the normal case. Given that learning to associate unrelated items qualifies as a "higher level" task and would therefore be expected to become more difficult for people when they have taken stimulants, one might surmise that the *AR*s approximate the normal situation. But even if the *AR*s show a response like that in the normal, it might be exaggerated in degree. From this view normal children would show some *SCL* elevation on stimulant, but *AR*s would be considered unduly susceptible to this effect of stimulants.

Event Rate and Learning by ADD Children

If the ADD deficit is comparable to the state that results in vigilance decrement, then manipulations that modify the vigilance decrement should modify ADD children's performance (even on nonvigilance tasks calling for much shorter duration of performance). Sykes, Douglas, Weiss and Minde, (1971) found that control children performed better with a 1½ second, than with a 1 second, presentation rate on a vigilance task involving targets added in a series. ADD children did no better at the slower rate. They concluded that the ADD children's attention span was so limited that the additional ½ second was simply not used.

Dalby, Kinsbourne, Swanson, and Sobel (1977) attempted a direct demonstration of hyperactive children's limited attention span in the context of a paired-associate learning task. Children were to learn associations between stimuli that were color slides of animals and responses that were points of a compass. Children favorably responsive to stimulant on paired associate learning were given these materials at three rates: every four, eight, or twelve seconds. The total study time, however, was held constant. According to Bugelski's (1962) total time principle, the amount learned is a function only of total study time and not of how it is subdivided. This indeed was found for the hyperactive children on stimulant. So, with regard to total time, they studied in a normal way. The same children on placebo did less well than on drug in all three conditions. However, the slower the presentation rate the worse they did. Dalby et al., suggests that the untreated hyperactives had an attention span (or concentration span) falling short of twelve or even eight seconds per item. Therefore, the longer the presentation, the more time was off task, and thus, the less efficient was the use of total study time.

As already discussed, Conte (1983) found that favorable responders when on placebo learned at a faster rate with rapid than slow presentation. On methylphenidate, this difference disappeared; the total time principle was reinstated. The adverse responders conformed to the total time principle in the placebo condition. Interestingly, on drug they did show a presentation rate effect, but in a direction opposite to that of the favorable responders; that is, they learnt better at the slower presentation rate.

These findings are consistent with the analogies drawn with the vigilance literature. Favorable responders are in a state that calls for a relatively high event rate to ensure maintenance of attention to the task. By raising the base level of activation of some behavioral control mechanisms, the stimulant abolishes this need. The adverse responders were not in the state in question in the first place. When they were given drugs, their behavior control mechanisms actually became overactivated, to the point that the total time principle was again breached, but in the opposite way. Now, the faster event rate was overstimulating, and the slower rate more conducive to optimal performance.

However, the findings can also be interpreted in the sense of documenting curtailed "concentration span" of untreated favorable responders (Sykes et al., 1981; Dalby et al., 1977), normal concentration of adverse responders and favorable responders on drug, and a different type of concentration deficit in the adverse responders on drug, in which task orientation to the new event takes a moment or two, thus penalizing the items presented relatively briefly (i.e., overfocussing on each item in the sense, cf. Kinsbourne & Caplan, 1979).

Conte (1982) pitted these two hypotheses against each other by the following design. In one condition, associates were presented every eight seconds. In the other, associates appeared for 8 or 12 seconds in random sequence (though any given associate would in consecutive reiterations of the list always appear for the same period of time). Total study time was held constant, so again the manipulation should make no difference to the amount learned. In fact hyperactive children on placebo did better in the faster condition, which is less taxing on concentration span and also presents events more frequently. However, if concentration span were the proper explanatory principle, then in the mixed duration list those items which were exposed for the shorter time (8 seconds) and more frequently should have been more rapidly learned than those items of longer duration (12 seconds) and lesser frequency. In fact the 12 second items were learnt at a faster rate by favorable responders in the placebo state. On drug that difference decreased. This outcome is more in accord with the event rate concept of control of learning ability.

A predilection for better functioning under circumstances in which more is happening could go far to explain manifestations of hyperactivity. In particular a low event rate could explain inattentiveness and impulsive, restless behavior could be seen as an attempt to generate additional events when events are occurring with suboptimal frequency.

Many more variables will have to be investigated before it can be concluded with certainty that the state during vigilance decrement has major commonalities with the state in ADD. At this stage we can note that in neither state has generalized arousal succeeded as an explanatory construct. Presentation rate manipulation is effective in both, but not via its differential arousing effects. We note from much literature (discussed in Broadbent, 1971) that it is relevant rather than overall event rate (just as it is relevant rather than overall stimulus salience) which controls the vigilance decrement. In other words, the more the task itself, in concrete instantiation, commands attention, the more likely is the long term observer to sustain attention to it. Further study will show whether this is true of ADD; the prediction is that frequency of relevant signals will control performance. If they have any effect at all, irrelevant signals, rather than being beneficial by maintaining arousal, should be detrimental in that they distract attention from the performance called for.

ADD and Temperament

Pursuing the possibility that ADD children cluster at one extreme of a dimension of temperament, we now ask, which temperamental extreme

7. A MODEL FOR THE ATTENTION DEFICIT DISORDER

would lead to the failure to sustain attention that characterizes much of the every day behavior (as well as laboratory performance) of the ADD child? A plausible case could be made for either impulsivity or emotionality as the relevant dimension of temperament (Buss & Plomin, 1975).

Impulsive people insufficiently weigh their decisions before committing themselves to action. This is the most critical symptom of hyperactivity according to Laufer and Denhoff (1957). An impulsive style, if extreme, is maladaptive in any setting. If moderate, it is maladaptive if limits are strict (for the child) or social sanctions complex and intangible (for the adult). Too little thought results in hasty, inaccurate solutions in formal problem solving in children (e.g., in the classroom) and in adults (e.g., in certain types of employment). The impulsive individual also may take excessive risks, infringe rules for immediate benefit, and display inability to delay gratification. These are some of the most common behavioral symptoms of hyperactivity. In hyperactivity, impulsivity is also considered the source of restlessness and overactivity, as rapid shifts in attention produce movement at a time during which the child is expected to maintain a posture of concentration on the task in hand.

Naturally, impulsivity is diversely expressed depending on the individual's other attributes of temperament, his social learning experience, and what society and his social group expect of him. If an impulsive individual happens to have a highly active temperament, he will more probably express his curtailed and chaotic thought processes in restless action than if his activity level is low. Whether he is high or low in sociability might determine whether he persists in his blundering interpersonal style and attention-gaining devices, or whether he withdraws from social situations (and particularly from peers) after a sufficient experience of rebuff. Social learning, both from role models and depending on reinforcement contingencies (whether consistent, immediate and concrete, or delayed, inconsistent, and nebulous) could have a differential impact on chronic impulsivity. Finally, social situations and stereotypic expectations related to a person's age and sex could modify impulsivity that otherwise could result in observable "hyperactivity". Though the range of overlapping clinical symptoms in ADD is wide, ADD could nevertheless result from a unitary constitutional deviance in cognitive style, because the variations may be due to interacting personality and environmental variables.

Now consider the other dimension, emotionality, and specifically individuals at the very low end of that dimension. Wender (1971) has described hyperactive children as experiencing relatively little fear or anxiety in anticipation of the possibility of punishment or non-reward (and possibly also less than the usual amount of pleasureable anticipation of rewarding events). In effect, reinforcements have less than the usual control over their behavior, and they may seem to act in disregard of potential hazard or punishment. Adults who typically behave in this way are called psychopaths.

A lack of emotionality may produce the behavior that seems to be the result of too little thought and thus be mistaken for impulsive behavior. For example, when instructed to concentrate on a task (such as classroom learning) which has little intrinsic interest, a child who does not fear punishment might readily relinquish concentration on that task and behave as if distracted, heedless of the teacher's displeasure. A lack of emotional responsiveness may lead to a high degree of noncompliance with the social structure, including physical activity at inappropriate times. An individual who lacks the normal emotional restraint of anxiety may be well aware of limits set by society, but choose to exceed them despite careful consideration of the outcomes. Thus, well thought out responses may seem to be premature or risky (i.e., "impulsive") to others. We now discuss some studies that suggest that the construct of ill-sustained attention is insufficient for the explication of ADD, and that inadequate control of behavior by a reward system might have to be implicated.

Although many have remarked that hyperactive children seem oblivious of the difficulties they experience and the trouble they cause, this could be attributed to defensiveness or motivated denial at the verbal level. We therefore devised a situation in which denial is not a confounding factor.

Dalby et al., (1977) interviewed children after they had within one day experienced two states, one drug, one placebo, in randomized drug-placebo sequence. Their performance and behavior was documented as being radically different between those two states. When at the end of the day they were asked to judge whether it was in the morning or afternoon that they had taken the effective pill, they responded with chance accuracy. It seems then that some self-evaluation is truly lacking and in any taxing performance it might be that self-evaluation leads to increased effort whereas its absence might result in bland contentment with inferior performance (and surprise at any criticism emanating from others).

A Possible Antecedent to the Attention Deficit

There are situations in which attentional explanations would seem forced. One such is a study by Freeman (1978) in our laboratory. He had ADD favorable responders learn their way through a Lykken maze. At each of twenty choice points only one of four locations was reinforced. Of the rest two yielded no consequence but the third resulted in an unpleasant noise through ear phones. This "punishment" normally results in incidental avoidance learning (Lykken, 1967). In parallel with the mastery of the correct sequence, subjects incidentally learn to reduce the proportion of their errors which impinges on punished locations.

Freeman found that hyperactives on stimulant did so too, but on placebo they did not. Untreated, they showed an incidental avoidance learning deficit. Paradoxically, adverse responders exhibited an opposite effect. On placebo they showed substantial incidental avoidance learning. On drug, this effect disappeared; their errors involved "punished" locations with chance frequency. This effect is analogous to the rate dependency discussed by Robin & Sahakian (1979). If the base state (placebo) is characterized by little avoidance learning, the drug increases it, if by much the drug cuts it down. It comes as no surprise to those acquainted with ADD children that negative consequences exert rather little control over their behavior. But does this apply to any negative consequence or more particularly to ones involving physical discomfort? In another experiment Freeman had subjects operate a marble dispensing machine. At each lever press a marble was delivered, exchangeable for two cents. Subjects were free to press the lever as they desired. But in one condition they were warned that "one press too many" (number unspecified) would result in them losing all their marbles. In the other condition it would result in a painful electric shock.

Neither consequence was in fact permitted to occur, but the design made it possible to observe subject's risk-taking behavior. Under risk of monetary loss favorable and adverse responses behaved similarly and stimulants decreased risk taking if it was high increased if it was low. But in the face of potential electrical shock, hyperactives made twice as many lever presses as controls. Stimulant medication corrected this greater risk-taking propensity.

It seems then that hyperactives are less apt to permit the risk of pain to control their behavior. In this situation, with avoidance learning, the possiblity of an attentional variable did not arise. One has to resort to a broader hypothesis of disinhibition (perhaps release of limbic systems from frontal control) rendering subjects more volatile and intractable as well as restless, impulsive, and inattentive.

Counterpoints to Hyperactivity

If, as has been suggested, the hyperactive deficit stations subjects toward one end of the behavioral continuum who is at the other end? Three populations are candidates for this position.

The first is the stimulant-overdosed hyperactive. His withdrawn behavior suggests a preference for unduly low event rates, but we have not yet demonstrated this experimentally. At least some ADD children who respond adversely to stimulants may be in the same situation: already internally generating "events" as rates comparable to those seen in stimulant-overdosed hyperactives, suggesting that the organism attempts to protect itself from a stimulus overload. The evidence for this is discussed by Kinsbourne (1980). There is also some evidence that children with autistic behaviors are as oversensitive to positively and negatively reinforcing situations as hyperactives seem immune to them (Richer & Nicholl, 1971).

SUMMARY

In summary, we have been able to use a laboratory based repeated measures design to highlight aspects of the ADD syndrome which have previously been suspected at the clinical level but not demonstrated experimentally. Our results to date incriminate attentional systems not in any primary way but as subject to the vagaries of an underactivated behavioral control system. Due to its weakness, it can constrain attention and restrain impulsive responding only when stimulated by vivid experiences and immediate tangible rewards.

REFERENCES

Achenbach, T. M. & Edelbrock, C. S. The classification of child psychopathology. *Psychological Bulletin,* 1978, *85,* 1275-1301.

Baker, C. H. Probability of signal detection in a vigilance task. *Science,* 1962, *136,* 46-47.

Baker, C. H. Signal duration as a factor in vigilance tasks. *Science,* 1963, *141,* 1196-1197.

Barkley, R. A. & Jackson, T. L. Hyperkinesis, autonomic nervous system activity and stimulang drug effects. *Journal of Child Psychology and Psychiatry,* 1977, *18,* 247-357.

Bax, M. & MacKeith, E. (Eds.) *Minimal cerebral dysfunction.* In: *Little Club clinics in developmental medicine* (Vol. 10). London: William Heineman, 1953.

Bradley, C. The behavior of children receiving benzedrine. *American Journal of Psychiatr,* 1937, *94,* 577.

Broadbent, D. E. The twenty dials and twenty dials test under noise conditions. *Medical Research Council Report.* Applied Psychology Unit, No. 160/51, 1951.

Broadbent, D. E. Noise, paced performance and vigilance tasks. *British Journal of Psychology,* 1953, *44,* 295-303.

Broadbent, D. E. *Perception and communication.* London: Pergamon Press, 1958.

Broadbent, D. E. *Decision and stress.* New York: Academic Press, 1971.

Buchsbaum, M. & Wender, P. H. Averaged evoked responses in normal and minimally brain dysfunctioned children treated with amphetamine. *Archives of General Psychiatry,* 1973, *29,* 764-770.

Bugelski, B. R. Presentation time, total-time and mediation in paired-associate learning. *Journal of Experimental Psychology,* 1962, *63,* 405-412.

Buss, A. H. & Plomin, R. A. *Temperament Theory of Personality Development,* New York: Wiley, 1975.

Cantwell, D. P. Familial-genetic research with hyperactive children. In: *The hyperactive child: Diagnosis, management, current research* (Ed.) Cantwell, D. P., Hollywood, N.Y.: Spectrum, 1975, 93-108.

Clements, S. E. *Minimal brain dysfunction in children: Terminology and identification.* Washington, D. C.: Public Health Service Publication, No. 1415, 1966.

Cohen, N. J. & Douglas, V. I. Characteristics of the orienting response in hyperactive and normal children. *Psychophysiology,* 1972, *9,* 238-245.

Cohen, N. J., Douglas, V. I., & Morgenstern, G. The effect of methylphenidate on attentive behavior and autonomic activity in hyperactive children. *Psychopharmacologia,* 1971, *22,* 282-294.

Conners, C. K. Minimal brain dysfunction and psychopathology. In: *Child personality and psychopathology: Current topics* (Vol. 2) (Ed.) Davids A. New York: Wiley, 1975.

Conner, C. K., Eisenberg, L., & Sharpe, L. Effects of methylphenidate (Ritalin) on paired-associate learning, Porteus-maze performance in emotionally disturbed children. *Journal of Consulting Psychology,* 1968, *28,* 14.

Conte, R. A behavioral and physiological analysis of the behavior of hyperactive children. Ph.D. dissertation, University of Toronto, 1983.

Corcoran, D. W. J. Doubling the rate of signal presentation in a vigilance task during sleep deprivation. *Journal of Applied Psychology,* 1963, *47,* 412-415.

Dalby, D. T., Kinsbourne, M., Swanson, J. M., & Sobol, M. P. Hyperactive children's underuse of learning time: Correction by stimulant treatment. *Child Development,* 1977, *48,* 1448-1453.

Davies, D. R., Hockey, G. R. J., & Taylor, A. Varied auditory stimulation temperament differences and vigilance performance. *British Journal of Psychology,* 1969, *66,* 453-457.

Davies, D. R. Parasuraman, R. *The Psychology of Vigilance.* New York: Academic Press, 1982.

Douglas, V. I. & Peters, K. G. Toward a clearer definition of the attentional deficit of hyperactive children. In: *Attention and the Development of Cognitive Skills,* (Eds.) Hale, G. A. and Lewis, M., New York: Plenum, 1980.

Duffy, E. *Activation and Behavior,* New York: Wiley, 1962.

Eason, R. G., Beardshall, A. & Jaffee, S. Performance and physiological indicants of activation in a vigilance situation. *Perceptual and Motor Skills,* 1965, *20,* 3-13.

Ebaugh, F. G. Neuropsychiatric sequelae of acute epidemic encephalitis in children. *American Journal of Disease in Childhood,* 1923, *25,* 89-97.

Eisenberg, L. The clinical use of stimulant drugs in children. *Pediatrics,* 1972, *49,* 709.

Ellis, H. C. & Ahr, A. E. The role of error density and set in a vigilance task. *Journal of Applied Psychology,* 1960, *44,* 205-209.

Flintoff, M., Barron, R., Swanson, J., Ledlow, A., & Kinsbourne. M. Methylphenidate increases selectivity in visual scanning. *Journal of Abnormal Child Psychology,* In press.

Flory, D. C. & Gilbert, J. The effects of Benzedrine Sulphate and caffeine citrate on the efficiency of college students. *Journal of Applied Psychology,* 1943, *27.*

Fraser, T. Vigilance and fatigue. Unpublished Ph.D. thesis. University of Edinburgh, 1957.

Freeman, R. An avoidance learning deficit in hyperactive children. Doctoral dissertation, University of Waterloo, 1978.

Goyette, C. H., Conners, C. K., & Ulrich, R. F. Normative data on revised Conners parent and teacher rating scales. *Journal of Abnormal Child Psychology,* 1978, *6,* 221-236.

Grunzke, M. E. The differential effects of visual and auditory feedback on a visual vigilance task under conditions of reward and nonreward. *Dissertation Abstracts,* 1966, *27,* 1637.

Hastings, J. E. & Barkley, R. A. A review of psychophysiological research with hyperkinetic children. *Journal of Abnormal Child Psychology,* 1978, *6,* 413-447.

Hebb, D. O. *A textbook of Psychology,* Philadelphia, Saunders, 1958.

Hopkins, J., Perlman, T., Hechtman, L., & Weiss, G. Cognitive style in adults originally diagnosed as hyperactives. *Journal of Child Psychology and Psychiatry,* 1979, *20,* 209-216.

Humphries, T., Swanson, J. M., Kinsbourne, M., & Yu, L. Stimulant effects on persistence of motor performance of hyperactive children. *Journal of Pediatric Psychology,* 1979, *4,* 55-56.

Jerison, H. J. & Wing, J. F. Human vigilance and operant behavior. *Science,* 1961, *122,* 880-881.

Kagan, J. Reflection—impulsivity and reading ability in primary grade children. *Child Development,* 1965, *36,* 609-628.

Kappauf, W. S. & Powe, W. E. Performance decrement in an audio-visual checking task. *Journal of Experimental Psychology,* 1959, *57,* 49-56.

Kinsbourne, M. The analysis of learning deficit with special reference to selection attention. In: *Specific Reading Disability Advances in Theory and Method.* (Eds.) Bakker, D. and Satz, P. Netherlands: Rotterdam University Press, 1970, 112-115.

Kinsbourne, M. The mechanism of hyperactivity. In: *Topics in Child Neurology*. (Eds.) Blau, M., Rapin, I., Kinsbourne, M. New York: Spectrum Press, 1977.

Kinsbourne, M. Do repetitive movement patterns in children and animals serve a dearousing function? *Journal of Developmental and Behavioral Pediatrics*, 1980, *1*, 39-42.

Kinsbourne, M. & Caplan, P. J. *Children's learning and attention problems*. Boston, MA: Little Brown & Co., 1979.

Kinsbourne, M., Swanson, J. M., & Herman, D. Laboratory measurement of hyperactive children's response to stimulant medication. In: *Minimal Brain Dysfunction: A Developmental Approach* (Eds.) Denhoff & Stern, L. New York: Masson, 1979.

Knights, R. M. & Hinton, G. G. The effects of methylphenidate (Ritalin) on the motor skills and behavior of children with learning problems. *Journal of Nervous and Mental Diseases*, 1969, *148*, 643.

Laufer, M. & Denhoff, E. Hyperactive behavior symptoms in children. *Journal of Pediatrics*, 1957, *50*, 463.

Loeb, M., Hawkes, G. R., Evans, W. O., & Alluisi, E. A. The influence of d-amphetamine, benactyzine, and chlorpromazine on performance in an auditory vigilance task. *Psychonomic Science*, 1965, *3*, 29-30.

Loeb, M. & Schmidt, E. A. A comparison of the effects of different kinds of information in maintaining efficiency on an auditory monitoring task. *Ergonomics*, 1963, *6*, 75-82.

Lykken, M. Neuropsychology and Psychophysiology in personality research. In: *Handbook of Personality Theory and Research* (Eds.), Borgatta, E. F. and Lambert, W. New York: Rand McNally, 1967.

Mackworth, N. H. Researchers on the measurement of human performance. Medical Re- *Journal of Psychology*, 1965, *19*, 111-117.

Mackworth, N. H. Researchers on the measurement of human preformance. Medical Research Council Special Report. #268, London, 1950.

Malmo, R. B. Activation: A neuropsychological dimension. *Psychological Review*, 1959, *66*, 367-386.

McGrath, J. J. Irrelevant stimulation and vigilance performance In: *Vigilance: A Symposium*. (Eds.) Buckner, D. N. & McGrath, J. J. New York: McGraw Hill, 3-21, 1963.

Neal, G. L. Some of differential pretask instructions on auditory vigilance performance. Paper presented at South-Western Psychological Association meeting. Houston, Texas, April, 1967.

Porges, S. W., Walter, G. F., Korb, R. J., & Sprague, R. L. The influences of methylphenidate on heart rate and behavioral measures of attention in hyperactive children. *Child Development*, 1975, *46*, 727-733.

Posner, M. I., Nissen, M. J., & Ogden, W. C. Attended and unattended processing modes: The role of set for spatial location. In Modes of Perceiving and processing information (Eds.) Pick, H. I. and Saltsman, E., Hillsdale, N.J.: Lawrence Erlbaum Associates, 1978.

Robbins, T. W. & Sahakian, D. J. "Paradoxical" effects of psychomotor stimulant drugs in hyperactive children from the stand point of behavioral pharmacology. *Neuropharmacology*, 1979, *18*, 931-950.

Rapoport, J. L., Buchsbaum, M. S., Weingartner, H., Zahn, T. P., Ludlow, C., & Mikkelson, E. J. Dextroamphetamine: Its cognitive and behavioral effects in normal and hyperactive boys and normal men. *Archives of General Psychiatry*, 1980, *37*, 933-943.

Richer, J. & Nicholl, S. The physical environment of the mentally handicapped: IV A playroom for autistic children and its comparison therapy project. *British Journal of Mental Subnormal*, 1971, *17*, 132.

Ross, D. M. & Ross, S. A. Hyperactivity: Research, Theory, Action. New York: Wiley, 1976.

Routh, D. K., Schroeder, C. S., & O'Tauma, L. A. Development of Activity level in children. *Developmental Psychology*, 1974, *10*, 163-168.

Satterfield, J. H., Atoian, G., Brashears, G. C., Burleigh, A. C., & Dawson, M. C. Electrodermal studies in minimal brain dysfunction children. In: *Clinical use of stimulant drugs in children* (Ed.) Conners, C. K., Amsterdam: Excerpta Medica, 1974.

Satterfield, J. H. & Braley, B. W. Evoked potentials and brain maturation in hyperactive and normal children. *Electroencephalography Clinical Neurophysiology*, 1977, *43*, 43-51.

Satterfield, J. H., Cantwell, D. P., & Satterfield, B. T. Pathophysiology of the hyperactive children syndrome, *Archives General Psychiatry*, 1974, *31*, 839-844.

Satterfield, J. H., Cantwell, D. P., Lesser, L. I., & Podosin, R. L. Physiological studies of the hyperactive child: *American Journal of Psychiatry*, 1972, *128*, 1418-1424.

Satterfield, H. J. H. & Dawson, M. E. Electrodermal correlates of hyperactivity in children. *Psychophysiology*, 1971, *8*, 191-197.

Shaffer, D. & Greenhil, L. A critical note on the predictive validity of "the hyperkinetic syndrome". *Journal of Child Psychology and Psychiatry*, 1978, *19*, 161-166.

Sokolov, E. N. Higher nervous activity and the problem of perception. In (Ed.) Simon, B. *Psychology in the Soviet Union*. London: Routledge and Kagan, Paul, 1957.

Solandt, D. Y. & Partridge, D. M. Research on auditory problems presented by naval operations. *Journal of Canadian Medical Service*, 1946, *3*, 323-329.

Sostek, A. J. Effects of electrodermal lability and payoff instructions on vigilance performance. *Psychophysiology*, 1978, *15*, 561-568.

Sprague, R. L. & Sleater, E. K. Methylphenidate in hyperactive children: Differences in dose effects on learning and social behavior. *Science*, 1977, *198*, 1274-1276.

Spring, C., Greenberg, L., Scott, J., & Hopwood, J. Electrodermal activity in hyperactive boys who are methylphenidate responders. *Psychophysiology*, 1974, *11*, 436-442.

Sroufe, L. A. Drug treatment of children with behavior problems. In: *Review of Child Development Research* (Ed.) Horowitz, F., Chicago: University Chicago Press, 1975, 347-407.

Sroufe, L. A., Sonies, B., West, W., & Wright, F. Anticipatory heart rate deceleration and reaction time in children with and without referral for learning disability. *Child Development*, 1973, *44*, 267-273.

Staton, R. D. & Brumback, R. A. Nonspecificity of motor hyperactivity as a diagnostic criterion. *Perceptual and Motor Skills*, 1981, *52*, 323-332.

Stennett, T. The relationship of performance level to level of arousal. *Journal of Experimental Psychology*, 1957, *54*, 54-61.

Stetor, R. M. Performance and physiological arousal during two vigilance tasks varying in signal presentation rate. *Perceptual and Motor Skills*, 1966, *23*, 691-700.

Strauss, A. A., & Kephart, N. C. Psychopathology and education of the brain injured child. (Vol. 2) New York: Grune and Stratton, 1955.

Strauss, A. A. & Lehtinen, L. E. Psychopathology and education of the brain injured child. (Vol. 1). New York: Grune and Stratton, 1948.

Swanson, J. M., Barlow, A., & Kinsbourne, M. Task specificity of responses to stimulant drugs in laboratory tests. *International Journal of Mental Health*, 1979, *8*, 67-82.

Swanson, J. M. & Kinsbourne, M. Stimulant related state-dependent learning in hyperactive children. *Science*, 1976, *192*, 1754-1755.

Swanson, J. M., Kinsbourne, M., Roberts, W., & Zucker, K. A time-response analysis of the effect of stimulant medication on the learning ability of hyperactive children. *Pediatrics*, 1978, *61*, 21-29.

Swanson, J. M., Logan, W., & Pelham, W. The SNAP rating scale for the diagnosis of the attention deficit disorder. Submitted.

Sykes, D. H., Douglas, V. I., Weiss, G., & Minde, K. K. Attention in hyperactive children and the effect of methylphenidate (Ritalin). *Journal of Child Psychology and Psychiatry*, 1971, *12*, 129-139.

Thomas, A. & Chess, S. *Temperament and development*. New York: Brunner/Mazel, 1977.

Thurston, C. M., Sobol, M. P., Swanson, J. M., & Kinsbourne, M. Effects of methylphenidate (Ritalin) in selective attention in hyperactive children. *Journal of Abnormal Child Psychology,* 1979, *7,* 471–481.

Webb, W. B. & Wherry, R. J. Vigilance in prolonged and repeated sessions. *Perceptual and Motor Skills,* 1960, *10,* 111–114.

Weinberger, R. S. & Ragan, J. Motor performance under three levels of trait anxiety and stress. *J. Motor Behavior,* 1978, *10,* 169–176.

Weingartner, H., Rapoport, J. L., Buchsbaum, M. S., Bunney, W. E., Ebert, M. H., Mikkelsen, E. J., & Caine, E. D. Cognitive processes in normal and hyperactive children and their response to amphetamine treatment, *Journal of Abnormal Psychology,* 1980, *80,* 25–37.

Weiss, B. & Lattes, V. G. Enhancement of human performance by caffeine and the amphetamines. *Pharmacology Review,* 1962, *14,* 1.

Weiss, G., Minde, K., Werry, J. S., Douglas, V., & Nemeth, E. Studies in the hyperactive child: VII Five-year follow-up. *Archives of General Psychiatry,* 1971, *24,* 409–414.

Wender, P. H. *Minimal Brain Dysfunction in Children.* New York: Wiley Interscience, 1971.

Wender, P. H., Reimherr, F. W., & Wood, D. R. Attention Deficit Disorder (Minimal Brain Dysfunction) in Adults. *Archives of General Psychiatry,* 1981, *38,* 449–456.

Wokoun, J. Vigilance with background music. Aberdeen Proving Ground, Maryland: Human Engineering Lab Report No. TM-16-63, 1963.

Zahn, T. P., Abate, F., Little, B. C., & Wender, P. H. Minimal brain dysfunction, stimulant drugs and autonomic nervous system activity. *Archives of General Psychiatry,* 1975, *32,* 381–387.

Zentall, S. Optimal stimulation as theoretical basis of hyperactivity. *American Journal of Orthopsychiatry,* 1975, *45,* 549–563.

8 Comments on Kinsbourne's Chapter

Anne D. Pick
Institute of Child Development
University of Minnesota

Children who acquire the label "hyperactive" or "attention deficit disorder" surely are numbered among the "Children with Special Needs" upon whom this symposium is focused. Kinsbourne has documented some of the problems hyperactive children face. He has made a compelling case for establishing a diagnostic criterion that is a more objective alternative or supplement to the behavior descriptions provided by teachers and parents. These descriptions, which are necessarily somewhat subjective, frequently are the primary basis for a decision to begin a treatment program consisting of powerful stimulant drugs. Kinsbourne's goal of establishing the direction and magnitude of a child's response to the drug with a task that reflects some skills necessary for learning in school is important since he and his colleagues have documented that more than one-third of children referred for hyperactivity react adversely to stimulant drugs (Dalby, Kinsbourne, Swanson, & Sobol, 1977). Furthermore, if the properties of the task are objectively specifiable, then the possibility exists for conceptualizing more precisely than at present the nature of the difficulties that come together under the label of "attention deficit disorder."

What would characterize tasks that are adequate tools for investigating the learning difficulties of hyperactive children, for making decisions about stimulant drug treatment, and for evaluating the efficacy of those drugs in remediating the learning difficulties? A first and obvious requirement of such tools is that they have high reliability. A second necessary property is validity; either the tasks should reflect important properties of the settings where change in the children's behavior and functioning is sought, or they should be predictive of behavior in that setting. It is unfortunate that many of the tasks adapted from psychological research for aiding decision-making about drug treatment and for evaluating the effects of such treatment have serious inadequacies in regard to one or both of the properties of reliability and validity. These inadequacies will be discussed in regard to three such tasks: paired associate learning, incidental learning, and the Matching Familiar Figures test.

It is the paired associate learning task that Kinsbourne and his colleagues use to define positive and adverse drug responders from among children referred for symptoms of hyperactivity. It was selected because "performance on it has been found to have a positive and highly significant correlation with performance in the classroom," and because "it can be used to test repeatedly with little practice effect (or transfer) . . . ." (Kinsbourne, Swanson, & Herman, 1979, p. 87). A positive feature of the task, and the presumed basis for its relation to school learning is thought to be that "The cognitive skills necessary for much of the learning in the traditional classroom, including the ability to persevere at a task imposed by an adult, are necessary to perform this task" (Kinsbourne, Swanson, & Herman, 1979, p. 88).

To what degree or in what ways does paired associate learning incorporate significant features of the learning tasks children must accomplish in school? There is some evidence on this point from a massive study of children's learning conducted by Stevenson and his colleagues about 15 years ago (Stevenson, Hale, Klein, & Miller, 1968). A large number of tasks were given to students in 15 classrooms in the third through the seventh grades. The tasks included paired associate learning, discrimination learning, incidental learning, verbal memory, probability learning, conservation, and anagrams. Among the questions to which Stevenson and his colleagues sought answers were the following: Are there significant interrelations in children's performance on different types of learning tasks? What is the relation of children's performance in brief, laboratory-like tasks to the long-term learning that occurs in school? Stevenson (1972) summarized the results of this study and other similar but much less extensive studies as follows: "Low positive intercorrelations tend to be found among different learning tasks, except when the tasks are similar in structure, or, in some cases, similar in content. There is little basis for assuming that learning represents a unitary function that operates in a similar manner across different types of learning tasks" (p. 326).

One finding of Stevenson *et al.*, (1968) was that paired associate learning tasks were related consistently to school achievement for children across grades three to seven, and of course, the fact of that relation is the basis for Kinsbourne's selection of paired associate learning as a criterion task for assessing the effects of drug treatment on learning. Across grades, in the study by Stevenson *et al.*, (1968) the significant correlations of paired associate learning and school achievement ranged in magnitude from r = .39 to r = .61 with an average r of .47 (see Table 23 p. 53). Thus, something over 20% of the variance of paired associate learning is shared with school tasks that have to do with children's evaluation, that is, the assignment of grades. In considering the use of this task as a diagnostic tool, and the finding that it reflects the effects of stimulant drugs for some children, it is worth while to speculate at least about what that shared variance might be, or about what third factor might be associated with both kinds of tasks. One hypothesis is that suggested by Kinsbourne, namely, that paired associate learning is a reasonable model of school learning in general. However, the findings of Stevenson and his associates of rather low interrelations among different types of learning tasks cast doubt on that hypothesis. Indeed it would be rather discouraging if paired associate learning were to provide a good model of school learning, for one of its features, as Kinsbourne has noted, is that it shows little or no transfer.

Another hypothesis about the common variance of paired associate learning and some school tasks is that the tasks share sheer boringness. This idea is consistent with the findings that stimulant drugs affect children's (as well as adults') performance on tasks that seem to require sustained control of attention. Of course, this hypothesis has not been specifically tested, but if it were to prove tenable, it should make us reconsider the implied goal of manipulating children's attention with drugs so as to make them more tolerant of dullness and boringness and meaningless tasks. An alternative course of action might be to turn our own attention to ways of structuring tasks for the purpose of motivating children to learn, and teaching them strategies for coping with necessary, boring tasks.

One of the findings of Stevenson *et al.* was that an anagrams task consistently was more highly related to school achievement and also to teacher ratings of such characteristics as "effective learner," "hard worker," than was paired associate learning. The average correlation coefficient for the school achievement measures and the anagrams task was .61 (Table 23, p. 53) compared to .47 for the paired associate learning task. The particular anagrams task that Stevenson *et al.* used required the children to construct as many words as possible from the word "generation" in eight minutes. To persist at such a task for eight minutes obviously requires the sustained attention that is difficult for hyperactive (and many other) children to maintain. However, the anagrams task also incorporates some requirements of problem-solving and thinking that seem absent from the paired associate learning task. Since the anagrams task is more highly related to school achievement than is the paired associate task, it may be that the anagrams task reflects some learning skills or strategies that are the same as those used for some of the things that children learn in school. In short, the greater validity of the anagrams task compared to paired associate learning, may give it an advantage over paired associate learning as a tool for assessing whether the school performance of children referred for symptoms of hyperactivity will likely improve when they are treated with stimulant drugs.

A second task adapted by Kinsbourne for investigations with hyperactive children is an incidental learning task. It was developed by Hagen and his colleagues and has been used extensively to study selective attention (Hagen, 1967; Hagen & Hale, 1973). In this task, children are shown a series of cards with pictures or line drawings on them. If there are two pictures on each card, one below the other, the children might be told to look at both pictures but to remember the pictures on top. Subsequently their recall is assessed—both for the pictures they were instructed to remember, that is, the central items, and for the pictures they were not specifically instructed to remember, that is, the incidental items. Also, their recall of picture pairs may be assessed by showing them a central item and asking which of the incidental pictures was on the same card. High incidental recall is assumed to reflect a high degree of attention to irrelevant information, whereas low incidental recall plus high central recall is assumed to reflect good selective attention.

Thurston, Sobol, Swanson, and Kinsbourne (1979) used the incidental learning task to assess the effects of a stimulant drug on hyperactive children's selective attention. Children who were favorable drug responders (i.e., whose performance on the paired associate learning task had improved with the drug compared to their performance with a placebo) recalled about the same number of central items with a placebo ($\overline{X} = 4.1$ of a possible 8) and with the drug ($\overline{X} = 4.8$). However, they recalled about two and a half times as many incidental pictures with the placebo as when they were under the influence of the drug, and they recalled twice as many pairs of pictures with the placebo as with the drug. The investigators suggested that the effect of the stimulant drug is to narrow the focus of attention and direct it more exclusively to the central pictures thereby decreasing the children's opportunity to learn the incidental pictures. Thus, with the stimulant medication the children showed greater selectivity of attention and learning, and Kinsbourne refers to this as an example of a demonstration "of attentional deficits corrected by stimulant drug". Yet, without the drug, the children learned and remembered more overall.

Perhaps the rationale of the incidental learning task as an assessment of so general a process as selective attention should be reconsidered. If this task does reflect the selectivity required for mastering school tasks, then Kinsbourne's interpretation of the children's attention as "improved" under the influence of the stimulant drug carries a rather startling implication, namely, that one educational goal for children is to *avoid* acquiring incidental information and knowledge in the settings in which they learn. It is unlikely that even those most convinced of the efficacy of stimulant drug treatment for hyperactive children would advocate such a goal.

The third task to be considered is the Matching Familiar Figures Test which was constructed by Kagan (Kagan, 1965; Kagan, Rosman, Day, Albert, & Phillips, 1964), and which has been used by legions of psychologists as a measure of children's cognitive style. For this task, children are shown a standard two-dimensional drawing, and a set of comparison drawings from which they are to select one identical to the standard. The procedure includes a dozen or more items, and the children's accuracy and response times for each judgment are measured. Typically, children are labelled as reflective who make few errors and have long latencies for making their judgments. Children are labelled as impulsive who make many errors and have short latencies for making their judgments. Pick and Pick (1970) reviewed the early evidence for the generality of the cognitive styles of reflectivity and impulsivity, and concluded that the measures of cognitive style have only a moderate degree of stability and have rather low relation to their criterion measures. Egeland and Weinberg (1976) investigated directly the reliability of the test as an operational measure of reflectivity and impulsivity for children of school age, and they found that 48% of kindergarteners, 36% of second graders, and 28% of fifth graders classed as impulsive or reflective on one occasion did not receive the same classification only one week later (cf. Tables 3, 4, 5, pp. 488-489). Block, Block, and Harrington (1974) could find little evidence for the construct validity of the cognitive styles of reflectivity and impulsivity although they did find that accuracy in the task (but not latency) was associated with personality variables related to their construct of ego resiliency. The low reliability of the Matching Familiar Figures task, and lack of evidence for the validity of the cognitive styles it is presumed to assess constrain seriously its usefulness as a tool for use in assessing effects of a drug treatment that is thought to affect attention. Its psychometric properties are simply unknown (or absent), and the aspects of children's functioning that it reflects are undocumented.

Since one goal of manipulating the attention of hyperactive children through drugs or other means is improvement in their school learning, alternative assessment tasks to those used by Kinsbourne might be ones taken from that setting, or at least constructed so as to incorporate specific components of school tasks. The issue of the usefulness or appropriateness of the tasks used to evaluate the effects of stimulant drugs really is an issue regarding the criterion for improvement during drug treatment. Although an explicit goal is improvement in school, and the assessment tasks are chosen, in part, for their presumed relation to school tasks, one rarely finds reference in the literature to whether children on stimulant treatment actually improve in their school performance, and Kinsbourne also does not discuss this issue. Children are thought to respond favorably who behave more "appropriately" in the classroom but do they learn more? Do their grades improve? One reason these are important questions is the phenomenon of state-dependent learning which has been documented by a number of investigators including Kinsbourne. Kinsbourne, Swanson and Herman (1979) had hyperactive children learn the paired associate task either with a placebo or under the influence of a stimulant drug, and then their retention was tested by relearning the task either in the same or different state. The children remembered the most material when they learned and then relearned while under the influence of the stimulant drug. However, the children who learned while under the influence of the stimulant drug, and then relearned the task without it remembered *less* information than did any other group of children. In short, when learning took place in the drug state, and a test for what had been learned, that is, a test for the use of that learning, was given in the placebo state, the children's performance was worse than if the drug had never been administered. These findings document the need for serious concern about the consequences for children's use of knowledge acquired in school and elsewhere when that learning occurs while they are under the influence of stimulant drugs.

A final issue to be considered here in regard to diagnostic and assessment tasks is the task-specificity of the response to stimulant drugs discussed by Kinsbourne and documented in his own research as well as that of other investigators. In a study from Kinsbourne's laboratory (Swanson, Barlow, & Kinsbourne, 1979) hyperactive children who were favorable and adverse drug responders on the paired associate learning task performed a boring vigilance task in a drug state and with a placebo. As Kinsbourne noted, both groups of children made fewer errors and responded more quickly when they were in a drug state than when they were not. Kinsbourne also noted that improved performance on vigilance tasks is a well-documented effect of stimulant drugs—both for children who are believed to be hyperactive and for children and adults who are not. However, the most striking effect found by Swanson, *et al.* was not the similarity of the children's behavior in the drug state, but rather a difference between the children who were favorable drug responders and those who were adverse responders. Specifically, the children who were favorable responders reacted more *slowly* than the adverse responders did either in the drug state or after a placebo. The average reaction time of the favorable responders in placebo and in drug states were about 900 msec and 800 msec respectively whereas those of the other hyperactive children in placebo and in drug states were about 700 msec and 630 msec respectively (p. 76). Thus children who are identified on one task, the paired associate learning task, as appropriate subjects for a drug treatment program, perform less well overall than other hyperactive children on the very kind of task that is known to reflect the effects of the drug. This fact makes all the more urgent a necessity to use tasks for diagnosis and evaluation that have known relations to school learning.

Kinsbourne's hypothesis that there may be different optimum event rates for different children is important for it directs us to consider the settings in which learning occurs, and the facts of state-dependent learning make such consideration imperative. Kinsbourne cites evidence that adults perform better on some tasks requiring sustained attention when there is extraneous stimulation that provides no information about the task. There is additional evidence (e.g., Turnure, 1970; Turnure & Zigler, 1964; Ellis, Hawkins, Preyer, & Jones, 1963) that has been available for nearly two decades that what would seem to be distracting information also facilitates children's concentration or attention to some tasks. Of course, there is a great deal of anecdotal evidence on the point, for example, a good many teenagers believe, or at least assert, that they concentrate better on their homework not just with the radio turned on, but blaring music of a genre and decibel level that are virtually intolerable for others within hearing range. Kinsbourne's hypothesis that the optimum rate of events for hyperactive children may be higher than for some other children has implications for the kinds of settings in which hyperactive children might learn more effectively. For example, hyperactive children might function better in a noisy classroom, or while walking about, or with a radio turned on instead of in what is assumed to be the ideal learning environment, that is, a silent room. Providing such settings would be far less intrusive—at least for the children involved—than is the daily ingestion of a powerful drug.

Several years ago, Sroufe (1975) noted in a review of the literature on the efficacy of stimulant drug treatment for the problems of hyperactive children that "In light of the fact that learning and other school problems are a major reason for referral for hyperactive children, it is unfortunate that little systematic research has been done on educational approaches with these children (p. 387). What is even more unfortunate is that Sroufe's observation is as accurate today as it was when he made it. Kinsbourne's hypothesis about the role of event rate in controlling attention in learning suggests potential alternative intervention to stimulant drugs for changing the problem behaviors that lead to children's referral for hyperactivity. It would be extremely informative for Kinsbourne's two-day diagnostic drug-placebo design to be carried out not with alternating drug and placebo medication, but instead, with externally manipulated frequency of events. Exploration of the specific event frequency hypothesis, and systematic research on educational approaches for helping hyperactive children can be important for many reasons. Not the least of these is the possibility of reducing the very large numbers of young children whose attention we now only try to manipulate through the use of powerful drugs.

REFERENCES

Block, J., Block, J. H., & Harrington, D. M. Some misgivings about the Matching Familiar Figures Test as a measure of reflection-impulsitivy. *Developmental Psychology*, 1974, *10*, 611-632.

Dalby, J. T., Kinsbourne, M., Swanson, J. M., & Sobol, M. P. Hyperactive children's underuse of learning time: Correction by stimulant treatment. *Child Development*, 1977, *48*, 1448-1453.

Egeland, B., & Weinberg, R. A. The Marching Familiar Figures Test: A look at its psychometric credibility. *Child Development*, 1976, *47*, 483-491.

Ellis, N. R., Hawkins, W. F., Preyer, M. W., & Jones, R. W. Distraction effects in oddity learning by normal and mentally defective humans. *American Journal of Mental Deficiency*, 1963, *67*, 576-583.

Hagen, J. W. The effect of distraction on selective attention. *Child Development*, 1967, *38*, 685-694.

Hagen, J. W., & Hale, G. A. The development of attention in children. In A. D. Pick (Ed.), *Minnesota symposia on child psychology* (Vol. 7). Minneapolis: University of Minnesota Press, 1973.

Kagan, J. Impulsive and reflective children: Significance of conceptual tempo. In J. Krumboltz (Ed.), *Learning and the educational process*. Chicago: Ran McNally, 1965.

Kagan, J., Rosman, B., Day, D., Albert, J., & Phillips, W. Information processing in the child: Significance of analytic and reflective attitudes. *Psychological Monographs*, 1964, *78* (1, Whole No. 578).

Kinsbourne, M. Toward a model for the attention deficit disorder. In M. Perlmutter (Ed.), *Minnesota Symposia on Child Psychology* (Vol. 16). Hillsdale, N.J.: Erlbaum, (in press).

Kinsbourne, M., Swanson, J., & Herman, D. Laboratory measurement of hyperactive children's responses to stimulant medication. In Denhoff & L. Stern (Eds.), *Minimal brain dysfunction: A developmental approach*. New York: Masson, 1979.

Pick, H. L., Jr. & Pick, A. D. Sensory and perceptual development. In P. Mussen (Ed.), *Carmichael's manual of child psychology* (Vol. 1). New York: Wiley, 1970.

Sroufe, L. A. Drug treatment of children with behavior problems. In F. D. Horowitz (Ed.), *Review of child development research*. Chicago: University of Chicago Press, 1975.

Stevenson, H. W. *Children's Learning*. New York: Appleton-Century-Crofts, 1972.

Stevenson, H. W., Hale, G. A., Klein, R. E., & Miller, L. K. Interrelations and correlates in children's learning and problem solving. *Monographs of the Society for Research in Child Development*, 1968, *33*, (No. 123).

Swanson, J. M., Barlow, A., & Kinsbourne, M. Task specificity of responses to stimulant drugs in laboratory tests. *International Journal of Mental Health*, 1979, *8*, 67-82.

Thurston, C. M., Sobol, M. P., Swanson, J., & Kinsbourne, M. Effects of methylphenidate (Ritalin) on selective attention in hyperactive children. *Journal of Abnormal Child Psychology*, 1979, *7*, 471-481.

Turnure, J. E. Children's reactions to distractors in a learning situation. *Developmental Psychology*, 1970, *2*, 115-122.

Turnure, J. E., & Zigler, E. Outerdirectedness in the problem solving of normal and retarded children. *Journal of Abnormal and Social Psychology*, 1964, *69*, 427-436.

9 A Longitudinal View of a Preschool Research Effort

David P. Weikart
High/Scope Educational Research Foundation

Longitudinal work is a relatively rare phenomenon that is subject to the vagaries of the times, theoretical fads, and changing political systems. It therefore demands an enduring commitment from the researcher. These and related issues are explored in this chapter, which is structured around the questions that have guided our longitudinal work since its inception. Our decision in 1960 to plan a preschool intervention effort was purely pragmatic. After working within the public schools as a school psychologist for several years, it became clear to me that the schools were basically closed to the kinds of substantive changes they would have to make to give children destined for failure a *real* opportunity for education. Thus, the initial decision to work at the preschool level was based on experience more than theory. The theoretical justification for such early educational intervention had to await the publication of J. McV. Hunt's book, *Intelligence and Experience* in 1961. The support for the notion that such a venture would suceed at all came from some thoughts expressed by Samuel Kirk (1958) in his reflections about an experimental program he operated for mentally handicapped children in the fifties and from several comparative psychology studies by Scott (1962) on critical periods in behavioral development among animals. Of course, as the social action of the sixties began, the concept of preschool as both a service and an educational effort became very popular, especially in relation to minority populations. Its effectiveness, however, had yet to be proven.

We established the Ypsilanti Perry Preschool Project to determine whether such an intervention could help children destined for failure. Complete results of the Perry Preschool work to date are published in a series of

High/Scope Foundation monographs (Weikart, Bond, & McNeil, 1978; Schweinhart & Weikart, 1980) and in other sources. Here I will present a very brief discussion of the major project processes.

Begun in 1962, the Ypsilanti Perry Project is a longitudinal experiment designed to reveal the effects of early intervention on disadvantaged children. The poorest children in a low-income black neighborhood in Ypsilanti, Michigan were selected for the longitudinal sample. A total of 123 children were included in the study and were choosen from five groups of children who were born between 1958 and 1962 and whose names appeared on the family census of the Perry Elementary School (the neighborhood school). They were referred by neighborhood groups, or were found in a door-to-door neighborhood search. The first criterion for selection was that the child's parents have low socioeconomic status. The second selection criterion was that the child's IQ, tested at project entry using the Stanford-Binet Scale, fall in the range of 70 to 85.

Children entered the project in five waves. Each wave of children was a year younger than the preceding wave, with the oldest born in 1958 and the youngest born in 1962. The project began in 1962 with the selection of a group of four year olds (designated Wave Zero) and a group of three year olds (designated Wave One). The sample was complemented over the next three years by the annual selection of additional waves of three-year-old children—Waves Two, Three, and Four. This wave design allowed the study to employ approximate replications of the basic treatment.

The study compares an experimental group that received a daily preschool program (with weekly home visits) for two years and a control group that received no intervention program. The ongoing study includes several major evaluation points for the program participants: yearly evaluations in preschool; in elementary school (grades K-3); at age 15 (the beginning of high school); at age 19 (after high school graduation); and at age 25 (after the expected critical period of family formation and rapid social growth). Most data through age 19 have now been collected.

Each year, children in the sample for that year were assigned either to the experimental group or to the control group in an essentially random manner so as to equate groups on the basis of initial cognitive ability, sex ratios, and socioeconomic status. The experimental group and the control group thus shared a variety of background characteristics. (See Table 9.1.)

Children in the experimental group attended a group preschool program 12½ hours a week (weekday mornings) and were visited by program staff along with their mothers at home 1½ hours a week. This routine was maintained for about 30 weeks a year, from mid-October through the end of May. The experimental group in Wave Zero participated in the program for one school year, the remaining waves for two school years. Children in the control group remained at home with their mothers until regular enrollment in kindergarten at age 5.

TABLE 9.1
Demographic Comparisons: Experimental Vs. Control Group

Category	Experimental Group	Control Group	p^a	Var
Number of cases (youths)[b]	58	65		
Gender: Percent female	43%	40%	—	
Age at entry—Wave 0	4.4	4.2	—	
Waves 1–4	3.3	3.3	—	
Number of children in family	5.7	5.8	—	
Siblings older than youth	2.8	3.0	—	
Stanford-Binet IQ at entry	79.8	78.5	—	
Median years of school of parents				
Mothers	10.0	9.5	—	
Fathers	8.6	9.0	—	
Families[d]				
Socioeconomic status[e]	8.00	7.92	—	
Receiving welfare assistance	55%	45%	—	
No parent employed	51%	34%	—	
Two-parent families	54%	51%	—	
Mother works	5%	9%	—	
Father works	46%	45%	—	
Employment level—Skilled	4%	2%	—	
Semiskilled	10%	3%	—	
Unskilled	32%	40%	—	
Female-headed families	46%	49%	—	
Mother works	4%	22%	.002	12.7%
Families 11 years later[c]				
No parent employed[f]	46%	40%	—	
Two-parent families	39%	42%	—	
Mother works	10%	6%	—	
Father works	32%	38%	—	
Female-headed families	61%	58%	—	
Mother works	17%	20%	—	
Housing				
Person/room ratio	1.20	1.25	—	
Neighborhood rating by parent:[c]				
Excellent	21%	15%	—	
Good	45%	46%		
Fair	13%	19%		
Not so good	13%	7%		
Poor	9%	13%		
Family moves since child started school[c] 0	15%	17%	—	
1	58%	54%		
2–4	27%	30%		

[a]The two-tailed p value, based on the chi-square test, was reported if less than .10, followed by the percent of variance accounted for by group membership.

[b]Data collected at project entry, 1962–65, unless otherwise noted.

[c]Data collected 11 years after program entry, 1973–1977.

[d]The 123 youths in the sample comprised 100 families due to siblings; 123 cases were used in these calculations because child conditions are being reported.

[e]SES = scores standardized within the sample for: average of parents' years in school, average of parents' levels of employment, and half of rooms per person in households.

[f]Labor force participation of unemployed persons was ignored in these calculations.

In almost two decades since the end of their preschool education, almost all the participants in the sample can still be located and assessed. This continuity is reflected in the very low rate of missing data across the 48 measures employed in the study through age 15. The median rate of missing data across these measures is only 5%; for only four measures do missing data exceed 25%. Such low rates of missing data have virtually no harmful effect on statistical analysis.

The goal of the Perry Preschool's educational program was to help children acquire the intellectual strengths they would need to do well in school. Throughout the operation of the program, the teachers and staff enthusiastically supported this goal and employed a variety of strategies in their attempts to meet it. In the first years, these strategies included teaching preschoolers the alphabet, colors, shapes as well as the more traditional nursery school emphasis on direct manipulation of materials. In the second year of the project, however, we learned about the Swiss psychologist, Jean Piaget, and were influenced by his explanation of how children's development is related to their experience. Piaget saw language and rational thought as closely related to sensory and motor experience. Also, we invited the Israeli psychologist, Sara Smilansky, to visit our project. She helped to crystallize the notion that the child should plan some of his or her own activities every day. The teacher's role in such an effort was to help the child think through and articulate these plans and activities.

The curriculum model used in the Perry Preschool Project (Weikart, Rogers, Adcock, & McClelland, 1971) initially featured educational extrapolations from Piaget's theories of child development—Emphasis on classification, seriation, number, space, and time. However, the fledgling curriculum model continued to evolve and active learning to increase the construction of knowledge by the child became dominant. The staff gradually embraced the notion of involving the child in the planning of program activities and recognized the importance of helping children learn directly through concrete experience and its expression in language. The resultant Cognitively Oriented Curriculum, as it is now conceived and practiced, is described in *Young Children in Action,* (Hohmann, Banet, & Weikart, 1979).

DOES PRESCHOOL EDUCATION MAKE A DIFFERENCE IN THE LIVES OF CHILDREN?

The Perry Preschool Project has had a significant and enduring positive impact on the scholastic performance and overall commitment to education of the children it served. Children who attended the preschool have also engaged in less antisocial behavior in the classroom or in the larger community than the control groups.

Our research shows that preschool education improved the children's cognitive ability during preschool, kindergarten, and first grade. (See Figure 9.1) The best evidence for this comes from comparisons between IQ's of the experimental group and the control group, since it might reasonably be assumed that the two groups would achieve similar scores had there been no intervention. The experimental group exceeded the control group by 12 IQ points after one and again after two years of preschool, by 6 points at the end of kindergarten, and by 5 points at the end of first grade (age 7). Contrary to earlier expectations, IQ's of the experimental group and the control group were equivalent by the end of second grade and thereafter. At eighth grade (age 14), for example, the Wechsler Intelligence Scale for Children was given instead of the Stanford-Binet because the former was judged to be more suitable for older children and provided subtest scores as well as a total IQ. No group differences were found in verbal IQ, performance IQ, or any of the subtests.

Within the domain of commitment to education, *children who had participated in our preschool education program showed increased motivation during elementary school.* Children in the experimental group were rated more highly in school motivation by their elementary school teachers (kindergarten, first, second, and third grades). At age 15, these children again placed a higher value on schooling, had higher aspiration for college, spent more time on homework, and had a higher self-rating of school ability than the control group. In addition, parents reported that youths who had attended the preschool were in more cases willing to talk about what they were doing in school; 65% of the experimental group parents, but only 33% of the control group parents said their child enjoyed talking about school-related matters. This greater willingness to discuss school-related issues might conceivably have been due to a better parent-youth relationship, with more communication in all areas; but upon examination, no broader differences were found between groups in quality of parent-youth relationship. The greater willingness of the experimental group to talk about school-related matters seems to indicate that the youths who had attended preschool were more committed to their school experiences and more willing to take credit for them.

Preschool education did contribute significantly, however, to increased school achievement during the elementary and middle school years. Group differences occurred at all points of measurement. At age 14, a highly significant difference occurred favoring the youths who had attended our preschool. (See Fig. 9.2) Reading, arithmetic, and language achievement subtests results followed a similar performance pattern over time. Further examination of the achievement test information at age 14 suggests that preschool education led not only to improved school achievement but also to greater persistence in carrying out academic tasks.

Turning to special education placement, the complete school records of

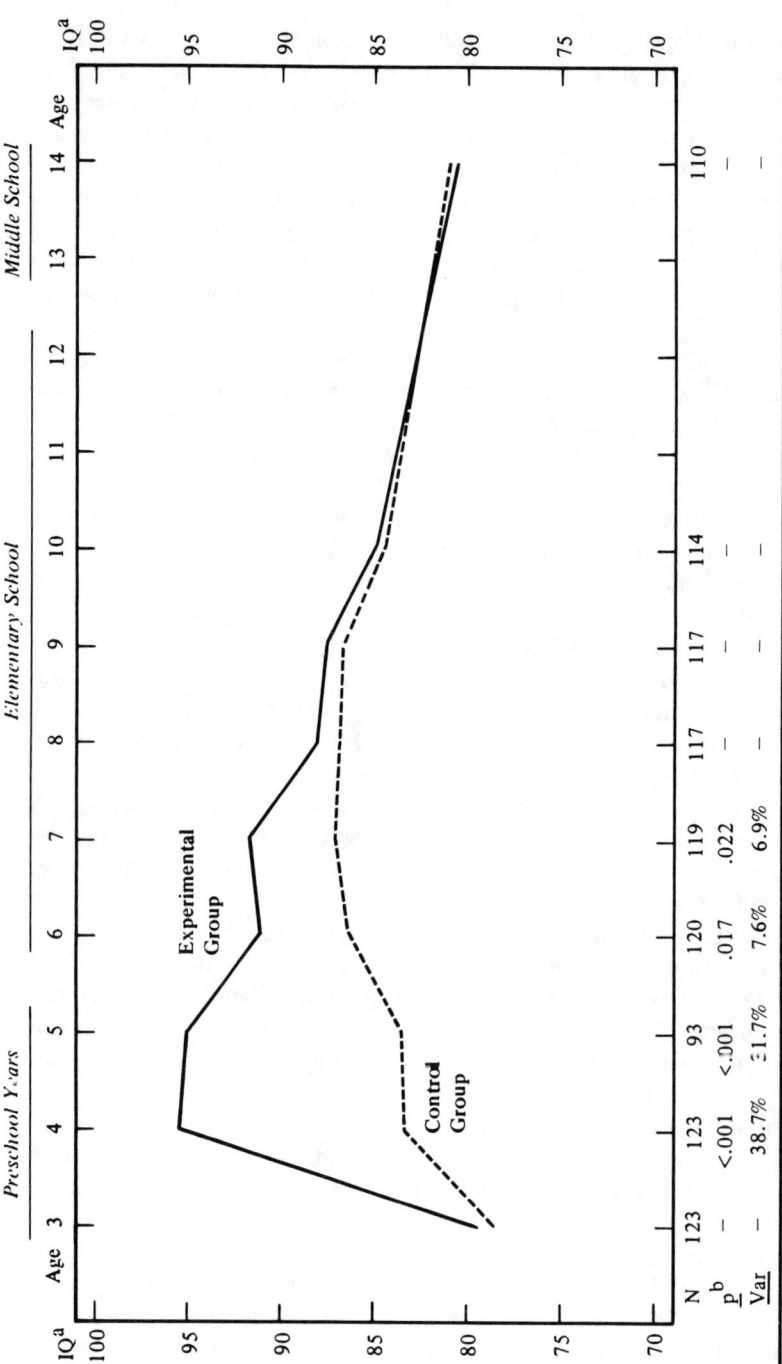

FIG. 9.1 Cognitive ability by group over time[a].

[a]Stanford-Binet tests, given at age 3 through 10, have IQs with a national population mean of 100 and a standard deviation of 16 (Terman & Merrill, 1960). WISC tests, given at age 14, have IQs with a national population mean of 100 and a standard deviation of 15 (Wechsler, 1974). The a_t, an index of consistency over time for these tests, was .921.

[b]p reported if less than .10, followed by the percent of variance accounted for by group membership.

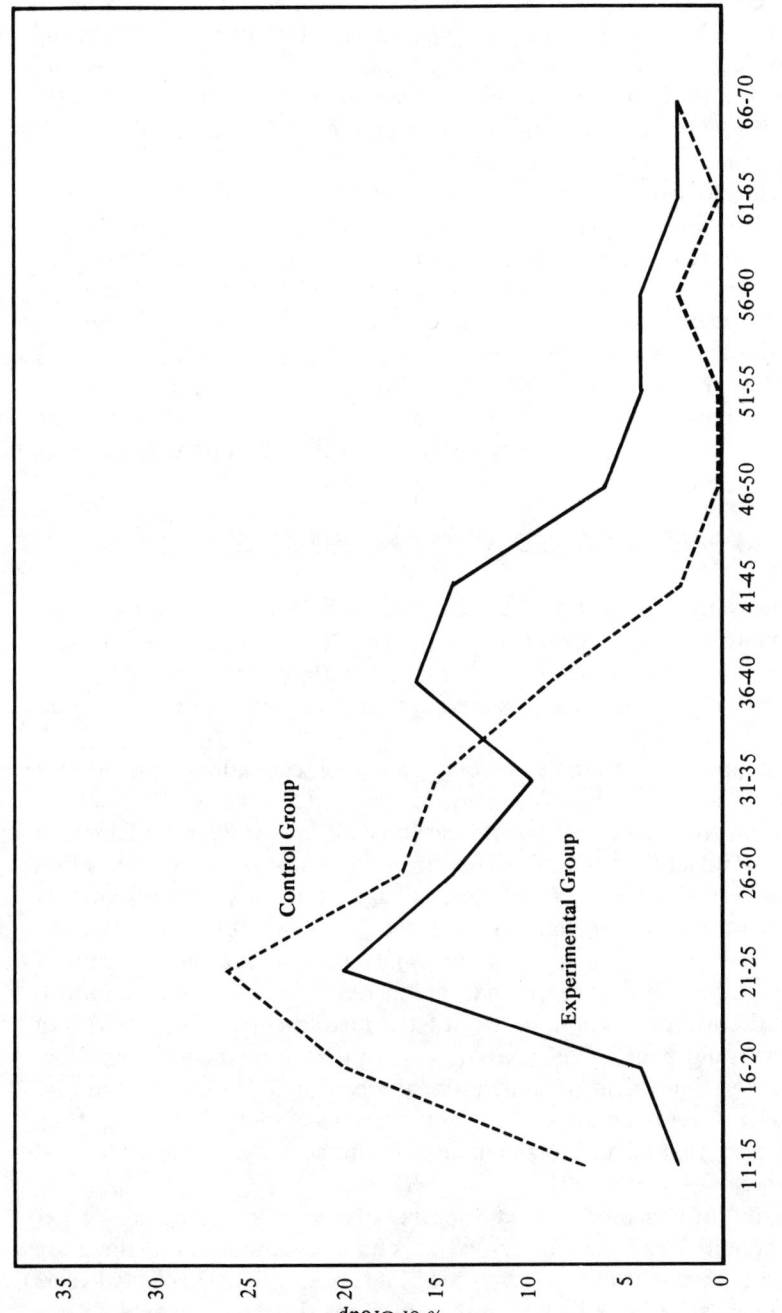

FIG. 9.2 Age 14 School achievement: Group distributions.

all members of the longitudinal sample were examined, from kindergarten through twelfth grade. *By the end of high school, 39% of the control group had received special education services for one year or more, compared with only 19% of the experimental group.* There were no group differences in the number of years retained in grade; as of eighth grade the sample as a whole averaged .13 years retained in grade.

We also discovered that *preschool education led to a decrease in teenagers' delinquent behavior;* we postulate that it did so by strengthening their bonds to schooling. In total self-reported delinquent behavior (see Fig. 9.3) there were two striking differences in group distributions: (1) combining nonoffenders and one-time offenders into one category, we found that 43% of the experimental group fell in that category as compared to only 25% of the control group; and (2) we found that 52% of the control group members as compared to 36% of the experimental group members fell into the category of chronic offenders—Those with five or more offenses.

IS PRESCHOOL EDUCATION COST-EFFECTIVE?

Early intervention programs that demonstrate returns to society on their initial investment ought to win the support of public and private investors concerned about the future of our society. The Perry Preschool Program, for one, has demonstrated a substantial return to society on its original investment.

For example, the benefits of our preschool education program far outweigh its costs. The benefits included were reduced costs of education, improved future wage earnings, and the value of time while the child was in preschool. The undiscounted benefits of two years of preschool education (in 1979 dollars) totalled $14,819 per child against the actual two-year program cost of $5,984 per child ($2,992 per year)—a 248% return on the original investment. The internal rate of return on the investment was calculated to be 3.7%. (The internal rate of return is a discount rate which indicates the average earning power of the investment in the project.) In other words, our benefit-cost analysis showed that investment in preschool education was equivalent to an investment receiving 3.7% interest after inflation over several decades. The cost estimate employed was the total resource cost, that is, the total public cost of the program plus the total private cost.

While the influence of a child's special education status on his or her lifetime potential earnings is verified by our longitudinal data, there are reasons to believe that our estimates are quite conservative. Projected years in special education were an underestimate of the difference in actual years of special education found in 1979. Dropout rates were assumed to be

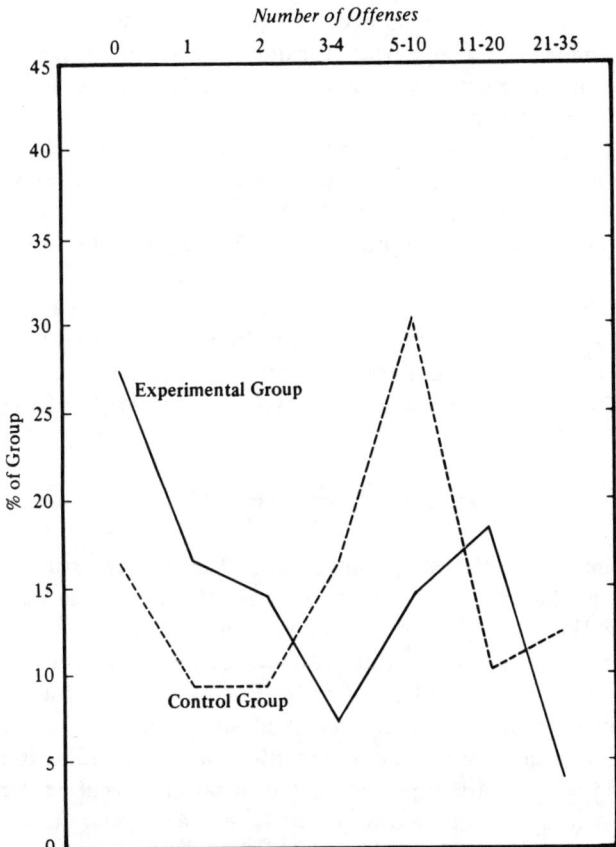

The experimental group scored less than the control group, median test, p = .022, Var = 5.4%.

FIG. 9.3 Self-reported delinquent behavior by group.

equivalent across groups, although there is a conceptual rationale and some preliminary data from the project to suggest that the dropout rate for the experimental group is lower than the control. Our preliminary information also shows that more members of the experimental group when compared to the central group are attending college.

Another potential benefit-cost of preschool education for the participants and for society is a reduced delinquency rate, resulting in savings for the victims of crimes as well as savings in police and court processing costs. There is evidence of a possible increase in labor-force participation on the part of the experimental group as compared to the control group, which would render even greater the marginal benefits in a projected lifetime earnings.

Additional savings may be realized through a decreased need for welfare assistance and other social services for individuals in the study who become self-supporting. These potential benefits remain to be calculated as part of a future benefit-cost analysis.

While the Perry Preschool Program was not part of a large, government funded program, there are many similarities between the Perry Program and programs such as Head Start. Both serve economically disadvantaged children and especially those judged to run a high risk of scholastic failure. The differences in cost between the programs are not great—the Perry Program cost $2,992 per year per child in 1979 dollars, whereas typical Head Start costs are $2,464 per year per child in 1979 dollars. As noted earlier, an economic analysis of the Perry Project revealed that the undiscounted economic benefits for two years of preschool were 248% of the cost.

HAVE WE FOUND THE ANSWER?

Perhaps the most interesting outcome of the 20 years of research and follow-up is that we have found an answer but still must meet more challenges. We know that preschool can make a difference in the lives of children and that difference touches areas of major concern to society as well as to the schools and the family. For example, reduced adolescent delinquency is important to all sectors of society not just the educational establishment. Increased school completion rates and indications of better job-holding patterns are important to the corporate executive. Less need for expensive school services is important to all taxpayers. And, of course, positive relations with their children is a goal of all parents. Preschool education does all these things—apparently, better than any other demonstrated and validated system available to us at this time.

How preschool does this is not a mystery. Preschool education opens the door fot the child to improved quality of interaction with all institutions: the schools, the employer, the community, and, especially the family.

The importance of commitment to schooling has been seen as a major preventive factor in delinquent behavior in other studies and the term "success flow" has been used to describe the positive relationship of the youngster with the institution (the school). The impact of preschool is not a "sleeper" effect, but a gradual accumulation of successful experiences that adults gradually notice and reinforce because the youngster is maintaining his "output." Thus, the preliminary finding that Perry Project children at age 19 who attended preschool go to court less frequently than children who did not participate in preschool "fits" the expected pattern of commitment from participants.

It is important to note, however, that preschool education is not *the* solution to the multitude of problems our society faces in jobs, learning, criminal justice, welfare, and so forth, but it is clear that it is *part* of the solution.

How Have Theoretical Fads Influenced Our Preschool Efforts?

It is clear that preschool education can be cost-effective and can make a big difference in the lives of children. But does a specific curriculum approach prove more effective than the others? A number of great social changes have swept the country and directly affected our work. In addition, other more specialized, but equally important changes have been occurring in the professional community. Perhaps the most interesting is the development of theoretical fads. Americans are always searching for the absolute "right" solution to a problem, and theory has become an important part of the game. Educational professionals have not been immune to this influence. In the late 1930's and 1940's, John Dewey and the theories of the progressive movement dominated early childhood and general education. The impact of Freudian theory on education was strongly felt in the 1950's. Finally, with the belated discovery of Piaget in the early 1960's, American educators hustled to adopt yet another way of programming their thinking. It is not surprising, then, to report that these stresses were felt in the Perry Project, too. We were "children of the times." Coming at the end of the Freudian reign, the first year of our program was dedicated to a search for a structure within which to present "learning." We rejected the open-flexibility concepts of the free play and social adjustment advocates because of our concern with the need to help children do well academically in school. With Hunt as our guide, we discovered Piaget and began adapting his theory of genetic epistemology to our early educational practices. This proved to be a promising but painful process for us.

The Piagetian influence led to some important changes in our preschool curriculum over a number of years. Our emphasis on preacademic activities was gradually replaced by an emphasis on discovering the strengths of each child, and viewing these strengths from the perspective of the child's developmental level. This was a decisive reorientation for us—a significant move away from our preoccupation with a child's *deficits* toward a focus on the child's *assets*. And the idea of representation, so critical in Piagetian theory, served as a basis for building the necessary links to traditional academic exercises in reading and mathematics.

The most significant curriculum change, however, was yet to come: the devolution of responsibility for initiating learning experiences from the teacher alone, to the child and teacher together. Our transition to the position of encouraging children to initiate their own learning began when we recognized the importance of children's planning in the educational process. It took many years for us to complete this transition—for at this stage the teaching staff still viewed children as being on the receiving end of the teaching-learning continuum. It was during this transitional process that we developed what is known now as the Cognitively Oriented Curriculum.

During this period, our teachers were trying to "teach" specific Piagetian tasks and relate them to children's developmental stages. Given what we know now, such teaching is hardly a realistic eductional goal, for both theoretical and practical reasons. But all Piagetian programs seem to have gone through this stage of direct teaching, either to accelerate a preschool child's development or to strengthen particular abilities that would help preschoolers when they entered school. Some programs even went so far as to create kits to "teach" classification, seriation, and so forth, or to diagnose children by means of Piagetian developmental tests so that remedial teaching could be undertaken. The Cognitively Oriented Curriculum, partly because of links to traditional nursery education, didn't stumble into that blind alley. However, our staff did aspire to "teach" basic Piagetian skills, and it wasn't until the next phase of curriculum development that the role of the child as "constructor" of knowledge became paramount.

In the early 1970's, we took a major step forward in the development of the Cognitively Oriented Curriculum with the organization of the classroom program around a set of key experiences. The key experiences were derived from developmental theory and the practical knowledge we had gained during a decade of work with young children. With these key experiences at their disposal, our teachers stopped asking children questions to which they (the teachers) knew the answers and began asking children to talk about what they were doing, thinking, and intending. Using this approach, teachers could explore the dimensions of the child's thinking instead of asking "test" questions to elicit predetermined responses. The teacher-child conversations became real. Gone was the "verbal bombardment" of the earlier period when the teacher would "surround the child with language." The new teaching focus was directed toward helping children use the preschool and home environment to accomplish their own activities and goals. Teachers used their knowledge of a particular child's developmental level to meet the needs of that child. As Banet (Hohmann, Banet, & Weikart, 1979) has written, "The point of Piaget's epistemology is that children abstract underlying truths through active encounters with reality, not through active encounters with genetic epistemologists."

When we started the Perry Project, the development of a curriculum was not one of our intended goals. As we entered into the actual operation of the program, however, it became apparent that we needed something more than was available from traditional sources. Influenced as we were by the social zeitgeist, we proceeded to operate the program with the support of the broad developmental theory we had gradually adopted and modified as our own.

OF THE THEORETICALLY DIVERSE SYSTEMS OF PRESCHOOL EDUCATION, IS ONE MOST EFFECTIVE?

During the follow-up phase of the Perry Project, the issue of quality of curriculum was examined in terms of various theoretical approaches. Traditional nursery educators questioned our development of a Piagetian-based curriculum while behaviorists were pushing highly structured solutions for solving the learning problems of disadvantaged children. The question, of finding a superior curriculum fit the American penchant for finding the best solution available, and was based on the assumption that one way would be best.

The Ypsilanti Preschool Curriculum Demonstration Project was an additional study of preschools, designed to compare the effectiveness, under carefully controlled experimental conditions, of three theoretically distinct approaches to compensatory preschool education. The three models represented the major approaches to early childhood education in operation during the late 1960's:

1. The *Cognitively Oriented Curriculum,* the "open framework" approach was developed by High/Scope staff in the Ypsilanti Perry Preschool Project. Piaget's theory provided the foundation for this model, which is based on the assumption that mental growth occurs through children's active exploration and manipulation of their environment to construct knowledge.

2. The *Language Training Curriculum,* a "programmed" approach was adapted from the work of Bereiter and Engelmann (1966). In this model, the academic problems of economically disadvantaged children were viewed as stemming from inadequate language development. Direct, programmed instruction was used to provide children with specific pre-academic skills in an atmosphere of "friendly competition" and positive reinforcement.

3. The *Unit-Based Curriculum,* a "child-centered" approach was based on traditional nursery school programs. The focus of this model was on the social and emotional growth of the child, and teachers were guided by their intuition and general knowledge of child development in formulating the curriculum.

The study involved 41 children, about equally divided among the three programs. The children were from families of low socioeconomic status living in Ypsilanti, Michigan. Their Stanford-Binet scores prior to preschool were low, with a mean of 81 points. Children entered the project in two waves, one wave beginning in 1967 and the other in 1968. Each child entered preschool as a two-year-old and remained in the program for two years. Children were assigned the three programs on a random basis.

Curriculum variables were carefully controlled in the Curriculum Demonstration Project so the outcomes could be attributed to program-related effects. All children attended half-day preschool sessions, five days a week, for two school years. A team of teachers, assisted by an adult aide and a student helper, were responsible for each classroom, and the staff/child ratio (including helpers) was maintained at 1 to 5. All three teaching teams were closely supervised and engaged in separate daily planning and evaluation sessions. In addition, teachers made home visits every two weeks, each visit lasting about 90 minutes, during which mothers were encouraged to help their children learn at home, using methods consistent with their children's preschool program.

The course of the project, anywhere from two to five teachers were responsible for implementing each curriculum model. Observational documentation of the programs indicates that, in all cases, activities conducted by teachers within the same program were much more similar than those conducted by teachers from different programs. This finding supports the conclusion that the Curriculum Demonstration Project compared curricula rather than teachers.

The Language Program, or programmed approach, adults verbally directed group of children in academic tasks. There was little spontaneous social interaction among the children themselves. The Cognitive Program, or open framework approach, was characterized by teachers interacting with children, both individually and in small groups, to support learning at the child's own level of cognitive development. In the Unit-Based Program, or child-centered approach, the emphasis was on socio-emotional growth and self-expression. Children in this program engaged in fantasy play and divergent activities.

At the end of the first year of the program, the three groups combined had an average Binet score of 104, a gain of 23 points over their entry level. By the end of the second year of preschool, the average gain had dropped to 17 points, but was still statistically greater than combined aptitude scores before preschool.

Binet scores at the end of preschool averaged 98 points; WISC scores at the end of fourth grade averaged 96 points. The 15-point gain from pretreatment to fourth-grade testing is not only statistically significant but also represents a meaningful increase in children's academic potential. At eighth grade testing, the 15-point gain from pretreatment was maintained, a remarkable finding more than a decade after treatment.

Approximatley one out of five children in the Curriculum Demonstration Project sample was not in his or her regular grade or class by the fourth grade. This number is close to the incidence of retention in grade or special-education placement of the experimental-group children who participated in the Ypsilanti Perry Preschool Project. Comparing these findings with the Perry Project control group, it appears that the children who attended these preschool programs have had much greater "actual school success" (i.e., regular grade and class placement) than the children who did not attend a preschool program.

There were almost no significant differences among children in the three Curriculum Demonstration Project Program on cognitive measures administered during the first five years of elementary school (K-4) and again at eighth grade. Language Program children tended to score highest and Unit-Based children lowest on the Binet and WISC.

Grade placement and linguistic and achievement measures administered after preschool also failed to reveal any significant differences in program impact among children in the three programs. There were no significant differences in rates of grade retention or special education placement, in scores of linguistic development or in academic achievement. There was a tendency, however, for Cognitive Program children to score the highest and Language Program children the lowest, on the achievement tests.

No consistent or meaningful program differences emerged in elementary school teachers' ratings of the Curriculum Demonstration Project children's behavior or parents' responses to interview questions at fourth grade. Also, children who entered preschool at different ability levels or who came from families of different socioeconomic status benefited equally from the Language, Cognitive, and Unit-Based programs in maintaining cognitive growth.

These results of the Curriculum Demonstration Project were difficult to accept, at least at first. Table 9.2 gives a picture of how the youngsters in the Curriculum Demonstration Project spent their time. The information was collected from an extensive time-sample study. It is clear from looking at the distribution of activities for the different models that the programs were in fact very different. The fact that children in with the Cognitive and Unit-Based programs engaged in far more fantasy or role play and divergent activities because of their self-defined goals is an important contrast to the Language Program curriculum where these activities hardly occurred at all. Time-sampling data such as these clearly support the fact that Curriculum Demonstration Project participants had different experiences. Looking then at the longitudinal outcomes found in elementary and junior high, it is surprising that there are and have been no differences in the children's performance across groups. The programs are structurally and experimentially different, but both the short-term and the long-term outcomes are the same.

Thus, the Ypsilanti Curriculum Demonstration Project produced a major

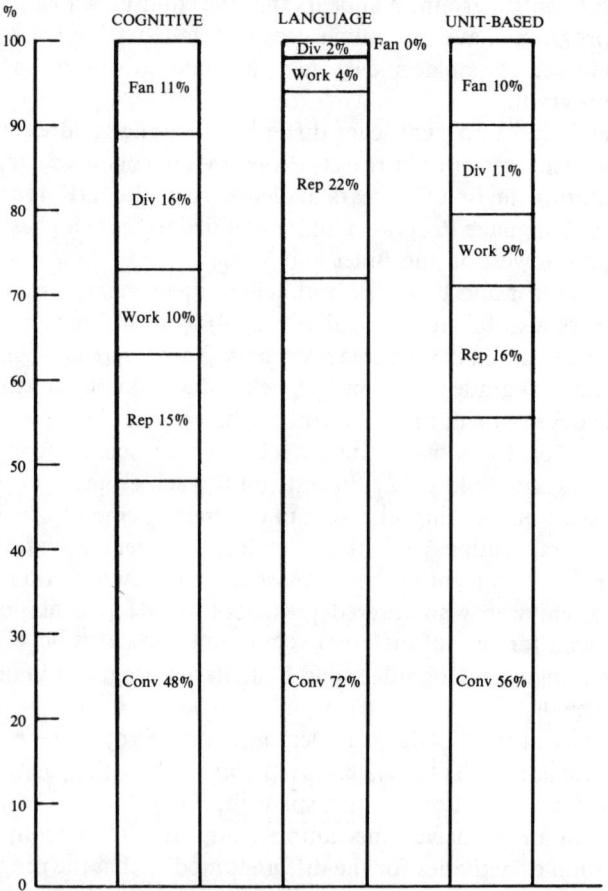

TABLE 9.2
The Curriculum Demonstration Project
Breakdown of All Interactions—Nature of Child's Activities

Fan = Fantasy or role play
Div = Divergent activity; child-defined goal
Work = Routine work
Rep = Kinesthetics; repetitive activity
Conv = Convergent activity; teacher-set goal

surprise. Neither during the operation of the project nor in the decade of follow-up (presently through age 15) has any one of these preschool curricula enabled the participating children to perform "better" than those in the other two programs. All program participants are doing equally well, following the pattern of performance established by the Perry Project experimental group youngsters. From these data, then, the answer to the question of whether one curriculum theory is better than another is "no." From

Curriculum Demonstration Project study it may be concluded that the curricula of high quality issuing from the broad range of possible theoretical approaches can be equally effective for children.

It is difficult to give up the notion that a particular curriculum is best or that somewhere in this wide world there is *the* correct curriculum just waiting to revolutionize education. But apparently there is none.

WHAT ARE THE ELEMENTS OF A SUCCESSFUL PRESCHOOL PROGRAM?

Yes, preschool education works. That is, it *can* work, which is a very different issue than whether or not preschool programs (and day care and family day care, etc.) *are* working. That such general programming works is not assured by the results of our studies and therein lies our major challenge. The results reported here were obtained in programs of the highest quality. If quality is so essential to success, then what is it and how is it obtained? The greatest surprise of the Curriculum Demonstration Project was that quality is *not* related to a specific curriculum.

Instead of waiting for *the* curriculum to arrive we must direct our energies to other issues that are more important than curriculum: the elements of a successful program that support the curriculum and that might be called "administration and management." We believe what made our three programs work equally well was that we insisted upon high operational standards for each. *First, we implemented a different, but theoretically consistent-curriculum in each program.* Such theoretical consistency is important, not so much for what it gives the children but for the discipline it provides for the teaching staff. Practical matters such as looking at the children's progress, orienting volunteers to work in the classroom, conducting home visits, organizing materials, working with other members of the team, being open to outside supervision, reading curriculum materials, and so on are all guided by the curriculum model. Typically, preschool programs have a broad and loosely humanist orientation at best, and usually only the intuitive interests of the teacher guide the program. A theory-based curriculum sets limits and forces decisions within those limits. It both permits certain actions and prohibits others. In the Curriculum Demonstration Project, each curriculum model forced the staff, albeit differently for each program, to focus, organize, and guide their work to provide effective programs for the participating children. Thus, to achieve high quality and aspire to the standards set by these successful preschool projects, a program must adopt a specific curriculum model.

Another major element of a successful program that we identified in looking at our administration and management systems was *the provision of consistent and ongoing supervision and inservice training to each program's staff within the specific theoretical curriculum framework.* Professionals often insulted by the term "supervision" and it is often rejected. Professionals often feel that they have received enough training and already know how to do their jobs. Yet we found that a supervisor must assist professional staff by constantly bringing key issues to the fore that might prevent a project from operating successfully. Such supervision can help the teaching staff see problems from the perspective of the theory underlying the curriculum. Additionally, the supervisor often can "translate" the theoretical generalizations to the daily practices in the classroom. Of course, no theory can be applied directly. The adaptation of theory to practice requires group discussions and the supervisor, in the role of trainer, can assist in introducing new topics and new solutions.

An important part of the supervisor's job in the Curriculum Demonstration Project, then, was to provide staff training. Programs of high quality must provide ongoing staff training to permit growth in the teachers' skills as they respond to the needs of the children. Often inservice training is offered to staff in a distant location, away from the program setting. In contrast, we found that if inservice training is provided within the program setting, with the needs of participating children as the direct challenge, dynamic curriculum growth occurs. Staff members are asked to apply theory in a practical manner to meet the needs of the children they serve.

Of course, the supervisor must also respond to the mundane needs of teachers. All types of administrative problems from inappropriate bus schedules to equipment needs often prevent effective operation of programs. In addition, the supervisor is responsible for resolving the personnel issues that teams have when working together. Questions of cooperation, dependency, work distribution, sick leave, and other absences that disrupt the classroom must be faced within the context of the curriculum and the needs of children. When these administrative elements are in place and functioning smoothly, the foundation for operating a program of the highest quality is in place.

A third necessary element for assuring quality in preschool programs concerns *fostering team teaching and planning by the staff.* A key to the success of both the Curriculum Demonstration Project and the Perry Project was people working together in a cooperative effort to help children and their families. Such cooperation was often difficult to achieve and occasionally impossible, but always an important ingredient to long-term program quality. On a very practical level, two adults are needed in the preschool, not to keep "class size" down, but to permit ongoing assistance to various children at several levels of intensity without interruption. In a team, adults can effectively teach individual children; without a team, adults become managers of groups.

A team has another important function. During the daily planning session, which must occur for the curriculum to be of service to children, the team must agree on how they are going to organize the day, solve the problems introduced by special children, and utilize materials in a reasonable fashion. The team also can read and make interpretations of the curriculum theory, identifying possible applications to practice. Discussions of when and how to introduce specific activities can also occur in this basically public forum.

This team process of cooperation and shared responsibility occurs within the context of the daily program, but the planning process must occur outside the actual program. The problem is to set aside a period of time for planning during which staff have no direct contact with children. Of all the things we found to be important in our successful programs, arranging for planning time was one of the most difficult tasks to accomplish and one of the most essential.

The fourth element for a successful preschool program is a *"catch bag" of components.* Included are involving parents in the educational process, having a stockpile of adequate supplies and equipment (this aspect can vary greatly in cost—"found" materials are just as good as purchased ones), and providing strong administrative support so that the teachers can focus on the classroom and not be stalled by system-wide problems. Finally, some system of program evaluation needs to be established. Outside adults should be included in meetings to evaluate the program. Systematic examination of student progress can be arranged not through testing and other standardized procedures, but through developmental or progress checklists systematically applied to children. The evaluation system should be simple and useful.

CAN LONGITUDINAL WORK SURVIVE CHANGES IN SOCIETY?

A fascinating component of effective longitudinal work in a social science field is its ability to survive the changing times. The Perry Project is a good example. The Perry Project operated outside the bounds of general social popularity. The project began in the early Sixties as a local attempt to solve a local problem of school failure and delinquency on the part of the disadvantaged segment of the school population. The advice I received as principal investigator from several outside consultants was not to initiate the project, because it would be harmful to children and their families. Of course, with the great social movement of the late Sixties coming to fruition with the "War on Poverty" legislation passed by Congress in 1965, preschool education suddenly became a national effort (through Head Start), and the public's attitude toward such programs shifted dramatically to favor such efforts. As things gradually tightened up during the Seventies both economically and philosophically, early education became less popular again and it has barely survived the early cuts in social programs that have been introduced by the Reagan administration. Interestingly enough, evidence of the cost-effectiveness of preschool programs of high quality has enabled them to become part of the social "safety net" formed by the conservatives. So, a program like the Perry Project began as a "suspect" activity, moved to the mainstream of one of the multitude of such efforts, and finally played a major role in legitimating preschool education through the research evidence of its cost-effective nature as a social investment.

Impossible to plan for in advance, but an accident of history finds that a carefully designed and executed project in a small midwestern city has the right data at the right time 20 years later to actually affect social policy at a national (and increasingly international) level. While I would like to claim the foresight and wisdom for achieving this success, it actually appears to be luck.

Nevertheless it is worth mentioning some of the special difficulties involved in carrying out longitudinal research. Such research receives much praise but few funds. Both government agencies and private foundations admire such efforts, but are wary of making the long-term funding commitments that such studies require. Thus, the researcher must constantly seek funds from all possible resources without any guarantee of success. In the Perry Project and our other early intervention efforts, we have found a wide range of funding sources for our work; fund-raising is a recurring process that begins again and again when we hear comments such as "Our agency policy has changed," or "We've done our share, now find others to help." The funding history of the Perry Project is a good example of the funding process just described. The following list is presented in historical sequence with the approximate length of the grant and the corresponding dollar amounts.

Perry Preschool Project Funding Sources

Basic operational funds

    1962–1967   Ypsilanti Public Schools
                    Washtenaw County Intermediate School District
                    State of Michigan Department of Special Education

Basic research

    1964–1967   Cooperative Research Grants, U.S. Office of Education ($120,000)

    1971–1974   The Spencer Foundation ($292,000)

    1975–1978   The Carnegie Corporation of New York ($322,000)

    1976–1980   Administration for Children, Youth and Families (through various channels) ($71,000)

    1981–1984   Office of Special Education, U.S. Department of Education ($480,000)

    1981–1982   National Institute of Mental Health, Center of the Prevention of Crime and Delinquency ($197,000)

The chart indicates more than three years were totally unfunded. So how did the data collection continue? "Begging, borrowing, and compromising" best describes our approach to such a dire problem. Some data collection was delayed. Staff were asked to increase their workloads. Reports were delayed until new funding sources were found. These and similar compromises were made to permit the longitudinal project to continue. We never "threw in the towel."

Of course, such tenacity depends on one or more individuals who must make an enduring commitment to the project. In our Perry and other preschool intervention projects, I have assumed this long-term commitment to become the "curator" of the projects and their data. At each phase, however, other talented individuals have been substantively involved in the intricate research process. The longitudinal work permits individuals to enter at one level of expertise, grow in experience and contribution over time, and exit at a much higher level of professional expertise. I am continually fascinated by this personal growth process. I have found over the years that it takes about three years for an individual to become involved fully and productively in the longitudinal studies. After working on the project anywhere from two years (seldom) to about seven years (frequently), staff either take on broader responsibilities within our Foundation or move on to other tasks elsewhere.

WHAT IS THE CHALLENGE OF THE 80's?

The Perry Project data demonstrate that high quality preschool education can alter the lives of children. We believe that early childhood education programs of high quality can be part of the solution of the major social problems of our times, and our data support this belief. These programs are well worth the investment, even in times of limited resources, because they are amazingly cost-effective. The challenge of the Eighties is to develop systems of early education that are consistently of the highest quality so that they can be widely disseminated and can guarantee delivery on their promise.

REFERENCES

Bereiter, C., & Engelmann, S. *Teaching disadvantaged children in preschool.* Englewood Cliffs, N.J.: Prentice Hall, 1966.
Hohmann, M., Banet, B., & Weikart, D. P. *Young Children in Action: A manual for preschool educators.* Ypsilanti, Michigan: High/Scope Press, 1979.
Hunt, J. McV. *Intelligence and experience.* New York: Ronald Press, 1961.
Kirk, S. A. *Early education of the mentally retarded.* Urbana: University of Illinois Press, 1958.

Schweinhart, L. J., & Weikart, D. P. Young Children Grow Up: The Effects of the Perry Preschool Program on youths through age 15. *Monographs of the High/Scope Educational Research Foundation,* 1980, No. 7.

Scott, J. P. Critical periods in behavioral development. *Science,* 1962, *138,* (3544).

Terman, L. M., & Merrill, M. A. *Stanford-Binet Intelligence Scale Form L-M: Manual for the third revision.* Boston: Houghton-Mifflin, 1960.

Wechsler, D. *Manual for the Wechsler Intelligence Scale for Children (revised).* New York: The Psychological Corporation, 1974.

Weikart, D. P., Bond, J. T., & McNeil, J. T. The Ypsilanti Perry Preschool Project: Preschool years and longitudinal results through fourth grade. *Monographs of the High/Scope Educational Research Foundation,* 1978, No. 3.

Weikart, D. P., Rogers, L., Adcock, C., & McClelland, D. *The Cognitively Oriented Curriculum: A framework for preschool teachers.* Urbana: University of Illinois - NAEYC, 1971.

10 Comments on Weikart's Chapter

Shirley G. Moore
Institute of Child Development
University of Minnesota

I would like to begin by applauding Weikart for his contributions to the literature on program evaluation in early childhood education. Not only was Weikart one of the first to investigate the efficacy of compensatory education for high risk young children, but his Perry Preschool Project, is, from a methodological standpoint, one of the best research studies of its kind to be published in the last 25 years.

The Perry Project is noteworthy in two important respects. First, Weikart was able to randomly assign successive cohorts of children to experimental (school) and control (non-school) groups with minor adjustments for sex of child and demographic variables. Although random assignment of subjects to conditions seems an obvious thing to do, it is extraordinarily difficult in field-based research when public relations and practical realities take precedence over the needs of the researcher. Second, the Perry Project has suffered very little attrition over the years, a state of affairs that is virtually unprecedented in program evaluation research. Attrition is a serious problem in evaluation studies because of dwindling populations over time, and suspected bias in the follow-up samples. If, for example, Head Start drop outs are biased toward children who did not adapt well to the school environment, or children whose parents care less about their school preparation and future achievement, the Head Start groups could look better after treatment and at follow-up than would otherwise be the case. Although the evidence from follow-up studies of Head Start suggests that attrition is not generally due to different reasons among the Head Start and control children, it is a potential problem that can be handled best by faithfully finding children for follow-up.

Weikart and his colleagues are to be complimented on other accounts as well. They have reported research on the Perry Project, and their models comparison work, in detail in High Scope Monographs and other places, subjecting their work to a level of peer review that is more stringent than that required for progress reports, government documents, and invited chapters. The most unique contribution Weikart has made to the field, however, is his analysis of the cost effectiveness of the Perry Project, an aspect of his research that was instrumental recently in keeping Head Start alive despite deep budget cuts in social and educational programs.

I would like now to discuss Weikart's work within the context of the larger body of research on early preschool intervention, including Head Start. I will not make a distinction between Head Start per se (i.e., those programs funded by the Office of Economic Opportunity) and other early childhood programs with similar purposes and serving similar populations of children. Over the past two decades there have been 25 or 30 major evaluation studies of the effects of educational intervention for children under six who are outside of the middleclass core culture in our society and in great danger of failing in our public schools. As we will see, Weikart's work is in reasonable accord with this literature.

Head Start evaluations have relied heavily on measures of IQ change, school readiness, and performance in the first year or two in the public schools to document program effects. Studies in this area have yielded essentially two kinds of results, either Head Start children perform better than control children on one or more of the major measures used (or better than would be expected by the passage of time) or there are no differences detected between the Head Start children and control or comparision children. Although it is difficult to know how many studies have been conducted in which no differences between groups were detected (since such studies typically are not published), the number of studies in which Head Start children outperformed their classmates appears to be well beyond chance. One would expect no more than two or three studies in 100 to show a pattern of results that would favor Head Start groups by chance alone. Furthermore, a chance distribution of results would have yielded about as many instances in which control children outperformed Head Start children, an event that is rare despite the fact that such results are publishable and were expected by some investigators in the field who felt that compensatory education would be harmful or offensive to low SES children and their families. Studies in which school and non-school children were judged to be comparable through other means than random assignment show a similar pattern of results to those in which children were randomly assigned to school and non-school conditions.

A discouraging aspect of this research, however, has been the finding, consistent with Weikart's Perry Project data, that the IQ superiority of

Head Start children does not last beyond the early grades—perhaps two or three years past the termination of their program participation—at which point these children drift back to the performance level of their companions who did not have a preschool experience. The convergence of the Head Start and non-Head Start children is due in part to a modest boost in cognitive performance shown by control children at the time they entered school at age five or six (another confirmation of school effects) and in part to the gradual decline in performance relative to norms by both Head Start and control children as they progress through the elementary grades. The drift is evident for the children who were enrolled in preacademic programs as well as for children in child-centered open classrooms (although in some studies children in the more highly structured academic programs maintain their gain somewhat longer).

In the opinion of many investigators, this pattern of results suggested that Head Start was on the right track, but that the intervention was too little and too late. Consequently, funds were made available for "Home Start", a program that extended the Head Start concept downward into the homes where parents of infants and toddlers were helped to provide an intellectually stimulating environment for their children under three. Evaluation studies of Home Start and other parent involvement programs are promising and, in the long run, may show more lasting effects than preschool center-based approaches alone. At this point, however, it is difficult to compare longevity of Home Start with that of center-based Head Start since longevity appears to be an artifact of the age at which the children are given the intervention. The superiority of Head Start children begins to fade when both Head Start and control children enter the elementary school. Home-based children, who participate in a program at age 2 or 3, may maintain their edge over control children for an extra year or two because neither group is yet in school. The question is not whether home-based children maintain their superiority for a longer absolute time, but whether they maintain it further into the elementary grades than Head Start children whose intervention came later. It is not clear, from the data, that Home Start has more persistent effects than Head Start, using this criterion, nor is it the case that home-based programs are superior to center-based programs in their immediate effects. Nevertheless, it is blatantly sensible to expect that early intervention involving the parent in the child's education would have some distinct long term advantages over later center-based intervention alone.

The most extensive longitudinal study of Head Start and Home Start to date was reported by a consortium of 12 investigators, of which Weikart is one, who submitted their project data for meta-analysis under the direction of Lazar and Darlington (1978) of Cornell University. All of these investigators had conducted and evaluated home-based and/or center-based programs for toddlers or preschoolers during the 1960s. Follow-up data on their project and control children were obtained in 1976–77 when their children ranged in age from 9 to 19.

The IQ measures for these children confirmed previous Head Start research in that differences that had favored the project children directly following intervention diminished year by year until by third or fourth grade there were few IQ differences of any consequence. The data were more encouraging for school performance, however. The consortium study indicates that project children were less likely than control children to be placed in special education classrooms as they proceeded through school. This finding was robust for a number of the individual projects as well as for the combined data. Also the school children were less likely to be retained in grade, an effect that was somewhat inconsistent for individual projects but reliable when data were combined across samples. Although achievement data are difficult to compare due to the multiplicity of measures and standards across schools and classrooms, the general thrust of these measures suggests that project children performed better than control children in mathematics and, to a lesser extent, on verbal tasks.

Weikart's own work now extends follow-up beyond the school milieu, indicating that Head Start children may adapt better to the demands of society as well as to the demands of the school. Further confirmation of these findings are needed, however; out-of-school follow-up data would be especially helpful from projects in which the school and non-school children were well matched at the beginning of the project, and in which attrition is unbiased.

It would appear that early childhood programs set in motion factors that generate adaptive behavior in at least some high risk children, and perhaps in their parents and teachers as well. This, in turn, leads to better management of the school environment by the children over time. How, specifically, this comes about is not clear. It has been suggested that Head Start findings can properly be interpreted as a Hawthorne effect and that providing helpful child care to mothers and friendly, supportive attention to children, with no specific program of school preparedness, would work just as well. Ironically, the fact that there were many failures to demonstrate the advantages of Head Start provides a partial answer to this interpretation. Apparently some classrooms were not providing experiences that were noticeably effective despite the commitment and fanfare that surrounded the opening of Head Start centers in most communities.

It has also been suggested that Head Start children were the beneficiaries of biased treatment by their teachers who, knowing that they had a preschool experience, expected more of them and treated them differently than non-Head Start children. This is a distinct possibility during the earliest school years. However, it seems an unlikely explanation for differences that become evident in the middle and upper grades of the elementary school since, by that time, Head Start children are distributed widely across many different schools and classrooms and would not be readily identified by their teachers.

Unfortunately, we have not learned as much as we could have, from Weikart's work and other studies, about the characteristics of programs that are, and are not, successful in helping high risk children in school. One reason for this is that our evaluation strategies have emphasized summative outcome measures at the expense of classroom observations and measures of educational process. It is clear from the observations that have been done, however, that models differ widely in program goals, curriculum, and style of teacher-child interaction, and that very different styles of education have had both successes and failures in one setting or another. As the models comparison work of Weikart and others suggests, no particular early childhood model has a corner on the market.

It would appear that to identify the significant characteristics of early childhood progams that work, we will need to look at aspects of programs that cut across styles of education and models rather than at those characteristics that distinguish models from each other. Weikart identified a number of promising variables—administrative know how, staff supervision and in-service training, daily planning, and teacher involvement in model development. I would like to add another variable to the list, teacher sensitivity. We have heard from our symposium presenters about the importance of sensitivity in mothers—the ability of mothers to respond appropriately to the cues given them by their babies and young children. School folklore suggests that a similar factor is an important predictor of teacher success. The role of the teacher varies from model to model but, whatever the model, teachers must operate on the basis of cues from the children themselves to determine whether a particular child feels secure in the school setting, understands what is being taught and what is expected of him or her, and is sufficiently motivated to participate fully in the school program. Teacher behaviors that promote these characteristics in children (thus assuring that each child *has* the treatment) are elusive and difficult to define. The current proliferation of observations of mothers and their children suggests using molar, qualitative constructs that tap dyadic interaction rather than relying on frequency counts of discrete, independent teacher behaviors.

In discussing the factors that distinguish successful from unsuccessful programs, Weikart addressed the importance of having a well conceived theoretical basis for program development. I agree. A theoretical orientation helps to give continuity to educational goals, and guidance in determining classroom practice. The rebirth of Piaget in the 1960s was a godsend to American early childhood educators because so much of what Piaget had to say about child development was relevant to the child's acquisition of physical and social knowledge during the early years, outside of the context of formal instruction. The Perry Preschool Project, under Weikart's leadership, was Piagetian in its theoretical orientation.

I would like to comment, however, on some of the pitfalls in relying as exclusively as we have in the past on psychological theories as a basis for educational philosophy and practice, and, in the process, make a pitch for equal attention to the empirical research in child development as a guide to model development and improvement. Educators tend to grasp at psychological theories like a drowning person grasps at a lifeline, espousing them prematurely and with a confidence that often is not fully justified. Piaget's notions of cognitive development were incorporated into practice by early childhood educators in the 1960s, well before aspects of the theory had been exposed to empirical verification by research scholars in this country. Although Piaget's own research led to some ingenious insights about cognitive development, his work did not provide a strong empirical base upon which to build an educational program. Twenty years of empirical research has helped to verify and refine his theory. As might be expected, some aspects of Piaget's theory have stood the test of time very well, but others have not—or have been extensively qualified. We now, for example, have a more elaborated conception of *stages* in cognitive development and of the factors that affect a child's ability to display mastery of a particular phenomenon (such as experience with the phenomenon and method of assessment). We also judge the young child to be less egocentric than Piaget did and better able to take the perspective of others, depending on how these behaviors are elicited from the child. As a result of this work, many psychologists studying cognitive development view the young child as more competent than Piaget seemed to believe, and although Piaget emphasized the importance of experience, other investigators place more emphasis on the quality of that experience than Piaget did. Educators who are pure Piagetian typically have not appreciated the advances in our understanding of children's cognitive development that have come about from the work of other psychologists. Nor are the purists likely to be aware of the contributions of investigators from other theoretical orientations who have emphasized the role of adults as mediators of cognitively enriching experiences, especially language experiences, to a far greater extent than did Piaget.

Theories of development serve several purposes for the psychologist only one of which is to synthesize and "make sense" of what is already known about behavior. Theories also guide speculation about that which we do not yet know with any degree of confidence. They lead to testable hypotheses which, in turn, either confirm or challenge parts of the theory. Psychological theories are themselves developmental, evolving over time and self-destructing in favor of more sophisticated formulations. Educators who espouse a theory should allow their practices to evolve and change with the theory, moving on to more enlightened versions of the theory—or even better theories—as more is known. Instead there is a tendency to ignore, deny, or discredit data that challenge one's theoretical orientation, leading to stagnant, unresponsive, and outdated educational practice. In the 1940s and 1950s, many early childhood educators espoused Freud's theory of psychosexual development and the role of the id, ego, and superego in personality development. As it turned out, Freud's theory did not fare well in the laboratory, nor did it lead to popular classroom decisions in the view of many teachers and parents. The theory gradually yielded to neoanalytic formulations that emphasized ego development, functional adaptations to social reality, and principles of social learning. These spinoffs have stood the test of empirical verification quite well and have provided a sound basis for educational practice. There were, however, many early childhood educators who held tenaciously to the tenets of psychoanalytic theory as postulated by Freud, translating them into practice despite evidence of their questionable validity in understanding normal young children.

As Weikart suggests, a well articulate theory of development is essential to provide an organizing framework for our knowledge of child development. But proponents of theories have an obligation to be among the most astute and informed critics of their own positions concerning children's development. Advances in research in cognition, language, social, emotional, and biological development in the past 15 or 20 years have increased our knowledge of developmental norms and our understanding of factors that affect the course of development and that govern behavioral change. Many of these advances have important implications for practice and should become a part of the working knowledge of the practitioner. In addition to data-based contributions to our knowledge, research scholars raise interesting questions about child behavior and propose new ways of conceptualizing and understanding behavior that are thought-provoking and challenging to the classroom teacher. It is this creative mix of theory and research that will give us our best shot at constructing good educational environments for high risk young children.

When all is said and done, should we invest in early childhood intervention programs? The data Weikart presents are supportive of this decision, but the evidence overall is inconsistent and frought with methodological problems. As a matter of public policy, we need to give serious consideration to the kind of error we are most willing to risk in interpreting early intervention research. We can conclude that early education is effective for high risk children, at least in many of its manifestations—and be wrong, or we can discount such programs as ineffective—and be wrong. The decision is as much one of values as of scientific integrity and judgment.

In the first instance, if we are wrong we will have squandered some precious resources for an educational program that is popular and attractive to communities and participants, but that has no long range consequences. In the second instance, if we are wrong, we will have given up a chance to intervene on behalf of children who need a special kind of help. Also we probably will have lost the opportunity to improve the performance of Head Start and Home Start since the further study of quality in programs will depend on the availability of programs to study.

It has been suggested by some scholars that an investment of our resources at the elementary level (in Follow Through and similar programs) would pay off even more, dollar for dollar, than an investment in early education. That is possible, especially given the general phenomenon that control children catch up to Head Start children when they enter school on at least some kinds of measures (although apparently not on others). This option becomes questionable, however, when one considers that low SES children from outside of the core culture in our society are beginning to diverge from their age mates in language development, general knowledge, and cognitive functioning by two and one-half or three years of age. By five, the differences are marked and of distinct educational significance.

The extent to which this pattern of development is due to differences in experience is not known at this time, but we have reason to suspect that early experience is a critical factor. Miller and Dyer's description of the everyday learning activities of children from which their school and non-school subjects were drawn for a Head Start models comparison study, gives an indication of the disparity in life style of middle class and low SES children in our society. They say, "Almost none of these children had been in a lake, river, or ocean, although about half had been in a swimming pool. From 80% to 90% of them had never visited a zoo, library, museum, farm, or airport, or been in a boat, train, or plane. Less than half had ever been on a bus trip, and only slightly more (56%) had been out of town in a car. Only 42% had had a birthday party, although about 60% had been to one and had had a birthday cake. Fewer than half had had a pet" (Miller & Dyer, 1975, p. 15).

There is little doubt that Miller and Dyer's children will enter school at a disadvantage without intervention and that early education programs can offer these children, and others like them, interesting, school-relevant experiences and the motivation to value and share what they are learning with a teacher and classmates. One would find it difficult to postulate a critical period for the kinds of experiences they lack, but on the other hand, there is little precedent in either education or child development for waiting until experiential deficits get to an optimal stage before doing something about them. The best guess is that the longer we wait, the more compounded the deficits will become and the more difficult catching up will be. It will appear to many that the more serious error we could make as a society would be to discount early intervention if such programs stand a chance of contributing significantly to the prevention of school failure in high risk young children. If Head Start and Home Start ultimately are determined to be cost effective, this error would be a particularly unfortunate one to have made.

The efficacy of early childhood education as a buffer against later school failure will be debated for some time to come. Different weightings of social values and scientific judgment will lead to different conclusions regarding the same evidence. The conclusion that early childhood programs contribute to the solutions of some of our more pressing social and economic problems, such as delinquency and chronic welfare, will almost certainly be challenged by skeptics. Weikart undoubtedly will be criticized for his hard sell attempts to convince business executives, politicians, educators, psychologists, and laymen, in this country and abroad, to fund high quality intervention programs for young children and their families for social and economic reasons as well as for educational and humanitarian reasons. It is to his credit, however, that he is willing to blend the role of scientist and social reformer in order to pursue a course of action in which he firmly believes.

REFERENCES

Lazar, I., & Darlington, R. B. *Lasting effects after preschool. A report of the Consortium for Longitudinal Studies.* Ithaca, N.Y.: New York State College of Human Ecology, Cornell University, 1978.

Miller, L. B., & Dyer, J. L. Four preschool programs: Their dimensions and effects. *Monographs of the Society for Research in Child Development*, 1975, *40*, (5-6, Serial No. 162).

11 Intervention to Protect Abused and Neglected Children

Michael Wald
Merrill Carlsmith
P. Herbert Leiderman
Carole Smith
Stanford University

INTRODUCTION

In the past twenty years concern over children who have been physically or sexually abused by their parents or who have suffered from gross parental neglect has increased enormously. In 1960, under ten thousand children were reported as abused or neglected (Gil, 1970). In 1978, social welfare and police agencies received nearly a million abuse or neglect reports (American Humane Association, 1979). State legislatures are constantly passing new laws seeking to improve government response to the problem (Antler, 1978).

During this time an ever-increasing amount of research related to abuse and neglect has been undertaken. At first, virtually all of the research focused on the parents who physically abused their children, as researchers attempted to explain why parents abuse children. The early studies primarily described the characteristics of known abusers (Steele & Pollock, 1968). Later research has compared abusive and non-abusive parents (Burgess & Conger, 1978; Egeland & Brunnquell, 1979). Some researchers also have tried to develop instruments that would enable prediction of abuse based on parental characteristics (Disbrow, Doerr, & Caulfield, 1977; Gray et al., 1978). While this body of research has not given any definitive answers about the causes of abuse, it has provided a better picture of those factors that predispose a parent to abuse a child (Kadushin, 1981; Parke & Collmer, 1975). Similar research recently has been undertaken focusing on parental neglect, although the lack of any common definition of neglect has limited the utility of such research (Polansky, 1981).

In recent years there also has been a significant increase in research focusing on the impact of abuse or neglect on children. While the data are still sparse, especially with regard to neglect, it seems clear that both abuse and neglect can have lasting consequences on the children (Elmer, 1977; Martin, 1976; Polansky, 1981). From such research we have learned that at least some abused and neglected children suffer severe emotional problems, language delays, difficulties in peer relations, as well as substantial physical problems. More recent studies have also shown some of the dynamics of abusing and neglecting families which may affect the child's future emotional development (Burgess & Conger, 1978).

There also have been a small number of studies examining the effectiveness of various types of intervention programs designed to prevent reabuse or continued neglect (Berkeley Planning Associates, 1977; Green, or how to keep parents from neglecting their children (Kadushin, 1981).

The research done to date, especially the more sophisticated and methodologically careful research undertaken in the past few years, will neglect. (Kempe & Kempe, 1978). However, most such studies have significant methodological weaknesses, including limited sample size, lack of baseline data and poor outcome measures (Zigler, 1980). Thus, we still know very little about how to prevent abuse from occurring or reoccurring or how to keep parents from neglecting their children. (Kadushin, 1981).

The research done to date, especially the more sophisticated and methodologically careful rsearch undertaken in the past few years, will help improve societal response to the problem. The research is particularly useful to agencies providing services to parents and children, since it provides a better idea of the dynamics leading to abuse or neglect and the programs that may help prevent reabuse or continued neglect. However, the research is of considerably less utility in answering the questions about public response to child abuse and neglect that must be addressed by the legal system, that is, by legislatures developing laws, and courts, police, and social agencies applying these laws.

From a legal perspective, four interrelated issues are central:

1. What situations justify intervention, against a parent's will, by state agencies in order to protect children?
2. What type of intervention is most appropriate when a child has been abused or neglected?
3. If children must be removed from their parents when, if ever, should they be returned?
4. What factors justify permanently terminating parental rights in order to prevent all further parental contact and to permit adoption of the child?

The first of these questions requires developing a definition of abuse and neglect that informs courts and public agencies of the instances in which coercive intervention may occur. The remaining questions deal with the types of responses which should be authorized and the situations in which particular responses are most appropriate.

There is virtually no research addressing these issues (Wald, 1976). Moreover, there is a substantial debate among child development professionals, as well as people from other disciplines, regarding the best policies with regard to each of these questions. On the one hand there are "interventionists" who believe that children are being severely damaged in a large number of homes and that without intervention to protect children from physical injury and emotional neglect, we are consigning a number of children to a bleak future (Polansky, 1981; Garbarino, 1977). Advocates of more intervention assume the beneficence and utility of state programs. They, therefore, seek to broaden the legal definition of abuse and neglect, to develop ways to identify problem families earlier and, ultimately, to establish systems for monitoring the care-giving of all families (Kempe, 1978).

However, other child development experts believe that any form of coercive state intervention, that is, intervention against the parents' will, is potentially detrimental to children and therefore that intervention is only justified to protect children from very serious physical harm or sexual abuse (Mnookin, 1973). The strongest opponents of intervention are psychoanalysts Anna Freud, Joseph Goldstein, and Albert Solnit. They have recently written that an adequate psychological relationship between a child and a parent can only be maintained in "the privacy of family life under guardianship by parents who are autonomous.... When family integrity is broken or weakened by state intrusion, [the child's] needs are thwarted and his belief that his parents are omniscient and all-powerful is shaken prematurely. The effect on the child's developmental progress is invariably detrimental" (Goldstein, Freud, & Solnit, 1979). Therefore, they assert, the family should be free from "state intrusion" in all but the most severe situations of abuse or physical neglect in order to safeguard the integrity of family ties crucial to the child's development.

As discussed more fully below, there is also substantial disagreement over what policies should be pursued once it is decided that a child is sufficiently endangered to justify some form of intervention.

It is not our purpose in this paper to try to resolve these issues. Instead, we want to explore the problems involved in developing research that will help policy-makers design good policy. The questions that need to be answered are relatively clear. In determining when and how to intervene we need to be able to:

1. Define the consequences in terms of a child's development that are likely to occur as a result of a given form or degree of abuse or neglect.

2. Determine what would be the consequences for the child of alternative interventions to protect the child, including the possiblity of no intervention at all.

For the last five years we have been designing and conducting a longitudinal study looking at the second of these questions, what type of intervention is appropriate if a child has been abused or neglected. The remainder of this paper examines the problem involved in developing research relating to this issue and describes our study.

WHAT TYPE OF INTERVENTION SHOULD OCCUR?

The Options

When intervention occurs to protect a child from abuse or neglect, (however defined), there are two basic options available to courts or other decision-makers: the child can be left with the natural parents and protected through monitoring the family and provision of services designed to mitigate the chances of reabuse or continued neglect or the child can be removed from the home and placed with relatives, in a family foster home, or in some type of residential group care. The removal can be permanent, designed to have the child remain permanently with new caretakers, or it can be temporary, with the goal being to return the child to the natural parent once it is determined that this can be done with only a minimal likelihood of reabuse (Wald, 1976).

In the 1960's, the main response of courts was to remove abused or neglected children and place them in foster homes (Mnookin, 1973). In recent years, a number of different treatment modalities have been tried in an effort to keep children with their parents. These include individual and group therapy, day care, crisis nurseries, and use of professional and lay home visitiors. Foster care has begun to be seen as a last resort. The shift in emphasis from foster care to keeping children at home has been based both on value judgments and clinical evidence about harmful effects from foster care. Yet there are almost no data that justify preferring one option over the other (Hubbell, 1981; Wald, 1976).

Factors Relevant to the Placement Decision

There are many factors which might be considered in deciding when it is best to remove a child. Obviously, a major consideration is the likelihood of the child being reabused or neglected if left at home and the impact on the child of such continued abuse or neglect. In this regard, however, it must be recognized that under current law and practice the terms abuse and neglect cover a broad range of actual or potential injuries to a child (Wald, 1975).

Physical abuse ranges from extreme brutality leading to severe injuries to cases of overdiscipline resulting in bruises on arms, legs, or other parts of the body, injuries which are unlikely to be permanent or lead to physical impairment. Neglect is even less well-defined. It ranges from inattention which leads to physical injury, for example, inadequate supervision of young children, to concerns over the social and emotional development of the child, caused by inadequate parental care, supervision, or lack of involvement with the child.

At least in one respect foster care would seem to have a clear-cut advantage over home placement. Removing the child is the least risky way of protecting the child from further physical abuse or neglect. Although some children are, in fact, injured by foster parents (Bolton, Laner, & Gai, 1981), the incident rate of reported abuse by foster parents is far lower than that of the general population (Gil, 1970). Moreover, a number of studies have found that reabuse by natural parents is fairly prevalent, even in situations where these parents have been in treatment programs (Cohn, 1979; Herrenkohl, 1980). Unfortunately, the existing research is not very helpful in identifying those parents most likely to reabuse or the programs most likely to minimize reabuse.

Depending on the definition of neglect, it is also likely that foster parents are less likely to be neglectful than natural parents, even if the natural parents are given good quality services. For the most part, foster parents do not leave children unattended; they virtually always provide adequate food or shelter; they send foster children to school; their households tend to be stable and their care regular. Thus, if the major goal is to protect the child from *physical* neglect, foster care may be a preferable alternative.

Unfortunately, from a policy perspective, the calculus is more complicated. While foster care can protect the physical needs of children, there are significant questions about its impact on a child's emotional development. If placement does have significant negative impact on the emotional or social development of children a policy designed only to avoid the risk of further abuse or neglect may be unwise, especially given the wide range of situations where intervention occurs.

Concern with placement has its roots in the theoretical work of child analysts like John Bowlby, who assert that separation from parents may have an extremely negative impact on children, even children from "bad" homes (Bowlby, 1965). From the research on attachment behavior, it seems clear that most children, even abused or neglected children, are attached to their parents (Egeland, Byron, & Sroufe, 1981). Interference with parental ties is extremely painful to children, at least in the short-run, and may have long-term consequences (Rutter, 1976). In addition, given the supposed temporary nature of foster care, it may be that foster parents are unwilling to make the type of emotional commitment to children which some experts in child development believe is essential for adequate development (Goldstein, Freud, & Solnit, 1973).

There is clinical evidence that some children view foster home placement as a punishment for something they did wrong (Littner, 1956). Moreover, children in foster care often must relate to three "caregivers" (natural parents, foster parents, social worker), all of whom have some stake in caring for them. Each of these adults may compete for power and responsibility. As a result, children placed in foster homes may experience identity problems, conflicts of loyalty, and anxiety about their future (Weinstein, 1960; Mandell, 1973).

Perhaps the greatest concern over foster care stems from the fact that such care is often quite unstable. Children who remain in foster care for longer than six months frequently are subjected to multiple placements (Fanshel & Shinn, 1978; Gruber, 1978). Multiple placements destroy the continuity and stability that children may need for adequate development.

Thus, there is reason to be concerned with the academic, social, and emotional development of children after they are placed in foster care. If placement leads to substantial deterioration in these areas, it may be better to run the risk of further physical abuse or neglect by the parents, at least in situations where the abuse or neglect is not life threatening or likely to lead to permanent impairment.

However, the evidence is by no means one-sided. Several studies of children who grew up in a foster home found no evidence of greater criminality, mental illness, or marital failure than the general population (Meier, 1966; Yarrow, 1964). Other studies have found that children in foster care do not have especially low self-esteem or poor self-concept or other problems often attributed to foster care (Lemmon, 1975; Seligman, 1979).

Moreover, there are two recent studies which indicate that the impact of foster care may be positive for at least some children. One study, conducted by Dr. James Kent, at Children's Hospital in Los Angeles, reviewed case records of over 500 neglected and abused children who were under court supervision in Los Angeles in January, 1972 (Kent, 1976). The cases were chosen so as to have an equal proportion of physically abused, sexually abused, and "grossly" neglected children. Using information found in the case records (a significant methodological problem), Kent found that a substantial number of children who had been in foster care at least a year were rated by their social workers as being better off—in terms of physical measures and social adjustment—*than at the time they entered foster care.*

A recent longitudinal study by David Fanshel and his colleagues as Columbia provides considerably more evidence in this regard (Fanshel & Shinn, 1978). Fanshel studied over 500 children placed in foster care in New York City in 1966. Each child's development was followed for five years.

Although their findings are complex, and difficult to draw any generalizations from, careful analysis of their data indicates that the well-being of many children improved in terms of physical development, IQ, and school performance upon entering foster care and that this improvement was maintained over a substantial period of time. Moreover, the fact that a child experienced multiple placements did not seem to have a negative impact on the child, at least with regard to the variables being measured.

In addition to the positive evidence about foster care there is also evidence indicating that abused and neglected children often suffer developmental problems beyond just physical injuries. As noted before, abused children are reported to have a number of emotional problems associated with the abuse, including very poor self-esteem' severe depression or other psychopathological symptoms; extreme behavior problems including firesetting, self-destructive behavior, abuse of animals, poor peer relations, and poor language development. Moreover, many abused children become abusing parents (Parke & Collmer, 1979). Removal may be necessary to stop this cycle. Neglected children are also reported to have a variety of problems beyond just poor physical health (Polansky, et al., 1974; Lagerberg et al., 1979). Recent studies also indicate that although abused and neglected children are "attached" to their parents, the quality of the attachment may be poor and disruption may not have a negative impact (Egeland & Sroufe, 1981; George & Main, 1979). While the research results are by no means uniform, they are at least as consistent as those describing problems among foster children.

Limitations in Exisiting Data

Unfortunately, the existing research has only limited value for policy purposes. With regard to the research on foster care, only Fanshel's study had adequate baseline data about the condition of the children when they first entered foster care. Most studies have no baseline data at all; those that do, derive the data from casework records, rather than from direct observation and testing of the children. These records have been shown to be highly unreliable (Borgatta & Cautley, 1966). Thus, it cannot be determined how the child's condition changed while in foster care. Moreover, none of the studies tell us how these children would have fared had they been left in their own homes. No study has compared foster children with "similar" children who remained at home. Similarly, very few studies report on the seriousness of the reabuse and the consequences for children left in their own homes. Again, we cannot know how these children would have fared had they been placed in foster care.

In addition, there are almost no data specifying which factors, such as the child's age, the nature of the abuse or neglect, the quality or stability of the foster placement, are useful in deciding the question of *under what circumstances* is foster care better or worse for an abused or neglected child.

Thus, the existing research does not permit us to determine which children do best in what type of placement or even the direction in which the law should lean. It appears that some children do well and some children do poorly in each setting. We do not know whether the ones who do well (or the ones who do poorly) are the overwhelming majority (or minority).

DEVELOPING RESEARCH TO GUIDE COURTS AND LEGISLATURES

The Nature of Legal Decisions

The types of decisions that must be made by courts and legislatures are quite different. Because legislatures have to make less specific decisions, it is likely that research will be more helpful at the legislative than the judicial level.

Legislation is written in general terms. In the area of abuse or neglect the task of the legislature is to determine whether intervention for a given type of harm, that is, physical abuse, sexual abuse, or severe emotional damage, is likely to be helpful more often than harmful (Wald, 1975). If so, the legislation can include such a harm in a general definition of abuse and neglect, thus enabling courts to make case by case decisions on whether to intervene in a given situation.

Similarly, with regard to home versus foster care the legislature has two questions to decide: (1) are there any situations in which removal should be required, and (2) if removal is not mandated should the law favor, *in general,* home or foster care. In the legal system decision-makers never approach a decision neutrally. Rather, the law establishes burdens of proof which dictate who has to provide the more persuasive case. With regard to the placement question, laws can be drafted that make it more or less difficult to remove a child from the natural parents by creating a presumption in favor of one option or the other. A presumption often is determinative in areas where there is little evidence to otherwise guide decision-makers.

Thus, to aid legislative decisions, research findings at least would have to indicate whether, *on average,* abused or neglected children do better in one setting or the other. Even more helpful would be findings that showed the average impact of alternative placements on certain categories of children—abused versus neglected, older versus younger, children from single parent homes versus two parent homes. Using such findings, presumptions could be created favoring different options for different classes of children (or homes).

Decision-making is far more difficult at the court and agency level. Virtually all legislation provides only general guidelines. In each individual case a judge or social worker must determine for the specific child the costs and benefits of each option. Presumably, this enables the decision-maker to take into account the full variety of factors, such as the extent of the harm, the attitude of the parents and child, the availability of resources that might be relevant to predicting the likely impact of alternative decisions. While in some instances the correct alternative may seem obvious, in many cases the predictions are extremely difficult to make. To help in these cases, decision-makers need information relevant to the particular combinations of characteristics of parents and children that may determine the likely impact of home versus foster care.

What is Researchable?

Although the ultimate legal standard entails value judgments, not just factual issues (Aber, 1980), it clearly would be valuable to have data that could help legislatures draft statutes and courts decide individual cases. However, as in many areas of social policy towards children, it is easier to determine what type of information is needed than it is to develop ways to obtain the data. There are a number of methodological problems that make it very difficult to do adequate research that would improve decision-making at either level.

Studying ideals versus the real world. It must first be recognized that it may not be possible to study certain options, which from a theoretical perspective, might be the most desirable options. For example, from a theoretical perspective, many of the problems associated with foster care, especially for very young children, stem from the instability of foster placements and the potential lack of strong emotional commitments developing between the foster parents and the child (or the breaking of such bonds when they do develop.) Therefore, an ideal study would include children left at home versus children who remain in a single, long-term placement or cases where the natural parents' rights to custody are permanently severed upon removal of the child and the child is adopted by another family. However, such cases are relatively rare, and involve unusual circumstances. As a practical matter, it would be extremely difficult to do an adequate study examining this option. Thus, we can only study "second best" options.

Even studies of existing options may have limited utility for judges and social workers. As discussed below, valid research on the placement issue requires comparing children left at home with comparable children in foster care. However, it is very difficult to get comparable groups. Judges are willing to leave children at home only when there are special treatment programs for the parents. Thus a study could compare the development of children left at home with "ideal" or very good treatment programs with comparable children in foster care. While such studies would shed light on the utility and desirability of such programs, which would be useful to legislatures deciding whether to fund such programs, the evidence from such studies does not tell a judge or a social worker what to do in places where such programs are not available.

Getting comparable samples. To provide policy relevant data, a researcher must compare the development of children left in their own home with a group of *comparable* children placed in foster care. If the two populations differed substantially at the time of the placement decision, in ways that might be systematically related to the impact of the actual placement on the child, inferences about what might have happened to either group of children had the opposite decision been made are tenuous and filled with ambiguity. One could describe the changes which take place and this would be a nontrivial advance over our current state of information. But, in the presence of large differences between the children or the home environments prior to a placement decision, one cannot draw conclusions about the effects of that decision.

This criterion is very hard to meet. It is not possible—for ethical and practical reasons—to get courts to assign children randomly to home and foster placement. Despite the ambiguity of existing data on both home and foster care, virtually all judges believe that they are obligated to make the best possible decision for each child based on whatever clinical factors are developed. It would clearly be impermissible to first identify children who could be left at home and then remove half. Such a policy would violate the parents' rights. A program which identified all children where the court ordered removal and left some at home may be ethically more acceptable, since foster care may be harmful, but most judges would not allow the additional risk to children.

Conceivably, these decisions are already being made in what amounts to a random process, for example, upon inspection it would turn out that there are no significant differences between *at least some of the children* placed and some of those left at home. This could be due to the difference in perspective among the various social workers who make recommendations to courts, reflecting different levels of tolerance for the risks involved in one choice or the other. While there is some evidence indicating that different judges and social workers do use different criteria for deciding whether to place a child (Phillips, Shyne, Sherman, & Haring, 1971), it is likely that, in any given jurisdiction, there will be significant differences between the children left at home and those placed in foster care. Since most courts and agencies adhere to the view that placement would be used only as a last resort, presumably either the family situation, the nature of the abuse and/or the development of the child will be worse for those children who are placed in foster care.

The most likely way to get "comparable" samples is by studying children from more than one jurisdiction (different counties or cities). It is possible that due to differences in resources, community or judicial attitudes, placement practices will vary significantly between jurisdictions. Researchers could then focus on that group of children who, although apparently similar, were treated differently.

The need for a longitudinal design. In order to compare the outcome of each alternative, it is essential to follow the children for a long enough period of time to take into account changes that are likely to take place as the child remains in foster care longer. It is clear that many children suffer short-term setbacks as a result of placement, in areas such as bowel control, sleeping, and eating (Littner, 1956; Robertson & Robertson, 1971). In other respects children may initially show improved behavior, what is sometimes called the "honeymoon" effect of placement, and then evidence deterioration as the placment continues.

Problems from foster care may set in at later points, depending on the age of the child. For example, confusion about identity might be related to a growing attachment to the foster parents or to decreased contact with the natural parent. Most significantly, the impact of multiple placements cannot be determined until the child has been in care long enough to experience multiple placements.

However, while it seems clear that any studies should be longitudinal, how long is long enough? Should the fact that the majority of children seem to be "doing better" in one or the other setting after six or twelve months be determinative of legal policy? Or is it necessary to follow the children for longer, even to adulthood? There are many reasons to believe that longer is better. It is unrealistic to expect most positive aspects of foster care to appear overnight. Many children will evidence the negative impact of separation for a lengthy period of time. Changes in school performance or lessening of emotional problems cannot be expected rapidly, especially if the problems are severe.

Time may also be needed to identify the negative consequences of either home or foster placement. Parents may reabuse children after services are withdrawn. Foster care becomes more unstable the long the child remains in care (Fanshel & Shin, 1978). Moreover, some theories maintain that the consequences of broken attachments will show up in adolescence, through increased delinquency, and in adulthood, as evidenced by an inability to establish adequate emotional relationships (Rutter, 1972). Thus, even relatively lengthy studies may only provide partial data.

Choosing suitable measures. If the only goal of intervention was to reduce the likelihood of reabuse, or continued physical neglect, choosing measures would be fairly simple. However, the concern over foster care focuses on the potential negative impact on the child's emotional and social development. The issue is whether any such effects outweigh the increased physical well-being. Therefore, one must decide the areas of emotional and social development that can and should be studied.

Choosing measures involves several important judgments. First, it must be decided what sorts of measures are likely to be relevant to policy-makers. Will judges or legislators be less likely to support foster care if children in care exhibit lower self-esteem? More bedwetting? Will they be willing to favor removal because children in foster care show greater social competence or increased IQ scores? Of course, for any possible social or emotional measure issues of magnitude are of great importance, but it may well be that certain aspects of development which are of interest to child development scholars may not seem important to policy-makers.

In addition, there may be measures which are of questionable relevance for policy purposes because the deficits being measured have few, if any, long-term consequences. For example, it may be that children placed in foster care evidence lower (or higher) self-esteem or that abused children left at home experience delays in gross motor development. However, it is far from clear what implications higher or lower self-esteem or delayed gross motor development has on the child's long-term well being. This is not to say that studies should not look at these or any other variables. The critical question is what types of measures are of sufficient importance to justify using as a basis for as critical a decision as home versus foster care.

Obtaining adequate sample sizes. Even if we can develop adequate dependent variables, researchers still face the problem of dealing with the large number of independent variables which might account for differences in outcome in the two groups. The problem is not severe with regard to the basic legislative question of whether the law should favor home placement or foster care. If it turns out that there are clear-cut differences on the most important dependent variables between the two groups, the legislature will have information directly relevant to the policy decision.

However, judges must decide which option is better for a specific child. Even at the legislative level it would be useful to know whether the overall findings hold true for various subpopulations. Obviously, better policy could be developed if we understood the conditions under which home or foster care were preferable, not just that *on average* one alternative seemed preferable.

Child development research and theory directs us to a large number of potentially critical independent variables. We obviously would want to look at the age, sex, and ethnicity of the child. Characteristics of both natural parents and foster parents must be important. Was the child placed in a single long-term placement, or in a series of different foster homes? What was the quality of the parent-child relationship at the time of intervention? The list is long.

THE "BAY AREA" STUDY

If we are correct in the previous analysis, an adequate policy-oriented study would require a longitudinal follow-up of a sizable number of abused and neglected children in both home and foster care where there is reason to believe that the children, and the situations leading to intervention, were comparable at the time of the initial decision. For the past five years we have been designing and conducting a study to meet these requirements.

The study, which began data collection in January, 1978, is comparing the development of 40 abused or neglected children left in their own homes with 30 children placed in foster care. The children are being followed for two years after the initial intervention. In addition, we are gathering data on 81 children who have never been found to be abused or neglected, who go to schools in the geographic areas from which our abuse or neglect cases are reported* Since we are still in the process of following our subjects, we do not have data on the ultimate questions. This section discusses the research design and some preliminary findings.

Finding Comparable Children

For policy purposes, the home and out of home samples must be comparable in at least three respects. First, the seriousness of the incidents leading to intervention must be comparable. In general courts tend to use removal in cases of more serious injuries. It is likely that the seriousness of the abuse or neglect is related to other factors we want to assess. For example, if seriousness is related to the likelihood of reinjury then we could not tell how the more seriously injured children would fare if left with their parents. Second, the home conditions and parental characteristics of the two groups must be comparable. Again, it can generally be expected that courts will remove children from more disorganized, less cooperative parents. If the home families were more responsive and amenable to services, or less likely to continue abusing or neglecting their children, findings about how children do when left with such parents would not tell us how the children

---

*Actually, two cases in this sample, which was designed to be comparable to our experimental sample, have subsequently been reported to the social work agencies as abused or neglected.

would do in more disorganized homes. Finally, the initial characteristics of the children must be comparable. If, for example, the out-of home group evidenced severe emotional problems which were only marginally helped by foster care, one could not tell whether the situation would have been better or even worse had the children been left at home without comparable children in the home group. Meeting this criterion is especially difficult methodologically since the focus of most intervention is either *injury* to a child or *parental* characteristics (e.g. the parent is a drug addict or leaves the child unattended). Typically, little information is gathered about the condition or characteristics of the children.

Insuring comparability in each of these realms raised a number of problems. With regard to the first variable, seriousness of injury or situation, we were fortunate in being able to conduct our research utilizing a "natural" experimental group. In 1977, the California legislature adopted new legislation regarding abused and neglected children (California Family Protection Act, 1977). In order to test the assumption that such children are better off if they can be kept out of foster care, the legislation created an experimental project in two counties, designed to minimize the need for removal. Specifically, the legislation changed the legal grounds for removal, limiting removal in these two counties to only the most serious cases of physical abuse or instances where the child was evidencing significant emotional problems. At the same time, it provided the experimental counties with a substantial amount of money to be used for services, such as homemakers, day care, and respite homes, designed to minimize the need for removal and to protect children left in their home. In the remaining California counties the standard for removal was left unchanged. This standard permitted removal whenever the home environment was detrimental to the child, even if the child had not suffered serious physical abuse or severe emotional damage.

As a result of this legislation, we assumed that there would be a group of children left at home in the experimental counties in situations where placement would occur in other counties. We therefore decided to try to isolate this group of children and draw our home population from one of the experimental counties and our foster case sample from neighboring counties, which had fewer services and were applying the old law.

In order to make sure the incidents leading to removal were in fact comparable, we eliminated cases where the extent of the physical abuse was so severe that courts would always remove the child. We also excluded cases where the threatened harm to the child was relatively minimal and the parent was willing to accept treatment services, since most courts would not consider removal in such situations. In addition, we did not take cases of sexual abuse because the incidence rates were too low to get enough cases in each setting. Finally, in keeping with the policy focus of the study we also eliminated all cases in which there was no real policy decision or the decision is not one of home versus foster care. For example, placement is always necessary when there are no parents available or where the parents refuse to keep custody.

We tried to deal with the second "match", the quality of the home environment, in two ways. First, we had the workers in the experimental county send us only cases where they had determined that removal would have been probable without the special services. In the other counties we selected cases where the workers indicated that the children would have been left at home if the county had services similar to those found in the experimental county. This assumed that to some extent workers were considering parental characteristics in their decisions. As it turned out some of our home cases also came from the non-experimental counties, in situations where the workers wanted to remove a child but could not find a placement. Since the availability of foster homes varies over time, these cases should be quite comparable to children placed at other times.

In addition to the screening by the agencies, two of the senior investigators read each potential case to determine whether, on the basis of both the incident and the characteristics of the home and parents, the cases from the various counties appeared comparable. A small number of cases of removal where the parent was severely disturbed were eliminated since home placement appeared impossible in these cases.

The hardest problem in determining comparability related to the children. At the time of intervention very little was known about the children. For the most part, we could not determine whether the children differed on characteristics other than age, sex and ethnic background. Thus, initially we assumed there should not be significant differences, if the seriousness of the incident and basic parental characteristics were similar. Perhaps courts or workers were responding to child-related variables but this seemed unlikely, since in most cases the children were seen only briefly (if at all) before the placement decision was made. We did eliminate one class of cases which singled out special children, cases where the recommendation was placement in a residential treatment facility. These children generally exhibited extreme behavior problems and it was unlikely that they would be left at home, regardless of the services available.

One other factor was utilized in choosing the sample, which was not directly related to our goal of obtaining comparable groups. The study population is comprised of children who were between 4 and 10 years old at the time of the intervention. Prior to beginning the study we had intended to include children between the ages of one and ten. There are very few reliable measures for children under one and such measures apply to only a limited range of attributes. Many of the cases involving children over ten, while cast as abuse or neglect, involve primarily child behavior problems, such as delinquency, and the children's preferences often play a major role in the decision. Thus we thought these cases would confound the basic study.

However, after conducting a pilot study, using children one to ten, we limit the age range even more. This decision was made in part on the basis of cost; an adequate sample for the age range from one to ten would require a budget several times that which was available. More important, we found in our pilot study that several measures which are only available for children who are at least five years old were very important. Observations of the children in the school playground setting, school attendance records, teacher ratings, and interviews with the children themselves, all emerged as extremely useful measures, leading us to limit the study to school aged children.

We believe that we were successful, for the most part, in obtaining comparable samples. With regard to the seriousness of the incident, 18/40 (40%) homes cases involved abuse, while 13/30 (43%) out-of-home cases involved abuse. Our preliminary analyses also indicates that the parents of both home and foster children were similar with respect to background factors such as marital status, history of drug or alcohol problems, and prior involvement with social services.

There were several significant differences regarding parental characteristics. First, black families were disproportionately represented in the foster care sample. This primarily reflected differences in the ethnic composition of the experimental and control counties. Several other factors, which turned out to be related to ethnicity, also distinguished the two groups. For example, the home cases had a somewhat greater proportion of intact families, the mothers were older at the time of birth of the study child, and the home families tended to have a more stable living pattern, measured by length of time at current residence and number of moves in past year.

There was also a mixed pattern with regard to the children. The children were comparable in age, sex, IQ and health. Obviously, the children differed in ethnicity. In addition, there was an interesting difference on two of the measures we used to evaluate the child's behavior, a social competence rating and a problem behavior scale (these are discussed below). Although most of the children in each setting had about the same scores, there was a small group of home placed children who appeared to be considerably more difficult for their parents to care for than the remaining home children or any of the foster children. Thus there may be a group of especially disturbed children in the home sample which require separate analysis.

Although these findings are still preliminary, they are generally encouraging. Yet despite the care spent in trying to obtain totally comparable samples we still have not overcome all the methodological problems and, as a result, the policy implications of the study may be less clearcut.

Length of Follow-Up

Our children are followed for two years from the time of the initial intervention. The two-year follow-up was chosen for several reasons. It is in the second year that foster care becomes less stable (Fanshel & Shinn, 1978). Thus a minimum of two years is needed to determine the negative impact of such instability. It is also after two years that the law in many states allows the courts to decide not to return children to their parents (Wald, 1976). Many commentators argue that this is too long a period and that termination should occur in six months to two years (Goldstein, Freud & Solnit, 1979). They argue that prolonging the decision is harmful to children. Therefore, we wanted to see whether there is a change in the condition of foster children in the second year.

It is certainly possible that an even longer follow-up would be desirable. Although only half of our sample has been followed for two years, major changes took place just as the child left the study in many of the cases. For example, several children changed custody, including moves to other states, just at the two-year mark. In some other cases the condition of the natural parents deteriorated dramatically at this time. In fact, for many children and parents in our sample, life consists of a series of crises and it seems likely that such crises will continue to occur throughout the child's minority.

Thus, any follow-up that did not last until adulthood would not give a full picture of the consequences of living in these families. It is questionable whether such a lengthy follow-up should be relevant for policy purposes, however. If a child were followed to adulthood it would be impossible to separate out the impact of the abuse or neglect from other factors. Many children who are not abused or neglected might grow up "better" in different homes. Does the fact that a child has been abused or neglected justify permanent termination of parental rights solely because the child may do better elsewhere?

The Dependent Measures

General considerations. In choosing measures we had several goals. First, we wanted to look at aspects of the child's well-being that would clearly be of interest to policy-makers. The major concerns of legislatures and judges are physical health and aspects of social functioning which may be related to "good citizenship", for example, poor school performance, antisocial behavior, severe emotional disorders. Second, we were interested in aspects of the child's functioning that might affect performance in these areas. For example, we collected data on school attendance on the assumption that successful school performance is conditional on at least minimal attendance. Attendance data are much more reliable than performance data for children of this age.

Third, we sought to obtain the child's perspective on the impact of the intervention. While the child's views may seem of obvious interest, in fact they are given little weight in placement decisions. Most judges and childcare workers believe that they must determine the child's best interest independently of the child's views, since the child may want to remain in, or return to, a "bad" home. We believe that the child's views are important, in and of themselves. Moreover, the child is the best source of information related to important theoretical issues, such as the impact of separation and living in a new family on feelings of attachment. Furthermore, in the chaotic world of many of the children, caretakers, teachers, and social workers all change frequently, leaving the child as the only source of information which remains constant over the two year period.

Finally, we were concerned about the child's peer relations. A number of studies report that abused and neglected children fare badly in retaining friendships and adapting to peer expectations (Pavenstedt, 1973; Sroufe, this volume; Roff, Sells, & Golden, 1972; Cowen, Pederson, Babijian, Izzo, & Trost, 1973). Poor peer relations in early childhood are a good predictor of later social problems and thus should be important to policy-makers. Moreover, foster care exposes children to new modes of social interaction.

We have tried to obtain measures on a regular basis throughout the two years, in order to see the changing impact of foster care. The children are interviewed every six months and received physical exams and cognitive tests at the initial interview and the one and two year follow-ups. The caretakers are interviewed every three months. If the child has a change of caretaker, the new caretaker is interviewed within four weeks and then at three-month intervals. We obtain teacher evaluations of the child yearly. In addition, the child is observed four times a year on the playground in an attempt to measure social behavior at school. This brief summary gives only a sketch of the procedures being used. Fuller descriptions will be presented in future papers.

Specific Measures

Physical screening examinations. A number of previous studies of abused, neglected, and foster care children have emphasized the prevalence of medical problems in these groups (Elmer, 1977; Martin, 1976; Swire & Kavaler, 1977). Therefore, we were interested in tracking the physical development of our sample. We used three approaches in assessing the medical characteristics of the children. First, we performed a physical screening examination at the initial interview and at two years. Second, we interviewed the child's parents or guardian to obtain a general account of the child's medical history and about any medical problems encountered during the study. Finally, with the permission of the child's legal guardian, we examined hospital, birth, and clinic records.

As with all of our measures, we have not yet done a full analysis of the data, especially the follow-up data. It is our preliminary impression, however, that the incidence of health problems is far lower among our sample than that reported in other studies. In fact, most of our children were in generally good health at the time of intervention and evidenced little change regardless of placement. This may be due to the fact that our sampling was fairly exhaustive,—that is, we included almost all cases which social agencies determined to be abused or neglected. Many earlier studies have selected populations, for example, through hospital referrals, and may have exaggerated the extent of physical difficulties characteristic of the entire population.

Measures of cognitive development. Our primary goal with respect to cognitive development is to identify changes in performance on cognitive tests and in actual school performance. While there are well-recognized problems in assessing cognitive development among low income children, we believe that intellectual functioning and school performance are important measures of a child's well-being.

All children receive either the Wechsler Preschool and Primary Scale of Intelligence or the Revised Wechsler Intelligence Scale for Children. Like the physical exams, these are done at the initial interviews and at one and two year follow-ups. In addition, we obtain the child's full school record each year, including grades and any standardized tests. We also ask the teacher to rate the child's academic performace since grades among schools are often non-comparable and many children miss, or are not given standardized tests.

Again, we have only preliminary data on the cognitive testing. At the time of the initial testing the scores of the children, as a whole, were comparable to those reported for children of similar ethnic and socio-economic backgrounds. In contrast, their school performance tended to be lower than that of their classmates.

Social development. We have also tried to measure changes in the child's social development, that is their ability to relate and interact with others. Three facts encourage a special interest in social development: (1) previous studies of abused or neglected children have found noticeable deficits in the level of social functioning of these children (Pavenstedt, 1973; Martin, 1976). (2) children who behave in a socially inadequate manner may be expected to be harder to deal with, which in turn may influence both the stability and duration of placement; (3) social development is largely determined by the amount and kind of interpersonal experience a child has (Hartup, 1982). Assuming that some growth and change are possible, the placement experience may be expected to have a stong and measurable impact on a child's social behavior and interpersonal skill.

We measure the child's social development in several ways. A number of different measures is necessary because it is likely that abuse and neglect and alternative placements will affect various aspects of the child's functioning in different ways. In fact, from a policy perspective, these data might prove difficult to utilize, since positive development on one dimension may be balanced by deterioration in another.

Problem behavior scale (PBS). Children identified as abused or neglected frequently exhibit behavior problems such as extreme aggressiveness, anxiety, or withdrawal (Martin, 1976). These behaviors may lead to additional difficulties for the child, whether with outside authorities, with peer interactions, or with interactions within a home setting. Foster care also has been reported to cause certain behavioral problems, such as bedwetting, sleep problems and anxiety.

Therefore, we developed a problem behavior scale, given to the primary caregiver at the time of initial intervention and every three months thereafter. The problem behaviors are divided into those involving normal peer interaction, those involving interaction with adult caregivers, and more aberrant behaviors such as vandalism and stealing. From this scale we hope to see whether foster placement alleviates any significant problems the child evidenced at intervention and whether it resulted in any other problems. We will also see whether certain problems associated with foster care, for example, bedwetting, are only temporary regressions. Finally, we learn whether problems of children left at home can be alleviated through intervention or merely the passage of time.

Social competence. The concept of social competence is an important one that has not been focused on in studies of abused and neglected children. While we certainly need to protect children from abuse and neglect, we should be more reluctant to remove children who are behaving competently at school, with peers and at home. Conversely, we may find that these children fare even worse in areas related to social competence than in physical health or cognitive skills. Previous studies relating social competency to behavioral and psychiatric outcomes have shown this concept to be predictive of poor psychiatric outcomes and poor academic achievement (Garmezy, 1970; Jones, 1976; Kohn, 1977). These studies have also shown that the presence of extreme incompetencies in many areas of functioning is stable across time and a major sign of vulnerability. An assessment of social competence should be an important measure of a child's level of adaptive functioning and should help identify those children who are at greatest risk for adaptive failure.

We are looking at the child's social competence in three ways. First, we ask the caretaker to complete a social competence scale focusing on the child's ability to adjust at home, in relations with the caretaker and other children in the household. Second, the child's teacher fills out a form each year, assessing the child's competence at school. Finally, we observe the child on the school playground a number of times each year. In these observations we are particularly interested in: (1) how much time was spent in interaction with peers; (2) an assessment of the quality of the interaction (e.g., competition, hostility, physical activity, highly structured activity); (3) identifying the child's role in the interaction, whether initiator-leader or follower.

In all these measures we are primarily interested in children who show extremely competent behavior or very dysfunctional behavior or who show major changes following intervention. These are the children of most relevance for policy purposes.

Our initial findings do indicate that many, although by no means all, of abused and neglected children seem to have substantial deficits in the area of social competence. A small group have great difficulty in parent-child interactions. A much larger number receive low ratings from their teachers, especially with regard to their peer relations.

Child interviews. Our final, and in many ways most important, source of information about social development is the children themselves. The child interview is designed to cover two principal areas. First, we are interested in the child's objective reporting of events and personal experiences in daily life. Second, we are interested in the child's interpretation of these experiences.

From the interviews with the children we obtain their description of the events of a typical day and their views and evaluations of their particular circumstances and experiences. We explore several areas of the children's phenomenological world: their neighborhood friendships, their home, school, social resources (e.g., what the child likes most about the neighborhood, whom the child can talk to when troubled). We also explore the children's personal feelings about themselves and their caretakers. Many of the questions were adopted from Zill's national survey of children (Zill, 1976), so that we can compare the response of our children with a broader national sample.

These interviews have been extremely useful. Most of the children are able to discuss their feelings about the experiences they are undergoing, and their perceptions provide a rich source of data. A portion of our success here may be due to the use of repeated visits to the family by the same interviewer, so that familiarity and rapport are developed. The children are willing to identify their preferred caretaker, talk about school and social problems, and indicate whether abusive or neglectful conditions are continuing. In addition, the interviews are a rich source of clinical material about the child's emotional state.

CONCLUSIONS

Through our project we expect to learn a considerable amount about the development of children who have been abused or neglected. Yet the results may shed only limited light on the legal issues we tried to address. We have found the methodological problems in getting truly comparable and large enough groups, following them for a sufficiently lengthy time, and obtaining consistently reliable data, to be very substantial. We experienced these problems even though we were fortunate to have a relatively large budget, a basically stable research staff, and total cooperation from people in the child welfare system.

The difficulty of doing sound research presents special dilemmas in the field of child abuse. As Zigler has recently written "[G]iven the embryonic and limited state of knowledge [about child abuse] that currently exists, it is not surprising that the literature is as replete with myths as it is with well-validated facts" (Zigler, 1980). Because of the lack of data, policy makers are prone to make much out of the limited data available. This has been true of most of the recent "reforms" in the foster care area.

Recognizing the need for data, many policy makers accept any data available, regardless of the limitations in the research. Therefore, it is critical that researchers doing policy-oriented research ask themselves which policy issues are researchable and what is necessary to adequately research the issue? It may also be necessary for researchers to invest substantial efforts in exploring whether an issue is researchable and to be willing to abandon efforts which are not producing reliable data.

We have tried in this chapter to examine the question "what is researchable" for one specific policy issue. We hope that the examination provides some insight not only on that issue, but also on the general problems involved in doing policy-oriented research of the type addressed in this Volume.

REFERENCES

Aber, J. L. III The Involuntary Child Placement Decision: Solomon's Dilemma Revisited. *Child Abuse: An agenda for action* (Eds. G. Gerbner, C. Ross, E. Zigler). New York/Oxford: Oxford University Press, 1980.

American Humane Association *National Analysis of Official Child Neglect and Abuse Reporting*. Englewood, Colo: American Humane Association, 1979.

Antler, S. Child Abuse: An emerging social priority. *Social Work* (January), 1978, *23*(1), 58–61.

Berkeley Planning Associates *Evaulation: National Demonstration Program in Child Abuse and Neglect*. Berkeley, Calif.: Berkeley Planning Associates, 1977.

Bolton, F. G. Jr., Laner, R. H., & Gai, D. S. For Better or Worse?: Foster parents and foster children in an officially reported child maltreatment population. *Children and Youth Services Review,* 1981, *3,* 37-53.

Borgatta, E. F., & Cautley, P. W. Behavioral Characteristics of Children: Replication studies with foster children. *Multivariate Behavioral Research,* 1966, *1,* 399-424.

Bowlby, J. (2nd ed). *Childcare and the Growth of Love,* 1965.

Bowlby, J. *Maternal care and mental health.* Geneva: World Health Organization, 1951.

Burgess, R. L. Project interact: A study of patterns of interaction in abusive, neglectful and control families. *Child Abuse and Neglect: The International Journal,* 1979, *3,* 781-791.

Burgess, R. L. & Conger, R. D. Family interaction in abusive, neglectful and normal families. *Child Development,* 1978, *49,* 1163-1173.

California Family Protection Act SB30 Cal. Leg. 1977 (West Cal. Code SS 300ff).

Cohn, A. H. & Follignon, F. C. Evaluation of child abuse and neglect demonstration projects, 1974-1977 (Vol. I & II). NCHSR Research Report Series, DHEW Publication No. (PHS) 79-3217-1, 1979.

Cowen, E. L., Pederson, A., Babijian, H., Izzo, L. D., & Trost, M. A. Long-term follow-up of early detected vulnerable children. *Journal of Consulting and Clinical Psychology,* 1973, *41,* 438-446.

Disbrow, M. A., Doerr, H., & C. Caulfield Measuring the components of parents' potential for child abuse and neglect. *Child Abuse and Neglect: The International Journal,* 1977, *1,* 279-296.

Egeland, B. & Brunnquell, D. An at-risk approach to the study of child abuse: Some preliminary findings. *Journal of the American Academy of Child Psychiatry,* 1979, *18*(3), 219-296.

Egeland, B. & Sroufe, L. A. Attachment and early maltreatment. (Abstract, Univ. of Minnesota). *Child Development,* 1981, *52,* 44-52.

Elmer, Elizabeth *Fragile families, troubled children: The aftermath of infant trauma.* Pittsburgh: University of Pittsburgh Press, 1977.

Fanshell, D., & Shinn, E. *Children in foster care.* New York: Columbia University Press, 1978.

Garbarino, J. The price of privacy in the social dynamic of child abuse. *Child Welfare,* 1977, *56*(1), 565-575.

Garmezy, N. Vulnerable children: Implications derived from studies of an internalizing-externalizing symptom dimension. In J. Zubin & A. M. Freedman (Eds.), *Psychopathology of adolescence.* New York: Grune and Stratton, 1970.

George, C. & Main, M. Social interactions of young abused children: Approach, avoidance, and aggression. *Child Development,* 1979, *50,* 306-318.

Gil, D. *Violence Against Children,* 1970.

Goldstein, J., Freud, A., & Solnit, A. *Beyond the best interests of the child.* New York: The Free Press, 1973.

Goldstein, J., Freud, A., & Solnit, A. J. *Before the best interests of the child,* New York/London: Collier MacMillan Publishers, 1979.

Gray, J. D., Cutler, C. A., Dean, J. G., & Kempe, C. H. Predication and prevention of child abuse and neglect. In *Proceedings of the 2nd National Conference on Child Abuse and Neglect.* Washington, D.C.: Children's Bureau, 1978, *1,* 346-354.

Green, A. A psychodynamic approach to the study and treatment of child abusing parents. *Journal of the American Academy of Child Psychiatry,* 1976, *15,* 414-429.

Gruber, A. R. *Children in Foster Care.* New York: Human Sciences Press, 1978.

Hartup, W. W. Two social worlds: Family relations and peer relations. In M. Rutter (Ed.), *Scientific foundations of development psychiatry.* London: Heinemann, in press.

Herrenkohl, R. C., Herrenkohl, E., Seech, M., & Egolf, B. The repetition of child abuse: How frequently does it occur? *Journal of Child Abuse and Neglect: The International Journal,* 1980, *3,* 67-72.

Hubbell, R. *Foster Care and Families: Conflicting Values and Policies,* Philadelphia: Temple University Press, 1981.

Jones, F. H. The Rochester adaptive behavior inventory: A parallel series of instruments for assessing social competence during early and middle childhood and adolescence. In J. S. Strauss, H. M. Babigian & M. Roff (Eds.), *The Origins and Course of Psychopathology.* New York: Plenum Press, 1976, 249-281.

Kadushin, A. & Martin, J. A. *Child Abuse: An internactional event.* New York: Columbia University Press, 1981.

Kempe, R. S. & Kempe, C. H. *Child abuse: The developing child,* Fontana Books, 1978.

Kent, J. T. A follow-up study of abused children. *Journal of Pediatric Psychology,* 1976, *25,* 31-00.

Kohn, M. *Social Competence, Symptoms and Underachievement in Childhood: A Longitudinal Perspective.* Washington, D.C.: V. H. Winston.

Lagerberg, D., Nilsson, K., & Sundelin, C. Life style patterns in families with neglected children. *Child Abuse and Neglect,* 1979, *3,* 483-490.

Lemmon, J. A. Self concept and the foster adolescent. (Doctoral dissertation, University of Illinois, 1975), *Dissertation Abstract International.*

Littner, N. *Some traumatic effects of separation and placement,* 1956.

Mandell, B. R. *Where are the children?* Lexington, Mass.: Lexington Books, 1973.

Martin, H. *The abused child.* Cambridge, Mass.: Ballinger Publishing Co., 1976.

Meier, E. Current circumstances of former foster children. *Child Welfare,* 1965, *44,* 196-206.

Mnookin, R. Foster care—In whose best interest? *Harvard Educational Review,* 1973, *43,* 599-638.

Parke, R. D. Collmer, C. W. Child abuse: An interdisciplinary analysis. In E. Hetherington, Ed., *Review of child development research.* Chicago: University of Chicago Press, 1975, *5,* 509-590.

Pavenstedt, E. An intervention program for infants from high risk homes. *American Journal Public Health,* 1973, *63,* 393-000.

Phillips, M. H., Shyne, A. W., Sherman, E. A., & Haring, B. L. *Factors associated with placement decisions in child welfare.* New York: Child Welfare League of America, 1971.

Polansky, N., Hally, C., & Polansky, N. F. *Child neglect: State of knowledge.* Athens, Ga.: Regional Institute of Social Welfare Research, 1974.

Polansky, N. A., Chalmers, M. A., Buttenwieser, E., & Williams, D. P. *Damaged parents: Anatomy of child neglect.* Chicago: University of Chicago Press, 1981.

Robertson & Robertson Young children in brief separation: A fresh look. *Psychoanalytic Study of the Child,* 1971, *26,* 264-000.

Roff, M., Sells, S. B., & Golden, M. M. *Social adjustment and personality development in children.* Minneapolis: University of Minnesota Press, 1972.

Rutter, M. *Maternal deprivation reassessed,* Penguin Education, 1972.

Rutter, M. Parent-child separation: Psychological effects on the child. In A. M. Clarke & A. D. B. Clarke (Eds.), *Early experience: Myth and evidence.* New York: The Free Press 1976.

Seligman, L. Understanding the black foster child through assessment. *Journal of Non-White Concerns in Personnel and Guidance,* 1979, *7,* 183-191.

Steele, B. F., & Pollock, C. B. A psychiatric study of parents who abuse infants and small children. In R. E. Helfer and C. H. Kempe (Eds.), *The Battered Child.* Chicago: University of Chicago Press, 1968, 103-138.

Swire, M. R. & Kavaler, F. The health status of foster children. *Child Welfare,* 1977, *56,* 635-650.

Wald, M. State intervention on behalf of "neglected" children: Standards for removal of children from their homes, monitoring the status of children in foster care, and termination of parental rights. *Stanford Law Review,* 1976, *28,* 625-706.

Wald, M. State intervention on behalf of neglected children: A search for realistic standards, *Stanford Law Review,* 1975, *27,* 985-1040.

Weinstein, E. A. *The self-image of the foster child.* New York: Russell Sage Foundation, 1960.

Yarrow, L. J. Separation from parents in early childhood. In M. L. Hoffman and L. W. Hoffman (Eds.), *Review of child development research.* New York: Russell Sage Foundation, 1964, 87-136.

Zigler, E. Controlling child abuse: Do we have the knowledge and/or the will? In *Child abuse: An agenda for action* (Eds. G. Gerbner, C. Ross, E. Zigler). New York/Oxford: Oxford University Press, 1980.

Zill, N. National survey of children. *Foundation for Child Development,* New York City, 1976.

12 Comments on Wald, Carlsmith, Leiderman, and Smith's Chapter

June Louin Tapp
Institute of Child Development
University of Minnesota

It is fitting that Wald's programmatic presentation was the finale of this year's Symposium. His provocative report encourages exploration of the macro issue of the relationship of science to society *and* the micro issue of the possibility of an interdisciplinary effort between psychology and law. Both issues speak to the need to relate child development principles and social policy perspectives at a multiplicity of levels: theoretical and methodological as well as empirical and practical.

In my chapter, I address four issues raised by Wald's proposal: The *first* deals with the precursors of a productive relationship between science and society (in this chapter, as represented by psychology and law); the *second* reacts to Wald, Carlsmith, Leiderman, and Smith's interdisciplinary attempt to move the enterprises of child psychology and legal policy beyond rhetoric to research; the *third* reviews implications for developmentalists and decision-makers in terms of roles and responsibilities; and the *fourth* contains a concluding note.

PRECURSORS FOR PRODUCTIVITY: THE MACRO ISSUES

The Historical Context

In the 1940s, Lewin (1947, 1948) stressed the importance of social action having a social psychology base; that is, social policy being based on science. He helped build a tradition that saw "psychological theory and research as a source as well as a resource for social change and social policy" (Campbell, 1971; Tapp, 1978, 1980, pp. 167-168). Lewin reasoned that the interdependence between theorist and practitioner or policy-maker was obvious and necessary: the theorist's special obligation was to provide a conceptual frame that could be used to solve social problems (Cartwright, 1978).

In the instance of psychology and law, researchers were to provide policy-makers, governmental authorities, and law operatives (i.e., police, lawyers, judges, legislators) with basic information and insight about human behavior from courtyard to courtroom. This orientation reflected the beliefs that (1) research should focus on the major responsibility and preeminent concern of both lawyers and psychologists—the establishment of norms and the assessment of established norms; (2) psychological perspectives are essential for conducting a just and comprehensive legal process; (3) psychologists can help reconceptualize legal system problems through empirical, systematic research not by appeals to authority, historical precedent, or logic; and (4) that such interdisciplinary efforts be made shortly and smartly (Tapp, 1969). Researchers over a decade have argued that translation and examination of psycholegal ideas would be distinctly more accurate, systematic, less naive, and fruitful, if done in active participation with lawyers (Tapp, 1969; Vidmar, 1980).

The apparent need for rapprochement between science and society was articulated in the 1940s by Lewin. It was identified for psychology and law in the 1960s by Tapp and reiterated in the 1970s for developmental psychologists by child psychologist Bronfenbrenner (1974) and family lawyer Wald (1976). In 1974, Bronfenbrenner challenged developmental psychologists to adopt a second axiom: Science needs social policy for its vitality and validity. Bronfenbrenner maintained that scientists' answers to policy-makers' questions were often too sparse or unrelated. Illustratively, Clarke-Stewart's (1977) useful review of research on child care in the family revealed that many ideas were reasonable and closely linked with available research "but they are not really designed to affect public policy" (Osofsky, 1979). Bronfenbrenner, Clarke-Stewart, and Osofsky all denote the irrelevancy of most developmental research to public policy questions.

In 1976, Wald told developmental psychologists that lawyers "do not have the data to tell us what is the 'right' policy. Yet decisions have to be made" (pp. 1-2). While Wald conceded that many questions related to the rights and best interests of the child are not answered "solely through research or data," he also observed that (1) scientific data can greatly influence the decision-making process, (2) lawyers need the insights and expertise of child researchers to clarify the goals of legal policy and get beyond the judge's (or legislator's) bias and background, and (3) that often existing data provide inadequate guidance to legislators or court officials on specific problems such as foster care, multiple placements, termination of parent rights, long- or short-term consequences of abusive or neglectful behavior. The paucity of research and the difficulty in writing legal standards prompted Wald to invite developmental psychologists (1) to join lawyers in facing the hard questions involved in drafting specific statutes, (2) to design research to provide treatment guidelines of use to judges and childcare workers, and (3) to frame questions and do research with lawyers in areas of concern to the legal system where presently there is little or no pertinent work.

The Necessary Conditions

In the 35 years of debate between Lewin's social science stance and Bronfenbrenner's and Wald's pleas to connect psychology to policy, four conditions have surfaced as characteristic of a productive relationship for science and society. They include styles of interaction, public and value concerns, theory and technology patterns, and hidden agendas.

Styles of interaction. For the benefit of both, the two representative fields must be interactive. The integrity and success of the research *and* the reform require that psychologists and lawyers be receptive to the interactive aspects of the scientific and social enterprises. To afford humankind generally—and children specifically—the best shot at healthy growth and development, psychology and law should select problems and advance solutions together. Unless they do so, a false dichotomy is perpetrated and an abyss created between "knowers" and "doers" (cf. Ryle, 1949). Scientists do not function only as compliers of bits of information, devoid of any values or interests, and policy-makers are not only as reformers, devoid of any critical or empirical capacities. At its best, science provides cogent empirical facts that form the basis for humane guidelines and decisions; at its best, public policy attempts to construct programs or procedures consonant with cultural values to better society. Tension arises between psychologists and lawyers when they neglect to recognize the necessity of interaction between knowers and doers.

Public and value concerns. Both psychology and law are public-oriented, as evidenced by their concern about social welfare. This is mirrored in psychology's self-definition as a science aimed to acquire knowledge about behavior for the benefit of humankind. Scientific researchers and social planners alike (psychologists and lawyers in our case) should continuously assess their evaluative and experimental efforts for methodological and ethical soundness. They must address, too, the educative aspect since knowledge facilitates understanding human development *and* creating a just legal order. Afterall, knowledge is power and public knowledge is public power.

To polarize psychology as conceptual, abstract, basic, private, and value-free *and* policy as practical, concrete, applied, public, and value-laden is to fail to see that both enterprises are embedded in the economics, ethics, philosophies, and politics of their times. Neither science or society operates *in vacuuo* unaffected by values or public pressures. The battles of Copernicus, Galileo, and Mendel affirm that resistances to scientific discoveries emanated from more than religious and ideological sources (Barber, 1961; Kuhn, 1962). Designations of "value-free" or "value-laden"—then as now—are frequently nourished within disciplines by those who would have scientists act as if they were totally private and value-free in their choice of research problems and research procedures.

The issue is to identify the value assumptions and public responsibilities of both researchers and reformers. Such recognition allows the scientist to function qua scientist empiricizing a particular problem and presenting important findings *and* the policy-maker to function qua policy-maker in taking evidence and making laws. This permits the scientist to be both expert and amicus; the policy-maker, both critic and advocate; and both to partake in making a bridge between science and society—in this case, connecting child psychology and legal policy.

If both psychology and policy are to flourish and benefit humankind, they need to see the vitality and validity of the two axioms (social policy needs science; science needs social policy) *and* the Janus (dual) nature of research (e.g., basic and applied, public and private, value-free and value-laden). At the same time, a science and society partnership must heed the following two potential dangers.

The technological advance over theory. Lured by the ease of technology as well as the sophistication of statistics, contemporary researchers often place science second to technological development and theory second to practice. For example, many investigators (at the student level and beyond) can multiply regress the effects of poverty on child abuse, but often cannot explain the etiology. Yet in the absence of theory, facts have no meaning (cf. Hempel, 1965; Parsons & Shils, 1951). In the absense of science, techniques (software or statistics) are mere gimmickry.

Decision-makers need data (evidence) to make policy. Science's statistically-sound probability statements *and* law's logically-derived doctrines (e.g., the reasonable man) are important data sources. But the manufacturing of reliable and valid evidence is most robust, parsimonious, and useful when considered within a theoretical framework. Decision-makers need not succumb to the dazzle of technology and fear the demand of theory. The option is both/and, *not* either/or. Nor should policy-makers expect lawyers to be more theoretically-sound and less technically-oriented than psychologists. Members of both disciplines may have suffered the advance of technology over theory.

Furthermore, defining social problems as technical issues is often an intellectual ruse to avoid theory construction or its confines. It can also be a maneuver to avoid changing the socio-economic structures. As importantly, it may be a myopic effort to use statistical or technical gadgetry to reject the possibility of remedying social ills through scientifically-based reform.

In the rush to become value-free, some psychologists may have become theory-free, creating a condition wherein technological advance has meant theoretical ignorance. Sophisticated technology need not mean abandoning theory. Neither the siren of statistics, the temptation of technology, the refuge of relevance, or the promise of policy should result in the abandonment of theory. Afterall, the search for a grand theory—or a series of mini-theories—to explain human behavior over time and place can provide an important framework for developing sound policy.

The hidden agendas of knowers and doers. Elsewhere I described lawyers' predilection to regard themselves as socially-responsible, value-laden gatekeepers of universal verities. They cannot comprehend psychologists' self-characterization as scientists free of value concepts and/or social responsibility (1969). Beyond psychologists' desire to be seen as value-free, and lawyers as value-laden, there are other value assumptions and hidden agendas that those studying the decision-making process must identify, especially in the area of child policy. The two agenda items most likely to confound the process are personal and professional.

On the *personal:* Zimmerman, Mattesich, and Leik's study (1979) of the effects on Minnesota legislators' (N = 201) attitudes about family policy revealed that stage in the family life-cycle was the strongest influence. Apparently legislators did not formulate policy solely on merits; they were influenced by personal and familial agendas. Zimmerman and associates found that legislators were more likely to make decisions on the basis of their role and place in family history rather than on non-familial/impersonal research data. It was not what one read, but whether one had children or grandchildren that was determinative. Psychologists working with policy-makers must recognize this hidden agenda effect and enter it as part of the decision-making process.

On the *professional:* Roberts (1980) argued that economics and employment are often bigger reasons for development of children's policies by experts than children's direct needs. He cited three examples where resolution of a conflict was in the interests of other than young children; they were unemployed teachers, empty school buildings, and expanded teaching staffs in early education. While "paychecks for adults and services for children are intertwined interests" (p. 154), Roberts recommended that "public policies on the child be based on child growth and development needs [not] on jobs for adults" (pp. 148-149).

As psychologists and lawyers examine and erect—or erase—programs for children, they must be guided in their research and reform by developmental principles and findings as an organizing base for policy formulation. Such efforts are best done when psychologists and lawyers work in concert to develop policy based on scientific principles and children's needs, not personal or professional ones. Developing professional guidelines and investigating research areas that comport with scientific and social values are essential if (1) both justice and knowledge are to advance, (2) the interactive and innovative effects of one field (profession) is to be felt by the other, and (3) both psychology and law are to remain receptive to viewing research *and* reform as experiments aimed to promote the human condition (Campbell, 1971; Tapp, 1971, 1974; Tapp & Levine, 1977).

CONTRIBUTIONS OF THE BAY AREA STUDY: THE MICRO ISSUES

The Approach

In a 1976 *Child Development* article, Wald told child specialists about lawyers' great need for new *and* translated developmental data to help create the "right" policies. At the 1981 Minnesota Symposium, moving beyond his own and others' rhetoric (e.g., Bronfenbrenner, 1974; Ellsworth & Levy, 1969; Tapp, 1969, 1976; Tapp & Levine, 1977), Wald described an important interdisciplinary event: One of the first psycholegal team efforts designed to "explore the problems involved in developing research that will help policy-makers design good policy" (Wald et al., this volume, 209). The topic of this rare but relevant research strategy, intended to inform reform, was the appropriate types of intervention in child abuse and neglect. The Stanford researchers selected this controversial area (cf. Goldstein, Freud, & Solnit, 1973, 1979; Katkin, Bullington, & Levine, 1974; Wald, 1980), cognizant of the debate about definitions and dispositions amongst policy-makers, psychologists, parents, and the public. The effort—replete with science, social, and legal implications—should reduce the gap between research and the formation of public policy for children and families.

In addition to the recommended interactive design (see above) between the disciplines, the Bay Area Study met other criteria important to a productive psycholegal research relationship. These included utilizing multiple conceptual frames, empirical modes, and professional styles *as well as* distinguishing the level of operation and communication for effective exploration and collaboration.

Past difficulties of psycholegal research may have been due to nonacceptance of theories, methods, and styles between disciplines (e.g., using children's perspective in intervention research and placement decisions) *as well as* non-equal relationships in the research enterprise (e.g., researcher-to-practitioner rather than practitioner-to-practitioner). A more satisfying interchange is possible also when the design calls for acknowledging differences in professional interests (e.g., relevance of "good citizenship" to policy-makers and a "lengthy follow-up" for child psychologists). In the Bay Area Study, interdisciplinary communication and collaboration occurred at the same level (i.e., researcher-to-researcher) assuring a more appropriate, compatible, efficient, and useful fit.

One advantage, actualized by the Wald team, to an interactive, interdisciplinary, and level-to-level research strategy is the multi-perspective in theory, method, and interpretation available to both fields. The utilization of a multi-oriented approach to the multi-faceted problems of child abuse and neglect is preeminent, especially if research and reform are to be viewed as experiments in the innovative, try-out sense recommended by many (Campbell, 1971; Federal Judiciary Center, 1981; Meehl, 1977).

The Stanford researchers also met the increasingly-applied criterion at the psychology-law interface of using real-life "experiments" (cf. Bronfenbrenner, 1974; Campbell, 1971; Cook & Campbell, 1979; Konecni & Ebbesen, 1980; Tapp, 1976, 1980). A legislatively-created condition (two jurisdictions with changed removal standards and the remaining counties in the state with an unchanged standard) provided a natural-field, real-life experiment.

Since no final analyses are in, and the data collection methods only sketched, the success of the Bay Area Study is yet to be judged. Nevertheless, the preparatory questions and preliminary results indicate a consideration of variables and procedures not employed to date on this topic. For example, the intention to go beyond physical to socio-emotional factors relevant to placement decisions (e.g., effects of reabuse plus stable, continuous relationships) stemmed from Wald's desire to make decisions based on a total child view and on research rather than value judgments or clinical evidence (albeit psychology's or law's). Furthermore, this position incorporated the developmentalist view of the importance of approaching the total child as a coherent entity (Sroufe, 1978, 1979). This stance revealed further the weight given to the child's contribution in the intervention (placement) decision; a contribution based on her constancy, comprehension, and competency. Using such a total child research strategy forced the investigators to deal with the interactive effects of developmental, legal, and familial systems (cf. Parke, 1977; Tapp, 1980; Tapp & Levine, 1977).

The multiple-perspective and total-child orientations also engendered more detailed considerations of psycholegal theoretical and methodological questions such as (1) the impact of the type of legal decision (i.e., if legislative, average data for general guidelines preferred; if judicial, particularistic data for individual application), (2) the complexity of controlled and comparable sampling, and (3) the suitability of cross-sectional time designs and cross-situational measures for determining long- and/or short-term policy consequences. These examinations required some intellectual risk-taking and some disciplinary decentering, given the actors in this research enterprise: legal and child development experts, academicians and practitioners, scientists and citizens. They also reduced some alleged barriers between law and psychology. For example, those related to orientation (practical *vs.* theoretical; value-laden *vs.* value-free; advocacy *vs.* inquiry) *and* those related to method (deductive *vs.* inductive; specific or individual *vs.* general or individuals; case study *vs.* experimental study) (Tapp, 1969). In so doing, they removed *de facto* many barriers to a functional psychology-law collaboration.

Wald discussed the difficulty of obtaining ideal research conditions and controls. He correctly concluded that some existing studies (even those on special programs) have limited utility, but afford data for decision-making. Rather than no information at all, such data may be useful in specific court cases or legislative statutes. This observation underscores the need for psychologists to summarize research trends and accept the utility of findings at a p value of .10 to policy-makers. Both these points have been well made by Moore (1981). Such issues reflect the debate and dilemma regarding the relationship, role, and responsibility of psychologists to policy-makers.

Problems and Possibilities

In addition to these observations on the Bay Area Study, other points, dealing with design, sample, instruments, and results, merit discussion. Included are suggestions germane to theoretical and methodological as well as empirical and practical issues.

Design

Given Wald's concerns about age, cost, time, match, and size in the Bay Area Study sample, as well as the requirement of a longitudinal followup, an overlapping design would have been an appropriate choice. Holtzman and associates' effective use of overlapping samples in a cross-cultural personality study (Holtzman, Diaz-Guerrero, & Swartz, 1975) allowed 12 years of child development to be covered in only six calendar years of repeated testing. The technique would permit easy identification of the most salient two-year span cognitively, emotionally, and socially while simultaneously providing a longitudinal analysis. Similarly, a more robust description of major changes and crises, characteristic of the target population between the crucial ages of five to seven (White, 1965) and 11 to 14 (Grisso & Vierling, 1978) would be expected.

An overlap between groups (e.g., 5, 8, 11 and continuing through 10, 13,

16) is powerful because it makes the study of curvilinear developmental trends and interactions longitudinally as well as cross-sectionally possible. Assuming adequate matched sampling, effects of repeated testing can be isolated so that data reflect developmental trends not methodological artifacts. Further, developmental differences can be distinguished from chronometric findings, but not at the cost of time, money, or an unduly restricted sample.

Such a design would have enabled the Stanford team to answer pressing theoretical and practical questions like: How long is long enough? What are the advantages of cross-sectional and longitudinal sampling techniques across counties? Is a psycholegal definition of abuse or neglect useful? Additionally, more attention could been have directed to the ethnic and economic confounds (i.e., disproportionate number of black and poor families). Again, such a design might account for the high incidence of problem behaviors and difficult care situations in the small but distinct group of children in home settings. The latter is a tantalizing finding, given that home families had more intact units and stable living patterns.

Sample Selection

Randomization. Wald described the problems in obtaining comparable samples. Given the absence of an overlapping longitudinal design, the psychological wisdom of a lifelong design, the instability of foster care placements over time, the issue of external validity, and the input of political pressures, *but* the presence of one legislatively experimental jurisdiction and several nonexperimental counties, it is curious that the investigators did not opt to randomize the sample of the Bay Area Study. While it seems impossible "for ethical and practical reasons to get courts to assign children randomly" (Wald et al., this volume p. 216), judges in equally-demanding ethical and practical situations do precisely that. Recently a report of Federal Justice Center's Advisory Committee on Experimentation in the Law (1981) maintained that only randomization assured fairness to the persons at risk, the society at large, and the experiment on trial.

Wald's dilemma is confusing and equivocal, given the following arguments: (1) "Decisions are already being made in what amounts to a random process" *and* (2) "Such a policy would violate parents' rights" (Wald et al., this volume p. 216). If the issue is the judge's disallowing "additional risk to children," it is even more imperative that systematic randomization rather than "sloppy" randomization to be used in a research study—even a natural field one—to assure the best interests of the child. Furthermore, in not opting for a randomization procedure, there may be inadequate attention to the rights of children. Protection of children and parental rights seem more likely in situations governed less by the biases of law operatives.

It is an empirical question whether clinical factors are another variable at best or an additional risk at worst. However, there is evidence that experts, operating within certain life-cycle orientations (Zimmerman et al., 1979), cannot guarantee fairness. Randomization of assignment to experimental situations—albeit foster care placement or studies of same—seem more likely to guarantee rights to children (e.g., due process) than "clinical factors."

Case criteria. The potentially different criteria used by the caseworkers and the senior investigators in obtaining the sample is also at issue. Wald noted the criteria necessary for policy purposes (incident seriousness, home conditions, parental characteristics, and initial child profiles). However, the "subjective" criteria used by the case-workers to select cases in the experimental county were not contrasted to other workers' or the senior experimenters'. The investigators employed yet another selection criterion if the county's services paralleled the experimental county's. Further, only two of the senior investigators reviewed potential cases for comparability. To date there are no reports on inter-judge reliabilities or the effects of differential training (e.g., case worker *vs.* experimenter) on case selection. Teacher ratings have comparable problems. Often standards are dissimilar between classes, let alone schools. Classrooms, school grounds, and grade levels all have "cultures" as do caseworkers and experimenters.

Instruments

Child interview. The inclusion of the child's perspective is commendable for methodological and ethical reasons. The constancy of the child's view, as the stable source of information over the two-year study period, provides an opportunity to attend to cogent short- and long-term developmental changes over age (or stage) and situation. Adoption of that research is consistent with recent developmental findings (cf. Damon, 1977; Levine, 1979; Melton, 1980; Tapp & Aliotta, 1976). Past inattention to this data source may mirror a noninteractive or unidirectional view of decision-making, whether at the child or adult level. Other studies, using reciprocal and/or interactive socialization models (Haggard & Mentschikoff, 1977; Konecni & Ebbesen, 1980; LeVine, 1980; Parke, 1977), emphasize the importance of assessing *all* actors in a social system; in this instance, all those involved in or affected by its rule-making or-maintaining.

The use of a child-centered interview instrument points also to the inadequacy of child-related research which does not query the person at risk. Certainly, in the area of rights, child placement is a case in point. This significant omission in past research may also reflect a skepticism about children's competency and comprehension (Skolnick, 1975).

Instrument development. Wald described four criteria used to choose the dependent measures (policy-makers' interest, child functioning, child perspectives on intervention, peer relations as social problem predictors) and demarcated the assessment schedule of child, caretaker, and teacher. However, he only sketched the procedures and promised a "fuller descriptions...in future papers" (p. 224).

The promise is not nearly as problematic as the very limited discussion on instrument development. For example, were the newly-devised measures empirically-derived or did they emerge *apiori*? What was the content or format of the child's interview, intended to probe objectively and subjectively "the child's emotional state" through daily-life events and personal experiences? What was the feedback effect on children taking the interview? This lack of information is less problematic for the physical (screening examination, medical histories, hospital records) or cognitive measures (Wechsler Intelligence scales) *than* for the social development and competence ones. The construction and validation of social development and social competence measures are of concern. The latter particularly is often a hard construct to define empirically. The present report on the measures plus the preliminary state of the data analysis afford only a minimal understanding of the instruments' success (reliability and validity) and the robustness of the findings.

Results

Health. The evidence of greater health in the cases studied was noteworthy. Whether it reveals an important difference in the samples drawn or the manner of selection is moot. Answers await a full analysis. However, preliminary impressions suggest that hospital referrals as a sample source may unduly exaggerate the "illth" (i.e., physical difficulties) of abused or neglected children. The finding, like the high incidence of abuse in the stable home families, is provocative. It requires further probing for practical, procedural, and policy reasons.

Separation as stress. Wald reported "clinical evidence" that children view foster home placement as punishment for wrong-doing *and* suffer identity problems, conflicts of loyalty, and anxiety about their future. Perhaps a reasonable experimental comparison or control group for an abuse study might be the children of divorce. Much non-clinical research shows that the divorce group have similar symptoms (Hetherington, Cox, & Cox, 1978, 1979; Luepnitz, 1978). This suggests there are theoretical and methodological advantages to considering a divorce group. For example, to document and interpret differences between groups of children exposed to stress-induced stimuli (i.e., abuse-related removal *vs.* divorce-related separation), researchers may need additional personality and social development theories to contrast abuse to divorce findings. At the methodological level, researchers could determine empirically if the stress stimuli of abuse, neglect, or divorce yield greater incidences of identity confusion, loyalty conflicts, and anxiety. While the present study does not address this comparative problem or possibility, it would appear to warrant some attention.

Promise

Although the Bay Area Study goals delineated by Wald and associates for developmental psychology and law, like the description of the employed measures and the preliminary data analyses show promise, the final applause and critique await the final analysis and report. Nevertheless, the study plan and announcement of preliminary trends permit lawyers and psychologists to see the possibilities stemming from interdisciplinary communication and collaboration. In time, for example, the researchers should be able to say whether foster placement alleviates social development problems evidenced at intervention time, whether so-called foster care problems like bedwetting are temporary, or whether there are major social competency changes following intervention.

On balance, the present report provides little hard (through clearly tantalizing) data in terms of substantive findings. But it has definitely demonstrated methodological as well as some theoretical advances. Further, the Bay Area Study's major contribution *now* is that it has helped dismiss the "myth of dissociation"—at least at the psychology-law interface (Tapp, 1974).

IMPLICATIONS FOR ROLES AND RESPONSIBILITIES

As one who pushed and watched, described and critiqued the evolution of psychology-law collaboration over a decade (Tapp, 1969, 1971, 1976, 1980, 1982; Tapp & Levine, 1977)), I submit that the interdisciplinary research effort by Wald, Carlsmith, Leiderman, and Smith is an important psycholegal event. The project bridges the gap between law and psychology, goes beyond rhetoric to research and results, suggests future directions, and augurs reciprocal socialization.

Bridging the Gap

The variety of issues (theoretical, methodological, empirical, practical) addressed in planning and executing this research revealed a sophistication rarely found to date in many psychology-law collaborations. This is especially the case in the area of child development and social legal policy, as both Bronfenbrenner (1974) and Wald (1976) discovered earlier. The present effort demonstrated exchange and cooperation between researchers from different disciplines who managed to reduce some barriers *vis-a-vis* method and orientation.

Beyond bridging the psychology/law gap, and learning to speak the other's patois, these researchers actively made "translations" about conceptual and procedural matters, sensitive to the interest, relevance, and need of both groups as well as to policy decisions for children's and parents' rights. The interdisciplinary team became tutored to be critically concerned about the continuous relationship of (1) basic to applied research, (2) child development principles to social policy issues, (3) psychological to legal theories and methods, (4) legal to social definitions of abuse, neglect, and rights, and (5) the role and responsibility of psychology to law. In so doing, they informed psychologists how policy needs should influence scientific decisions while simultaneously advising law operatives how developmental data should influence judicial to legislative dispositions. In short, they worked both sides of the scientific and social streets; they saw the validity and vitality of reciprocal science and social policy axioms.

Operationally, the Bay Area Study investigators demonstrated the tensions *and* advantages of scientific-societal cooperative efforts while at the same time challenging psychologists and lawyers to meet each other's demands. Wald captured the dilemma for psychologists and lawyers: "Recognizing the need for data, many policy-makers accept any data available, regardless of the limitations in the research. Therefore, it is critical that researchers doing policy-oriented research ask themselves 'which policy issues are researchable?' and 'what is necessary to adequately research the issue?' (p. 228). "These observations clarify the role and responsibility of both disciplines to be empirical, experimental, educative, and ethical—preferably at the same time on the same point: "Together we *can* be more systematic, *and* more committed to documenting events descriptively, and *may* be more willing to ask questions from more than one perspective" (Tapp, 1974; Tapp & Levine, 1977, p. 368).

Beyond Rhetoric To Research and Results

While Wald's paper is primarily a proposal, containing only preliminary analyses, the limited findings are sufficiently provocative and tempting to make us all eager for the final analysis and arrival of a full report. Even the preliminary results show the relevance to judicial and legislative decision-making of a psycholegal study designed to yield informed social policy. Without recounting any findings in detail, those dealing with the health of the sample, social and cognitive competencies, and the child's conceptions of abuse and neglect exemplify the potential *and* power of empirical, dual-perspective undertakings to make available new information and insights.

Future Directions

The preliminary results underscored the importance of focusing on how research is used. They also suggest how little is known about the process of decision-making at all levels. Beyond stimulating thoughts about an investigation of decision-makers, the Bay Area Study also evoked ideas about a study comparing the children of abuse/neglect to the children of divorce. The multi-faceted quality of such problems as abuse, neglect, and divorce at the child's level (and parole and sentencing at the adult level) reveal the importance of using a multi-disciplined perspective that encourages and enhances a multi-method, multi-theory, and multi-variant research strategy.

Reciprocal Socialization

Over a decade ago, I was concerned that lawyers not become psychologists or the converse (1969). I have continued to voice concern that psychologists not become the empiricist captive of lawyers *and* that neither discipline lose its identity to become the intellectual handmaiden [sic] of the other (1969, 1976, 1978, 1980). Instead, I recommended exchange and cooperation, persuasion and instruction, collaboration and critique. Such communication ensures unfeigned interdisciplinary respect and full-fledged partnership, not one-shot deals that disregard mutual social and scientific roles and responsibilities.

A CONCLUDING NOTE: ANOTHER PERSPECTIVE

In an age where the U.S. government's official expected loss in the event of nuclear holocaust is anywhere from four-and-one-half to 100 million persons, perhaps the calculus of one million abused or neglected children seems miniscule and negligible. None of the figures is acceptable. All three reckonings are frightening, inhumane, and irresponsible. They underscore the need for psychology and law to be socially- and scientifically-responsible *and* responsive to children (and parents) who experience abuse and/or neglect—whatever the form.

At this point in history, lawyers and psychologists alike need a combination of competence, collaboration, and courage to overcome the pessimism that rejects the necessity of science *and* the possibility of remedying social issues through informed research-based reform. The interdisciplinary policy-oriented research of Wald and colleagues is a worthy first attempt that incorporates these qualities.

REFERENCE NOTES

1. Levine, F. J. *The legal reasoning of youth: Dimensions and correlates.* Unpublished Ph.D. dissertation, University of Chicago, 1979.
2. Moore, S. *Research and practitioner: What do we have to say to each other?* Presentation to J. L. Tapp's class on "Children and Youth in Society," University of Minnesota, 1981.
3. Tapp, J. L., & Aliotta, J. *Developmental, legal, and social aspects of rights-consciousness.* Unpublished manuscript, University of Minnesota, 1976.

REFERENCES

Barber, B. Resistance by scientists to scientific discovery. *Science,* 1961, *134,* 596–602.
Bronfenbrenner, U. Developmental research, public policy, and the ecology of childhood. *Child Development,* 1974, *45*(1), 1–5.
Campbell, D. T. Legal reforms as experiments. *Journal of Legal Education,* 1971, *23,* 217–239.
Cartwright, D. Theory and practice. *Journal of Social Issues,* 1978, *34*(4), 168–180.
Clarke-Stewart, A. *Child care in the family: A review of research and some propositions for policy.* New York: Academic Press, 1977.
Cook, T. D., & Campbell, D. T. *Quasi-experimentation: Design and analysis issues for field settings.* New York: Rand McNally, 1979.
Damon, W. *The social world of the child.* San Francisco: Jossey-Bass, 1977.
Ellsworth, P. C., & Levy, R. J. Legislative form of child custody adjudication: An effort to rely on social science data in formulating legal policies. *Law and Society Review,* 1969, *4*(2), 167–233.
Federal Judiciary Center. *Experimentation in the law: Report of the Federal Judiciary Center Advisory Committee on Experimentation in the Law.* Washington, D.C.: U.S. Gov't Printing Office, 1981.
Goldstein, J., Freud, A., & Solnit, A. J. *Beyond the best interests of the child.* New York: Free Press, 1973.
Goldstein, J., Freud, A., & Solnit, A. J. *Before the best interests of the child.* New York: Free Press, 1979.
Grisso, T., & Vierling, L. Minors' consent to treatment: A developmental perspective. *Professional Psychology,* 1978, *9*(3), 412–427.
Haggard, E. A., & Mentschikoff, S. Responsible decision making in dispute settlement. In J. L. Tapp & F. J. Levine (Eds.), *Law, justice, and the individual in society: Psychological and legal issues.* New York: Holt, Rinehart & Winston, 1977.
Hempel, C. G. *Aspects of scientific explanation and other essays on the philosophy of science.* New York: Free Press, 1965.
Hetherington, E. M., Cox, M., & Cox, R. The aftermath of divorce. In J. H. Stevens, Jr., & Mathews (Eds.), *Mother-child, father-child relations.* Washington, D.C.: NAEYC, 1978.
Hetherington, E. M., Cox, M., & Cox, R. Family interactions and the social, emotional,

and cognitive development of children following divorce. In V. C. Vaughan & T. B. Brazelton (Eds.), *The family: Setting priorities.* New York: Science and Medicine Publishers, 1979.

Holtzman, W. H., Diaz-Guerrero, R., & Swartz, J. D. *Personality development in two cultures: A cross-cultural longitudinal study of school children in Mexico and the United States.* Austin, Texas: University of Texas Press, 1975.

Katkin, D., Bullington, B., & Levine, M. Above and beyond the best interests of the child: An inquiry into the relationship between social science and social action. *Law and Society Review,* 1974, *4,* 669-687.

Konecni, V., & Ebbesen, E. B. A critique of theory and method in social-psychological approaches to legal issues. In B. D. Sales (Ed.), *Perspectives in law and psychology Vol. II: The trial process.* New York: Plenum Press, 1980.

Kuhn, T. S. *The structure of scientific revolutions.* Chicago: University of Chicago Press, 1962.

Lewin, K. Group decisions and social change. In E. Maccoby, T. M. Newcomb, & E. L. Hartley (Eds.), *Readings in social psychology.* New York: Holt, Rinehart & Winston, 1947.

Lewin, K. *Resolving social conflicts: Selected papers on group dynamics.* New York: Harper & Row, 1948.

LeVine, R. A. Anthropology and child development. *New directions for child development,* 1980, *8,* 71-86.

Luepnitz, D. A. Children of divorce: A review of psychological literature. *Law and Human Behavior,* 1978, *2*(2), 167-179.

Meehl, P. E. Law and the fireside inductions: Some reflections of a clinical psychologist. In J. L. Tapp & F. J. Levine (Eds.), *Law, justice, and the individual in society: Psychological and legal issues.* New York: Holt, Rinehart & Winston, 1977.

Melton, G. B. Teaching children about their rights. In J. S. Henning (Ed.), *Children and the law: Empirical and theoretical approaches to children's rights.* New York: Thomas, in press.

Osofsky, J. D. Do we value our children enough to change our child-care policies? (Review of *Child care in the family: A review of research and some propositions for policy* by A. Clarke-Stewart.) *Contemporary Psychology,* 1979, *24*(2), 118.

Parke, R. D. Socialization into child abuse: A social interactional perspective. In J. L. Tapp & F. J. Levine (Eds.), *Law, justice, and the individual in society: Psychological and legal issues.* New York: Holt, Rinehart & Winston, 1977.

Parsons, T., & Shils, E. (Eds.) *Toward a general theory of action.* Cambridge, Mass.: Harvard University Press, 1951.

Roberts, F. Child growth and development: A basis for policy. *Education and Urban Society,* 1980, *12*(2), 147-161.

Rogers, C. M., & Wrightsman, L. S. Attitudes toward children's rights: Nuturance or self-determination? *Journal of Social Issues,* 1978, *34*(2), 56-67.

Ryle, G. *The concept of mind.* New York: Barnes & Noble Books, 1949.

Skolnick, A. The limits of childhood. In R. H. Mnookin (Ed.), Children and the law. *Law and Contemporary Problems,* 1975, *39*(3), 38-77.

Sroufe, L. A. The coherence of individual development: Early care, attachment, and subsequent developmental issues. *American Psychologist,* 1979, *34*(10), 834-841.

Sroufe, L. A. Attachment and the roots of competence. *Human Nature,* October, 1978, *1*(10), 50-57.

Tapp, J. L. Psychology and the law: The dilemma. *Psychology Today,* February, 1969, *2*(9), 16-22.

Tapp, J. L. Reflections. In J. L. Tapp (Ed.), Socialization, the law, and society. *Journal of Social Issues,* 1971, *27*(2), 1-16.

Tapp, J. L. The psychological limits of legality. In J. R. Pennock & J. W. Chapman (Eds.), *The limits of law: Nomos XV.* New York: Lieber-Atherton, 1974.

Tapp, J. L. Psychology and the law: An overture. *Annual Review of Psychology,* 1976, *27,* 359-404.

Tapp, J. L. Linkages and liaisons as the mission: The SPSSI connection, *SPSSI Newsletter,* November, 1978, pp. 1; 4.

Tapp, J. L. Psychological and policy perspectives on the law: Reflections on a decade. *Journal of Social Issues,* 1980, *36*(2), 165-192.

Tapp, J. L. Reflections on a decade of law and psychology in the United States. In J. Gunn & D. Farrington (Eds.), *Abnormal offenders, delinquency, and the criminal justice system: Current research in forsenic psychiatry and psychology.* Chichester, England: John Wiley & Sons, 1982.

Tapp, J. L., & Levine, F. J. (Eds.) *Law, justice, and the individual in society: Psychological and legal issues.* New York: Holt, Rinehart & Winston, 1977.

Vidmar, N. The other issues in jury simulation research: A commentary with particular reference to defendant character studies. *Law and Human Behavior,* 1980, *3*(1/2), 95-106.

Wald, M. S. Legal policies affecting children: A lawyer's request for aid. *Child Development,* 1976, *47*(1), 1-5.

Wald, M. S. Thinking about public policy toward abuse and neglect of children: A review of *Before the best interests of the child. Michigan Law Reviw,* 1980, *78,* 645-693.

Wald, M., Carlsmith, M., Leiderman, P. H., & Smith, C. Intervention to protect abused and neglected children. In M. Perlmutter (Ed.), *Minnesota Symposium* on *Child Psychology: Volume 16.* Hillsdale, N.J.: Lawrence Erlbaum Associates, 1983.

White, S. Evidence for a hierarchical arrangement of learning processes. In L. P. Lipsitt & C. C. Spiker (Eds.), *Advances in child development and behavior.* New York: Academic Press, 1965.

Zimmerman, S. L., Mattesich, P., & Leik, R. K. Legislators' attitudes toward family policy, *Journal of Marriage and the Family,* 1979, *41*(3), 507-517.

Author Index

A

Abate, F., 153, 154, *166*
Aber, J. L., 215, *228*
Achenbach, T. M., 43, *78,* 139, 142, *162*
Adamson, L., 3, 20, 22, 24, *33*
Adcock, C., 178, *196*
Ahr, A. E., 152, *163*
Ainsworth, B., 131, *135*
Ainsworth, M., 132, *135*
Ainsworth, M. D. S., 38, *39,* 46, 47, 50, 71, *78*
Albert, J., 171, *174*
Aliotta, J., 242, *247*
Allen, L., 93, *127*
Alluisi, E. A., 148, *164*
Als, H., 3, 20, 22, 24, *31, 33,* 96, *126*
Altshuler, K. Z., 102, *126*
Antler, S., 207, *228*
Arend, R., 46, 48, 58, 61, *78, 79,* 112
Asher, S. R., 56, *78*
Atoian, G., 153, *164*

B

Babijian, H., 224, *229*
Bakeman, R., 3, 4, *31*
Baker, C. H., 151, *162*
Banet, B., 178, 186, *195*
Barber, B., 236, *247*

Barkley, R. A., 140, 151, 153, *162, 163*
Barlow, A., 147, 148, 150, *165,* 172, *174*
Barron, R., 144, 147, *163*
Bax, M., 140, *162*
Beardshall, A., 153, *163*
Bee, H. L., 3, *31*
Beebe, B., 22, 24, *33*
Behar, L. B., 56, 68, 69, *78*
Beller, E. K., 56, 60, *78*
Benezra, E., 103, *126*
Bennett, S. L., 22, 24, *33*
Bereiter, C., 187, *195*
Bergman, A., 45, 48, *79*
Bergman, P., 71, *78*
Berkowitz, L., 3, *31*
Birch, H. G., 70, 71, *79,* 88, *91*
Blehar, M., 38, *39,* 46, 47, 50, 71, *78,* 131, *135*
Block, J., 44, 48, 64, *78,* 171, *174*
Block, J. H., 44, 48, 64, *78,* 171, *174*
Bolton, F. G., Jr., 211, *228*
Bond, J. T., 176, *196*
Borgatta, E. F., 213, *229*
Bowlby, J., 44, 46, 77, *78,* 211, *229*
Brachfeld, S., 3, *32*
Bradley, C., 142, 147, 149, *162*
Braley, B. W., 140, *165*
Brashears, G. C., 153, *164*
Brazelton, T. B., 3, 20, 22, 24, *31, 33*

Breger, L., 44, 45, *78*
Bridger, W. M., 13, *33*
Broadbent, D. E., 151, 152, 158, *162*
Bronfenbrenner, U., 234, 238, 239, 245, 247
Brown, J., 3, 4, *31*
Brumback, R. A., 142, *165*
Brunnquell, D., 131, *135*, 207, 229
Buchsbaum, M. S., 140, 146, 148, *162, 164, 166*
Bugelski, B. R., 157, *162*
Bullington, B., 238, *248*
Bunney, W. E., 148, *166*
Burgess, R. L., 207, 208, *229*
Burleigh, A. C., 153, *164*
Buss, A., 70, *78*, 159, *162*
Buttenwieser, E., 208, *230*

C

Caine, E. D., 148, 158, *166*
Callaghan, J., 3, *31*
Campbell, D. T., 234, 238, 239, *247*
Cannady, C., 102, *126*
Cantwell, D. P., 87, *91*, 140, 143, 153, *162, 165*
Caplan, P. J., 148, *164*
Carlsmith, M., 238, *249*
Cartwright, D., 234, *247*
Caulfield, C., 207, *229*
Cautley, P. W., 213, *229*
Chalmers, M. A., 208, *230*
Chandler, M., 88, *91*
Chapple, E. D., 2, 3, *31*
Chess, S., 70, 71, *79*, 88, *91*, 141, *165*
Cicchetti, D., 4, *31*, 120, *126*
Clarke-Stewart, A., 234, *247*
Clausen, J., 106, *126*
Clements, S. E., 140, *162*
Clifton, R., 4, 13, *32*
Cohen, N. J., 153, *162*
Cohen, S. E., 4, *33*
Cohn, A. H., 211, *229*
Collins, J. T., 103, *126*
Collmer, C. W., 207, 213, *230*
Conger, R. D., 207, 208, *229*
Conner, C. K., 147, *163*
Conners, C. K., 143, 147, 153, 154, 156, *162, 163*
Conte, R., 147, 154, 155, 157, 158, *163*
Cook, T. D., 239, *247*
Corcoran, D. W. J., 153, *163*
Cowen, E. L., 224, *229*

Cox, M., 243, *247*
Cox, R., 243, *247*
Crichton, L., *79*
Cutler, C. A., 207, *229*

D

Dabiri, C., 5, *32*
Dalby, D. T., 147, 157, 160, *163*
Dalby, J. T., 167, *174*
Damon, W., 242, *247*
Darlington, R. B., 199, *205*
Davies, D. R., 152, *163*
Dawson, M. C., 153, 154, *164*
Dawson, M. E., 153, *165*
Day, D., 171, *174*
Dean, J. G., 207, *229*
Deinard, A., 71, *78*
Demos, V., 2, 18, 20, 24, *32*
Dempsey, J., 4, 5, 13, *32*
Denhoff, E., 154, 159, *164*
Diamond, G. R., 2, 18, 20, 24, *32*
Diaz-Guerrero, R., 240, *248*
Disbrow, M. A., 207, *229*
DiVitto, B., 3, *31, 32*
Doerr, H., 207, *229*
Douglas, V. I., 95, 101, 102, 103, 104, *126*, 143, 147, 148, 153, 156, *162, 163, 165, 166*
Duffy, E., 151, *163*
Dunst, C. J., 3, *31*
Dyer, J. L., 204, *205*

E

Eason, R. G., 153, *163*
Easser, B. R., 101, 102, *127*
Ebaugh, F. G., 140, *163*
Ebbesen, E. B., 239, 242, *248*
Ebert, M. H., 148, *166*
Edelbrock, C. S., 139, 142, *163*
Edelbrock, C. S., 139, 142, *162*
Egeland, B., 71, 72, *78, 79*, 131, *135*, 171,
Egolf, B., *29*
Eisenberg, L., 147, *163*
Ekman, P., 5, *31, 33*
Ellis, H. C., 152, *163*
Ellis, N. R., 173, *174*
Ellsworth, P. C., 235, *247*
Elmer, E., 208, 224, *229*
Emde, R., 71, *78*
Emerson, P., 71, *79*
Engelmann, S., 187, *195*

Erickson, M. F., 132, *135*
Erikson, E. H., 44, 46, 63, *78*
Escalona, S., 71, *78*, 86, *91*, 105
Evans, W. O., 148, *164*

F

Fanshell, D., 212, 217, 223, *229*
Field, T., 2, 3, 4, 5, 8, 10, 13, 16, 17, 20, 22, 24, 25, 26, 29, *31, 33,* 38, *39*
Flintoff, M., 144, 147, *163*
Flory, D. C., 149, *163*
Fogel, A., 2, 18, 20, 24, *32*
Follignon, F. C., *229*
Forsythe, A. B., 4, *33*
Fraser, T., 151, *163*
Freedman, D. C., 102, *126*
Freeman, R., 147, 160, *163*
Freud, A., 209, 212, 223, *229,* 238, *247*
Friesen, W. V., 5, *31*

G

Gaensbauer, T., 71, *78*
Gai, D. S., 211, *228*
Galbraith, G., 106, *127*
Garbarino, J., 209, *229*
Garmezy, N., 91, *91,* 226, *229*
George, C., 213, *229*
Gewirtz, J., 38, *40*
Gibson, D., 121, 122, *126*
Gibson, E., 103, *126*
Gil, D., 207, 211, *229*
Gilbert, J., 149, *163*
Goldberg, S., 3, *31,* 39, *40*
Golden, M. M., 224, *230*
Goldstein, J., 209, 212, 223, *229,* 238, *247*
Goulder, T. J., 131, *135*
Gove, F., 48, 58, *78*
Goyette, C. H., 143, *163*
Gray, J. D., 207, *229*
Green, A., 208, *229*
Greenacre, P., 105, *127*
Greenberg, L., 153, 154, *165*
Greenberg, N. H., 3, *32*
Greenfield, P. M., 104, *127*
Greenhil, L., 142, *165*
Greenspan, S., 86, *91*
Grisso, T., 240, *247*
Gruber, A. R., 212, *229*
Grunske, M. E., 152, *163*
Gunnar, M., 38, *40*

H

Hagen, J. W., 103, *126,* 170, *174*
Haggard, E. A., 242, *247*
Hale, G. A., 168, 170, *174*
Hallock, N., 4, 5, *32*
Hally, C., 213, *230*
Haring, B. L., 216, *230*
Harmon, R., 71, *78*
Harrington, D. M., 171, *174*
Harris, D., 102, 105, *127*
Harter, S., 122, *127*
Hartup, W. W., 225, *229*
Hatch, J., 4, 13, *32*
Hawkes, G. R., 147, *164*
Hawkins, W. F., 173, *174*
Hebb, D. O., 151, *163*
Hechtman, L., 143, *163*
Heider, G., 86, *91*
Hempel, C. G., 236, *247*
Henker, B., 102, *128*
Herman, D., 145, *164,* 168, 172, *174*
Herrenkohl, E., 211, *229*
Herrenkohl, R. C., 211, *229*
Hetherington, E. M., 243, *247*
Hinton, G. G., 153, *164*
Hockey, G. R. J., 152, *163*
Hogan, R., 132, *135*
Hohmann, M., 178, 186, *195*
Holtzman, W. H., 240, *248*
Honzik, M. P., 93, *127*
Hopkins, J., 143, *163*
Hopwood, J., 153, 154, *165*
Hubbell, R., 210, *230*
Humphries, T., 146, *163*
Hunt, J. McV., 175, *195*
Hymel, S., 56, *78*

I

Ignatoff, E., 3, *32*
Izzo, L. D., 224, *229*

J

Jackson, T. L., 153, *162*
Jaffe, J., 22, 24, *33*
Jaffee, S., 153, *163*
Jerison, H. J., 151, *163*
Joffe, L., 131, *135*
Johnson, K., 102, 104, *126, 127*

Jones, F. H., 226, *230*
Jones, O. H. M., 3, 4, *32*
Jones, R. W., 173, *174*

K

Kadushin, A., 207, 208, *230*
Kagan, J., 3, *33*, 103, *127*, 143, *163*, 171, *174*
Kaplan, B., 103, *128*
Kappauf, W. S., 152, *163*
Karrer, R., 106, *127*
Katkin, D., 238, *248*
Kavaler, F., 224, *230*
Kempe, C. H., 207, 208, 209, *229, 230*
Kempe, R. S., 208, 209, *230*
Kent, J. T., 212, *230*
Kephart, N. C., 140, *165*
Kershman, S. M., 3, *33*
Kinsbourne, M., 139, 140, 144, 145, 146, 147, 148, 150, 156, 157, 158, 160, 161, *163, 164, 165*, 167, 168, 170, 172, *174*
Kirk, S. A., 175, *195*
Klein, G. S., 44, *78*
Klein, R. E., 168, *174*
Knights, R. M., 153, *164*
Kogan, K. L., 3, 4, *32*
Kogan, N., 103, *127*
Kohn, M., 226, *230*
Konecni, V., 239, 242, *248*
Kopp, C. B., 72, *78*, 94, 95, 97, 101, 102, 103, 104, 105, 106, 111, 119, 121, *126, 127*
Korb, R. J., 153, *164*
Korner, A., 71, *78*
Krakow, J. B., 72, *78*, 101, 102, 103, 104, 117, 119, 121, *126, 127*
Kubicek, L., 3, *32*
Kuhn, T. S., 236, *248*

L

Lagerberg, D., 213, *230*
Laner, R. H., 211, *228*
Langhorst, B. H., 2, 18, 20, 24, *32*
Lattes, V. G., 149, *166*
Laufer, M., 154, 159, *164*
Lazar, I., 199, *205*
Ledlow, A., 144, 147, *163*
Lehtinen, L. E., 140, *165*
Leiderman, P. H., 29, *32*, 238, *249*
Leik, R. K., 237, 242, *249*
Lemmon, J. A., 212, *230*
Lesser, L. I., 153, *165*
Lesser, S. R., 101, 102, *127*

Levine, E. F., 102, *127*
Levine, F. J., 238, 239, 242, 244, 245, *247*, *249*
Levine, M., 238, *248*
LeVine, R. A., 242, *248*
Levy, R. J., 238, *247*
Lewin, K., 233, *248*
Lewis, M., 35, 39, *40*
Lidz, T., 101, 105, *127*
Lieberman, A. F., 47, 71, *78*
Little, B. C., 153, 154, *166*
Littner, N., 212, 217, *230*
Lockie, M. S., 3, *31*
Loeb, M., 148, 151, *164*
Loevinger, J., 44, 45, *78*
Logan, W., 143, *165*
Loney, J., 87, *91*
Lourie, R., 86, *91*
Ludlow, C., 146, *164*
Luepnitz, D. A., 243, *248*
Luria, A. R., 105, *127*
Lykken, M., 160, *164*

M

MacKeith, E., 140, *162*
MacTurk, R. H., 3, *33*
Mackworth, N. H., 148, *164*
Mahler, M., 45, 48, *79*
Main, M., 46, *79*, 213, *229*
Malmo, R. B., 151, *164*
Malone, C. A., 95, 101, *127*
Mandell, B. R., 212, *230*
Marcus, S., 85, *91*
Martin, H., 208, 224, 225, 226, *230*
Martin, J., 38, *40*
Martin, J. A., 207, 208, *230*
Massie, H. N., 3, *33*
Masterson, J., 87, *91*
Matas, L., 10, 18, *35*, 46, 48, 61, *79*, 112
Mattesich, P., 237, 242, *249*
McCall, R. B., 93, 121, *127*
McCarthy, M. E., 3, *33*
McClelland, D., 178, *196*
McFarlane, J. W., 93, *127*
McGrath, J. J., 152, *164*
McNeil, J. T., 176, *196*
McQuiston, S., 3, *33*
Meehl, P. E., 239, *248*
Meier, E., 212, *230*
Meiselman, K., 89, *91*
Melton, G. B., 242, *248*

Mentschikoff, S., 242, *247*
Merrill, M. A., 180, *196*
Mikkelsen, E. J., 148, *166*
Mikkelson, E. J., 146, *164*
Milich, R., 87, *91*
Miller, L. B., 204, *205*
Miller, L. K., 168, *174*
Minde, K. K., 143, 148, 156, *165, 166*
Mischel, W., 100, *127*
Mnookin, R., 209, *230*
Mock, 147
Moore, S., 240, *247*
Morgenstern, G., 153, *162*

N

Neal, G. L., 152, *164*
Neilon, P., 51, *79*
Nelson, K., 104, *127*
Nelson, M., 106, *127*
Nemeth, E., 143, *166*
Nicholl, S., 161, *164*
Nilsson, K., 213, *230*
Nissen, M. J., 144, *164*
Nyman, B. A., 3, *31*

O

Offer, D., 88, *91*
Offer, J., 88, *91*
Ogden, W. C., 144, *164*
Osofsky, J. D., 234, *248*
Oster, H., 5, *33*
O'Tauma, L. A., 140, *164*

P

Parke, R. D., 207, 213, *230*, 239, 242, *248*
Parmelee, A. H., 94, *127*
Parsons, T., 236, *248*
Partridge, D. M., 148, *165*
Patterson, C. J., 100, *127*
Pavenstedt, E., 224, 225, *230*
Pawlby, S., 3, 22, 29, *31, 33*
Pederson, A., 224, *229*
Pederson, F., 39, *40*
Pelham, W., 143, *165*
Perlman, T., 143, *163*
Peters, K., 102, *126*
Peters, K. G., 147, *163*
Phillips, M. H., 216, *230*
Phillips, W., 171, *174*

Piaget, J., 104, *127*
Pick, A. D., 171, *174*
Pick, H. L., Jr., 171, *174*
Pine, F., 45, 48, *79*
Plomin, R. A., 70, *78*, 159, *162*
Podosin, R. L., 153, *165*
Polansky, N., 213, *230*
Polansky, N. A., 208, 209, *230*
Polansky, N. F., 213, *230*
Pollock, C. B., 207, *230*
Porges, S. W., 153, *164*
Posner, M. L., 144, *164*
Powe, W. E., 152, *163*
Preyer, M. W., 173, *174*

R

Rader, N., 103, *126*
Ragan, J., 156, *166*
Rapoport, J. L., 146, 148, *164, 166*
Redl, F., 88, *91*
Reimherr, F. W., 143, *166*
Rexford, E. N., 101, *128*
Rheingold, H., 38, *40*
Ricciuti, H. N., 104, *128*
Richer, J., 161, *164*
Robbins, L., 51, *79*
Roberts, F., 237, *248*
Roberts, W., 147, *165*
Robertson, 217, *230*
Robertson, 217, *230*
Robins, L., 87, 90, *91*
Robinson, J. A., 102, *126*
Roff, M., 224, *230*
Rogers, C. M., *248*
Rogers, L., 178, *196*
Rose, S. A., 13, *33*
Rosen, M., 131, *135*
Rosenberg, D., 46, *79*
Rosenblum, L., 35, *40*
Rosman, B., 171, *174*
Ross, D. M., 137, *164*
Ross, H., 38, *40*
Ross, S. A., 137, *164*
Routh, K., 140, *164*
Rubenstein, J., 39, *40*
Rutter, M., 211, 217, *230*
Ryle, G., 235, *248*

S

Sackett, G. P., 106, *128*
Saltzman, E., 104, *127*

AUTHOR INDEX

Sameroff, A., 88, *91*
Sander, L., 45, 46, *79*
Sander, L. W., 96, *128*
Satterfield, B. T., 140, *165*
Satterfield, H. J. H., 153, *165*
Satterfield, J. H., 140, 153, 154, *164, 165*
Schaffer, H., 70-71, *79*
Schein, J. D., 130, *135*
Schildroth, A. N., 130, *135*
Schmidt, E. A., 151, *164*
Schmidt, K., 13, *33*
Schroeder, C. S., 140, *164*
Schweinhart, L. J., 176, *196*
Scott, J., 153, 154, *165*
Scott, J. P., 175, *196*
Seech, M., *229*
Seligman, L., 212, *230*
Seligman, M., 37, *40*
Sells, S. B., 224, *230*
Serafica, F. C., 120, *126*
Sersen, E. A., 106, *126*
Shaffer, D., 142, *165*
Sharpe, L., 147, *163*
Sherman, E. A., 216, *230*
Shils, E., 236, *248*
Shinn, E., 212, 217, 223, *229*
Shirley, M., 51, *79*
Shuman, H., 4, 5, *32*
Shyne, A. W., 216, *230*
Sigman, M., 4, *33*, 94, *127*
Singleton, L. C., 56, *78*
Skolnick, A., 242, *248*
Sleater, E. K., 149, *165*
Smith, C., 238, *249*
Sobol, M. P., 147, 157, 160, *163, 165,* 167, 170, *174*
Sokolov, E. N., 10, *33*, 144, *165*
Solandt, D. Y., 148, *165*
Solnit, A. J., 209, 212, 223, *229*, 238, *247*
Sonies, B., 153, *165*
Sostek, A. J., 29, 32, 155, *165*
Sprague, R. L., 149, 153, *164, 165*
Spring, C., 153, 154, *165*
Sroufe, L. A., 4, 10, 12, 16, 18, *31, 33*, 45, 46, 48, 51, 58, 61, 71, 72, 73, *78, 79*, 112, 147, 153, *165*, 173, *174,* 211, 213, 224, *229*, 239, *248*
Stayton, D. J., 132, *135*
Staton, R. D., 142, *165*
Steele, B. F., 207, *230*
Stennett, T., 151, *165*
Stern, 153

Stern, D. N., 3, 22, 24, *33*
Stetor, R. M., *165*
Stevenson, H. W., 168, *174*
Stingfield, S., 56, *78*
Stoller, S., 2, 17, 20, 24, *33*
Strauss, A. A., 140, *165*
Streissguth, A. P., 3, *31*
Stringer, S., 3, *32*
Sullivan, H. S., 45, *79*
Sundelin, C., 213, *230*
Swanson, J., 144, 146, 147, *163*, 168, 170, 172, *174*
Swanson, J. M., 143, 145, 146, 147, 148, 150, 157, 160, *163, 164, 165*, 167, 172, *174*
Swartz, J. D., 240, *248*
Swire, M. R., 224, *230*
Sykes, D. H., 148, 156, *165*

T

Tant, J. L., 103, *128*
Tapp, J. L., 234, 237, 238, 239, 240, 244, 245, 246, *247, 248, 249*
Taraldson, B., *79*
Taylor, A., 152, *163*
Terman, L. M., 180, *196*
Thomas, A., 70, 71, *79*, 88, *91*, 141, *165*
Thurston, C. M., 147, *165*, 170, *174*
Ting, G., 4, 5, 13, *32*
Tinsley, B. R., 56, *78*
Trevarthen, C., 2, 22, 24, *33*
Trilling, L., 85, *91*
Tronick, E., 3, 20, 22, 24, *31, 33*
Trost, M. A., 224, *229*
Trybus, R. J., 131, *135*
Tulkin, S., 3, *33*
Turnure, J. E., 173, *174*

U

Udsky, A., 106, *126*
Ulrich, R. F., 143, *163*
Uzgiris, I. C., 103, *128*

V

VanEgeren, L. F., 3, *31*
Vaughn, B. E., 18, *33*, 56, 71, 72, *78, 79*, 101, 103, 117, 119, 121, *126, 127*
Vernon, M., 131, *135*
Vidmar, N., 234, *249*
Vierling, L., 240, *247*

Vietze, P., 3, 29, *32, 33*
Vygotsky, L. S., 105, *128*

W

Wald, M., 209, 210, 214, 223, *230, 231,* 238, 241, *249*
Wald, M. S., 234, 245, *249*
Walker, J. A., 3, *33*
Wall, S., 38, *39*, 46, 47, 50, *78*, 131, *135*
Walter, G. F., 153, *164*
Ward, M., 73, *79*
Waters, E., 10, 12, 18, *33*, 38, *39*, 46, 47, 48, 50, 56, 61, 71, 72, *78, 79*, 131, *135*
Webb, W. B., 151, *166*
Wechsler, D., 180, *196*
Weikart, D., *79*
Weikart, D. P., 176, 178, 186, *195, 196*
Weinberg, R. A., 171, *174*
Weinberger, R. S., 156, *166*
Weingartner, H., 146, 148, *164, 166*
Weinstein, E. A., 212, *231*
Weiss, B., 149, *166*
Weiss, G., 143, 148, 156, *163, 165, 166*
Wellman, H. M., 104, *128*
Wender, P. H., 140, 143, 147, 153, 154, 156, 159, *162, 166*
Werner, H., 103, *128*
Werry, J. S., 143, *166*
West, W., 153, *165*
Whalen, C. K., 102, *128*
Wherry, R. J., 151, *166*
White, S., 240, *249*
Widmayer, S., 3, 29, *32*
Williams, D. P., 208, *230*
Wineman, D., *91*
Wing, J. F., 151, *163*
Wippman, J., 48, 61, *79*
Wise, S., 3, 20, 22, 24, *33*
Wokoun, J., 152, *166*
Wood, D. R., 143, *166*
Wright, F., 153, *165*
Wrightsman, L. S., 248
Wunsch, J. P., 16, *33*

X,Y,Z

Yarrow, L., *39, 40*
Yarrow, L. J., 212, *231*
Yu, L., 146, *163*
Zahn, T. P., 146, 153, 154, *164, 166*
Zentall, S., 151, *166*
Zigler, E., 106, 122, *127, 128*, 173, *174*, 208, 228, *231*
Zill, N., 227, *231*
Zimmerman, S. L., 237, 242, *249*
Zucker, K., 147, *165*

Subject Index

A

Abused and neglected children,
  adult outcome, 88-89, 213, 235
  attachment, 211-213
  behavior problems, 213, 226
  definition problems, 208-209, 211
  emotional development, 208, 213
  foster care, 210-227, 234-235, 238-247
    and attachment, 211-213
    changes over time, 223
    child's views, 224, 227, 242
    and emotional development, 211
    factors in placement, 210-213, 219-222
    and IQ, 213, 225
    long-term effects, 217
    multiple placements, 212, 235
    and physical development, 213, 224-225
    research issues, 214-219, 240-243
    and school performance, 212-213, 222, 225
    and self-esteem, 212
    and social development, 211, 225
  hyperactivity, 87
  intervention issues, 208-227, 238-246
  language development, 208, 213
  legal issues, 208-209
  parent characteristics, 207-208, 219
  peer relations, 208, 213, 224
  physical problems, 208, 213, 224-225, 243
  research and public policy, 209-210, 214-215, 238
  school measures, 222, 225
  self-regulation, 95
  social competence, 226-227
Acting-out behavior, *see* Externalizing behavior
Activation band model of infant responsivity, 10-13, 36-37
Anticipatory behavior, 86-87, 90-91
Arousal modulation, infant, 10, 18-20, 25, 27
Attachment assessment,
  predictive value, 48, 68-70
  using strange situation, 69-70
Attachment classification
  and affect expression, 61-62
  and aggression, 71-72
  and classroom behavior problems, 62-64, 71
  and compliance, 132-135
  and dependency, 60-61, 64, 71-72
  and ego control, 64-65
  and ego resiliency, 58-59, 64-65
  and empathy, 63
  and externalizing behavior, 64-65
  and impulse expression, 61-62
  and internalizing behavior, 64-65
  and peer relations, 71
  and self-esteem, 59-60, 64

259

and self-regulation, 131-135
and social competence, 62
Attachment relationships,
  abused and neglected children, 211-213
  anxious, 48-51, 60, 63-68
    behavior problems, 60
    and compliance, 134-135
    differentiation, 63-68
    see also Attachment relationships, avoidant; Attachment relationships resistant
  avoidant, 47, 49-52, 59-76, 86
    and aggression, 71-72
    classroom behavior problems, 71
    dependency, 71-72
    overcontrol, 49, 64
    peer relations, 71
    preschool behavior patterns, 52
    undercontrol, 64
  biological predisposition, 45, 47
  and competence, 48-51
  effect on latter development, 45-52, 58-77, 85-91
  maladaptive, see Attachment relationships, anxious; Attachment relationships, avoidant; Attachment relationships, resistant
  resistant, 49-52, 59-76, 86
    preschool behavior patterns, 52
    undercontrol, 49, 64
  secure, 46-47, 50, 58-63, 86-87, 89
    and compliance, 133-135
Attention deficit disorder (ADD), 137-162
  arousal model, 153-156
  DSM-III behavior checklist, 138-139, 142-143
  nature of attentional weakness, 144-145, 150-151
  origin of term, 142
  subtyping, 142, 144-145
  vigilance model, 155-158
  see also Hyperactivity
Attention, sustained,
  and arousal, 152-153
  effect of stimulants, 151
  effect of task, 151-152
  and self-control, 100-103, 107, 112, 117-119, 123-125, 130
Autism
  and parent-infant interaction, 3, 12-13

B,C

Behavior disorders, aggressive,
  adult outcome, 86-87, 90
  intervention, 87, 89-91
Blindness,
  and parent-infant interaction, 3
Block Q-sort, 48-49, 55-56, 58-59, 64-68
Borderline personality organization, 87-89
Cerebral palsy
  and parent-infant interaction, 3-4
Classroom behavior problems
  and attachment classification, 62-64, 71
Coherence, developmental, 51-52, 68-70, 73-74
Communication disorders
  and self-monitoring, 105
Compliance, 93, 98-100, 109, 111-112, 115-117, 131-135
  and attachment classification, 132-135
  development of, 98-100
  and self-control, 109, 111-112, 115-117

D,E,F

DSM-III, 137-138, 142-143
Deafness
  and impulsivity, 105, 130-131
  and parent-infant interaction, 3
  and self-regulation, 101-102, 105, 130-131
Delay of behavior
  and self-control, 109-115
Dependency, 45, 47, 52, 60-61, 64
  and attachment classification, 60-61, 64
Developmental delay,
  and self-control, 107-125
Disadvantaged children,
  developmental differences, 204
  early experience, 204
  preschool intervention, 173-195, 197-205
    and college attendance, 183
    cost-benefit analysis, 182-184
    and delinquency, 182, 184-185
    and dropout rate, 183
    evaluation measures, 201
    and grade retention, 182, 189, 200
    Head Start, 184, 197-205
    Home Start, 199-200, 204
    home visits, 176, 188
    and IQ, 179, 188, 198-200

and labor-force participation, 183
and language development, 189
outcomes of different curricula, 189–191
program evaluation, 175–195, 197–205
and school achievement, 179, 184–185, 189, 200
and school motivation, 179, 184–185, 189
and special education placement, 179–182, 189, 200
Down's syndrome,
cognitive development, 121–122
infant stimulation thresholds, 4
and parent-infant interaction, 3–4, 12–13
and self-control, 107–125
Efficacy, development of, 38–39
Ego control, 44, 55, 64–65
and attachment classification, 64–65
Ego resiliency, 44, 48–49, 55, 58–59, 64–65
and attachment classification, 58–59, 64–65
Externalizing behavior, 51–52, 64–65, 86–91
and attachment classification, 64–65
and self-regulation, 101–102
Failure to thrive,
and parent-infant interaction, 3

H,I

High-risk infants, 1–30, 35–39
arousal modulation, 18–20, 37
disturbed interaction, 1, 3–30, 35–39
long-term effects, 4
infant gameplaying, 16–20
see also Postterm infants, Preterm infants
Hyperactivity,
adult outcomes, 87
arousal, 153–156
behavioral variability, 137–139, 141–142
and child abuse, 87
concentration span, 157–158
developmental changes, 142–143
and emotionality, 159–161
and impulsivity, 143–144, 159
and inattentiveness, 142–145
laboratory study, 141–161
neurological models, 139–141
brain damage model, 139–140
developmental lag model, 140–141
self-regulation, 95, 101–104

and stimulant drugs, 143–151, 153–158, 161, 167–173
determining optimal dosage, 149
effect on incidental learning, 147, 170–171
effect on laboratory tasks, 146–149, 167–173
effect on matching familiar figures, 143–144, 147, 171
effect on paired-associate learning, 147, 154–158, 168–170
explanations of divergent effects, 145, 149–150
implications for school performance, 167–173
measurement of effects, 167–173
physiological effects, 154–155
task specificity of effects, 172–173
and temperament, 141, 158–161
see also Attention deficit disorder
Hyperkinesis, see hyperactivity
Impulse expression, preschool, 57, 61–62
and attachment classification, 61–62
Impulsivity, 101–102, 105, 130–131, 143–144, 159
and deafness, 105, 130–131
and hyperactivity, 143–144, 159
and language development, 105
Infant gameplaying, 15–20, 27–29
Interaction coaching, 1, 9–10, 20–29
gameplaying, 27–29
individual differences, 29
maternal attention-getting, 10, 25–27
maternal imitation, 9–10, 22–24, 36
maternal repetition, 24
maternal silencing, 24, 37
socioeconomic and cultural differences, 29
Internalizing behavior, 51, 64–65, 86–87
and attachment classification, 64–65

L,M

Learning disabilities
and self-regulation, 95
Longitudinal research
on abused and neglected children, 217, 219
funding problems, 194–195
and social change, 193–194
and social policy, 194, 217, 219
Maternal seductiveness, 73

SUBJECT INDEX

Mental retardation,
  developmental hypothesis, 106
  infant stimulation thresholds, 4
  self-regulation, 95
Minnesota Preschool Affect Checklist,
  56–57, 80–83

O,P

Overstimulation, maternal, 3–4, 8
Parent-infant interaction, 1–30, 35–39
  affective displays during, 5–15
  child's contribution, 35–36
  child's control of, 37–39
  disturbed, 1–30, 35–39
    gaze aversion during, 1, 3–5, 15–20, 22–29
    long-term effects, 4
  heart rate during, 3, 5, 8, 17–18
  infant autonomic arousal, 17–18
  normal, 1–2, 5–21
Postmaturity syndrom, see Postterm infants
Postterm infants
  arousal modulation, 18–20
  disturbed interaction, 5–20
  and infant gameplaying, 16–20
  responsivity, 13–15
  stimulation thresholds, 13, 16
Preschool adaptation,
  assessment, 54–58, 63–68, 72–74
    teacher, 55–56, 65–68
  and child's life circumstances, 72
  individual patterns, 43–44, 63–70, 72–77, 85–91
    clinical implications, 85–91
  and intelligence, 42
  intervention programs, 73, 76–77, 85–91
  and parental impulse management, 72–73
  prediction difficulties, 72–74
  and teacher intervention, 73, 76–77, 90–91
Preschool classroom ecology, 57–58
Preschool curricula, 178, 185–191
  child-centered approach, 187–191, 199
  child-initiated learning, 185–186
  Cognitively Oriented Curriculum, 186–191
  comparison, 187–191, 201–203
  need for empirical research, 202–203
  Piagetian, 185–191, 202
  preacademic, 187–191, 199
  theoretical influences, 185–191
Preschool programs, successful,
  administration and management, 191–193
  parent involvement, 193
  program evaluation, 193
  teacher sensitivity, 201
  team teaching, 192–193
  theoretical consistency, 191, 201–203
Preterm infants,
  arousal modulation, 18–20, 25, 27
  disturbed interaction, 4–29
    long-term effects, 4
  and infant gameplaying, 16–20
  information-processing limitations, 10, 24–25, 27
  interaction coaching, 22–29
  stimulation thresholds, 4, 12–13, 16
  unresponsiveness, 3, 12–15
Psychoanalytic theory,
  evolution of, 44–45
Psychology and law, 233–247

R,S

Research and public policy, relationship, 209–210, 233–247
Respiratory distress syndrome (RDS), see Preterm infants
Schizophrenia
  and parent-infant interaction, 3
  prediction from early behavior, 51
Self-control, 96–97, 99–125
  age-related changes, 121, 124
  and cognitive development, 122
  and cognitive strategies, 100–101, 103–104
  and compliance, 109, 111–112, 115–117
  and delay of behavior, 109–115
  and developmental delay, 107–125
  and Down's syndrome, 107–125
  and handicapped children, 100–125
  and language, 100–101, 105, 107, 112, 119–120, 123–125
  normal and handicapped children compared, 107–125
  and sustained attention, 100–103, 107, 112, 117–119, 123–125, 130
Self-esteem,
  in abused and neglected children, 212
  and attachment classification, 59–60, 64
Self-monitoring, 93–94, 98–99, 105, 129–131
  and communication disorders, 105, 130
  in handicapped children, 94, 129–131
Self-regulation, 93–125, 129–135
  in acting-out children, 101–102
  and attachment classification, 131–135

and deafness, 101–102, 105, 130–131
development of, 94–125
  caregiver influence, 94–95
  and cognitive development, 94–95, 98–100, 130–131, 133–135
  developmental phases, 96–100
    control, 96–99
    neurophysiological modulation, 96–97
    sensorimotor modulation, 96–98
    see also self-control
  and hyperactivity, 95, 101–104
  and learning disabilities, 95
  and mental retardation, 95
  in neglected children, 95, 101–102
  and self-awareness, 99
  and social/emotional factors, 131–135
Social competence,
  in abused and neglected children, 226–227
  and attachment classification, 62
Stimulant drugs,
  effect on hyperactivity, 143–151, 153–158, 161
  effect on normal sustained attention, 151
Stimulation modulation, maternal, 4, 18
Stimulation thresholds, infant, 4, 10–11, 12–13, 16

T,U

Teacher-child relationships, preschool, 56, 75
Temperament,
  and attachment, 70–72, 88
  and behavior disorders, 88
  and hyperactivity, 141, 158–161
  infant, 35–37, 47
  and preschool adaptation, 42–43
Unresponsiveness, infant, 3–4, 12–15